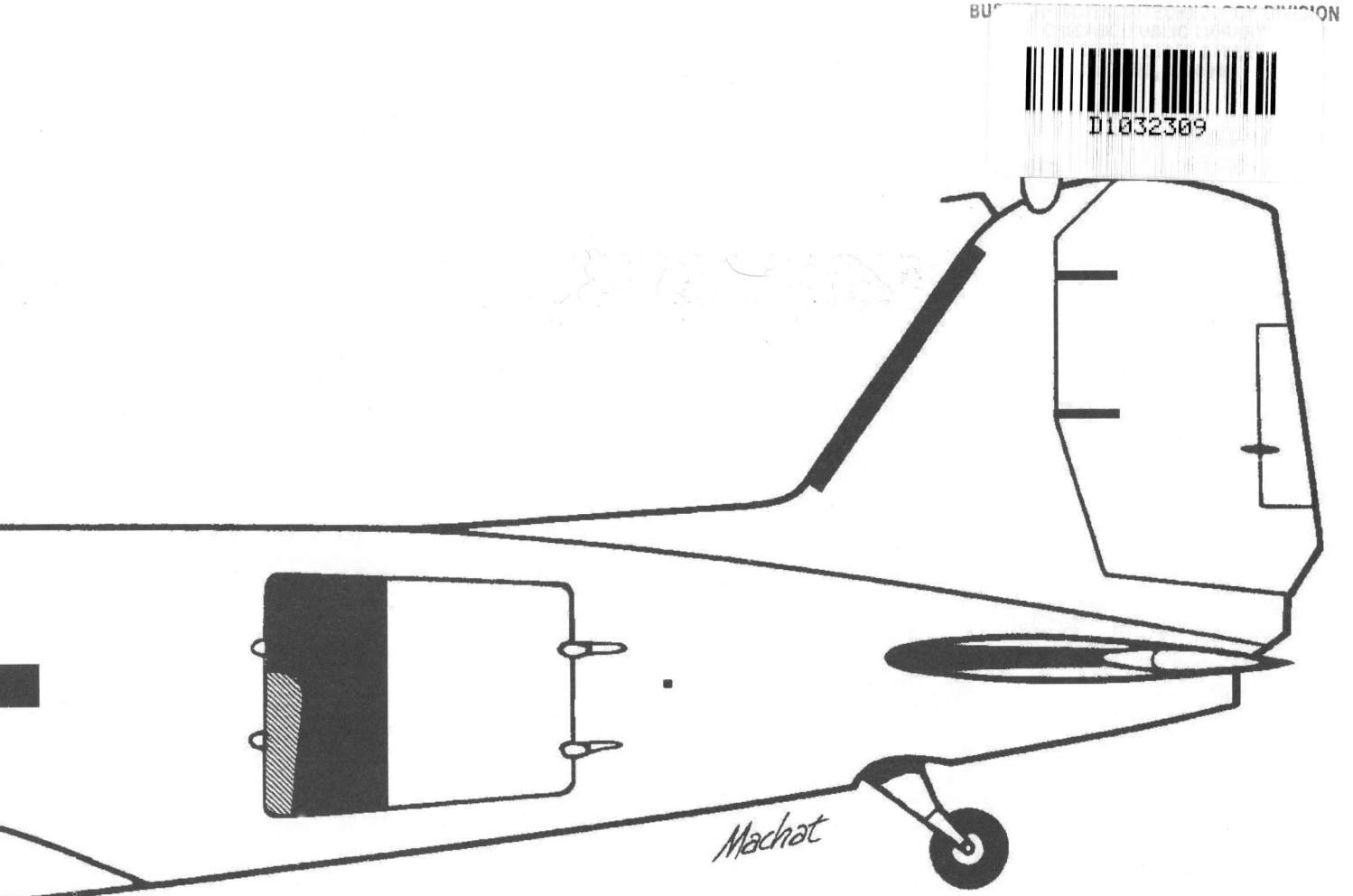

Machat

GUNSHIPS
The Story of Spooky, Shadow, Stinger and Spectre

Wayne Mutza

specialtypress
PUBLISHERS AND WHOLESALERS

SPECIALTY PRESS
PUBLISHERS AND WHOLESALERS

Specialty Press
39966 Grand Avenue
North Branch, MN 55056
Phone: 651-277-1400 or 800-895-4585
Fax: 651-277-1203
www.specialtypress.com

Edit by Mike Machat
Layout by Monica Bahr

ISBN-13 978-1-58007-123-9
Item No. SP123

Library of Congress Cataloging-in-Publication Data

Mutza, Wayne.
  Gunships : the story of Spooky, Shadow, Stinger, and Spectre / by Wayne Mutza.
    p. cm.
  Includes bibliographical references and index.
  ISBN 978-1-58007-123-9
  1. Gunships (Military aircraft)--United States--History--20th century. 2. AC-47 (Gunship)--History. 3. AC-119 (Gunship)--History. 4. Spectre (Gunship)--History. 5. Vietnam War, 1961-1975--Aerial operations, American. 6. United States. Air Force--History--Vietnam War, 1961-1975. I. Title.
  UG1242.G85M88 2008
  358.4'3--dc22
                        2008043107

Printed in China
10 9 8 7 6 5 4 3 2 1

Front Cover: *Poised for the kill, the menacing shape of the 105mm Howitzer-equipped Lockheed AC-130H Spectre Gunship is depicted in the aircraft's typical 30-degree left-bank attack attitude.*

Back Cover Top Right: *Little did the innocent nickname Sweet Pee give away the truly lethal mission description of this Douglas AC-47 Spooky Gunship belonging to the 3rd Special Operations Squadron.*

Back Cover Top Left: *Taking the gunship concept to the next level, the jet-augmented Fairchild AC-119K Stinger allowed for more internal space and weaponry. Shown here is Ship 910 of the 415th Special Operations Training Squadron.*

Back Cover Bottom: *In a dazzling display of defensive aerial countermeasures, an AC-130H launches an array of high-intensity flares creating what is called an angel effect. The flares would serve as decoy targets for heat-seeking anti-aircraft missiles instead of their homing into the AC-130's engine exhaust.*

Title Page: *This AC-130U means business, as attested to by its deadly combination of two 20mm Vulcan cannons, a 40mm Bofors cannon, and the formidable 105mm Howitzer. Large external fuel tanks mounted under-wing combined with inflight refueling capability allow for the ultra-long endurance required on these missions.*

Front Flap: *The Scorpion's deadly sting is depicted on this 18th Special Operations Squadron patch as being representative of the ultimate effects of a Fairchild AC-119K Stinger Gunship mission.*

Distributed in the UK and Europe by
Crécy Publishing Ltd
1a Ringway Trading Estate
Shadowmoss Road
Manchester M22 5LH England
Tel: 44 161 499 0024
Fax : 44 161 499 0298
www.crecy.co.uk
enquiries@crecy.co.uk

TABLE OF CONTENTS

ACKNOWLEDGMENTS

When first discussing the possibility of doing this book with the staff of Specialty Press, it seemed a monumental task. But I've always welcomed a challenge, and have long harbored a fondness for writing and aviation history. Dispelling any doubt I may have had about creating an accurate and comprehensive account of fixed-wing gunships was just knowing that people I've counted on in the past would come through again. And come through they did, in stellar fashion. This book would not have been possible without their research assistance or allowing me to tap their rich photo collections. Adding to their ranks were the many systems pioneers and gunship crewmen who found it important to document this history—their history. These veterans are the core resources for material that could only come from those who climbed aboard gunships to carry out their duties. The countless lives they saved stand as testimony to their skill and dedication. To them this book is dedicated. They are Robert Atkinson, Anton "Tony" Bautz, John Bessette, Doug Blair, Charles A. Boatwright, Alfred C. "Ace" Bowman, William Bryden, Jack Chandler, Jay A. Collars, Wendell Cosner, Michael Friel, David Galvan, Fred Graves, James W. Green, William Hamilton, Don Jay, Lee Keyser, John H. Lamb, Randall G. Lawrence, Robert A. Leach, James Mattison, Trooper McVey, Larry Mersek, Albert A. Nash, Richard Noble, Thomas Novak, David E. O'Mara, William Petrie, Edward L. Pinkham, Robert Price, Donald Savel, Roy A. "Tony" Simon, Robert Stein, Ralph "Ed" Thien, Bill Wait, and Henry Zeybel.

Also vital to this project was the input of Ralph D. Kimberlin, Ronald W. Terry, and John F. Harvell, pioneers of the gunship program who overcame seemingly insurmountable odds, and who became largely responsible for its success.

I am indebted to noted aviation authors Robert F. Dorr, Lennart Lundh, and Larry Davis. For generously allowing me access to their photo collections, special thanks go to Stephen H. Miller, Robert Brackenhoff, David W. Menard, Norm Taylor, Luc Hornstra, Sunil Gupta, David A. Hansen, and Tom Hansen. Author Kenneth Conboy provided insight to the more obscure applications of gunships, and Sakpinit Promthep and Analayo Korsakul expanded my knowledge of gunships in Thailand. I'm grateful for the diligent research done by Ron Thurlow and John Konek, and for NC-123K material from Alan Renga of the San Diego Air & Space Museum. Despite limited assistance available from the Air Force Special Operations Office at Hurlburt Field due to worldwide commitments, 2nd Lt. Lauren K. Johnson and SrA. Stephanie Jacobs came across with material detailing the AC-130. Important technical information was provided by David C. Hook, Pamela Braithwaite of the Air Force Association, and Michael D. Rowland of the Aviation Flight & Technology Museum. Special mention is due Thomas R. Weigt, President of Basler Turbo Conversions, LLC, for his assistance in providing insight to the firm's present day adaptations of the famed C-47. I'm indebted to Francy and her efficient staff at Allied Digital Photo for their kind attention to my photo needs. And I thank my wife, Deb, for her unwavering support of my work.

INTRODUCTION

Gunships, quite simply, are powerful aerial weapons that were born of a need to impede the flow of troops and supplies the enemy needs to wage war. The military labels this process "interdiction." Gunships, among a host of tactical strategies, would prove to be the most effective element of interdiction campaigns, and the most formidable means of defending ground forces. Interdiction exists to some degree in any armed conflict. However, it wasn't until World War II that it became instrumental to the outcome of hostilities. Interdiction took many forms, but in the air it reigned supreme. If an aircraft could carry sufficient fuel and armament, and find the enemy, it could then attack, often where ground and naval forces could not.

During World War II, interdiction by air in the European theatre was effective, but it was a different story in the Pacific theatre where the Japanese moved most supplies by sea. When it was discovered that Japanese transports were relatively impervious to Allied aircraft guns, light and medium bombers were re-armed with heavy gun packages—and the word "gunship" was first heard in military vocabularies.

Night interdiction came into play during the Korean War, mainly as a result of advances in radar technology. Crucial among such systems was Short Range Navigation, or SHORAN, an electronic navigation and bombing system using precision radar beacons to pinpoint and attack targets. Equipped with SHORAN, Douglas B-26 Invaders became the premiere night interdiction aircraft of the Korean

The distinction between gunship and attack aircraft has never been clear. In general terms, many aircraft not officially designated gunships certainly qualify. The Douglas A-1 Skyraider, for example, had its day in the sun as a heavy weapons platform. Able to carry its own weight in ordnance, the venerable "Spad" took the war to the enemy during the Korean and Southeast Asian conflicts. Like many of the gunships of the Vietnam War that supposedly had seen their heyday, the Skyraider was a key member of the "antique air force," whose purpose was counterinsurgency. This A-1, carrying a partial load of fire bombs, like many of the AC-47D and AC-119G/K gunships, was passed to the Vietnamese Air Force. (Tom Hansen)

conflict. After Cold War operations and having been exported to more than a dozen Allied air arms, Invaders would play an equally important role in the conflict in Southeast Asia.

The B-26 would serve its usefulness until replaced by another Douglas stalwart, an aircraft mistakenly thought to have reached its twilight—the legendary C-47. A small group of visionaries would give the rugged, reliable, and versatile C-47 yet another lease on life and a virtually new identity, most popularly called the "Spooky Gunship." With dogged determination, these aviators and engineers married a simple vintage flying maneuver, called a pylon turn, with large aircraft capable of carrying lots of ammunition and staying on station for long periods of time. The result would be astounding. So revolutionary and successful was the design that it was applied to two other U.S. Air Force cargo aircraft: Lockheed's C-130 Hercules and Fairchild's C-119 Flying Boxcar. Since endurance, and not speed, was

essential over the target, the obvious choice for dynamic gun platforms was radial-engine aircraft. Although such throwbacks to previous wars did not fit into the Air Staff's blueprint for a modern all-jet air force, they proved painfully necessary in the emerging dimension of warfare labeled "counterinsurgency," popularly termed COIN.

As the situation in Southeast Asia worsened, the order was given; President Kennedy in 1961 directed that counterinsurgency forces be established. The Air Commandos, who had gained fame in Burma during World War II, were resurrected, including in their "antique air force," the AC-47 gunship. Motivated by Spooky's success, Air Force leaders sought bigger and better gunships, which led to the development of AC-130 and AC-119 variants.

But what constitutes a gunship? To many, the term evokes images of imposing aircraft equated with battleships. In fact, in its infancy the AC-130 program was even called *Project Gunboat*, a label that recently has

Loaded for war in 1967 and resplendent in its non-standard scheme of emerald green over medium gray, this A-26K Counter Invader was a gunship through-and-through. Yet, the Air Force categorized it as an attack aircraft, reserving the "Gunship" designation for cargo haulers with side-firing guns. (Tom Hansen)

been revived to identify the newest of the breed. Yet, to others, gunships are identified as nimble, fearsome attack helicopters, and justifiably so. In fairness, the term can be applied to any aircraft considered heavy hitters that can take a sizeable chunk of war to the enemy, decimating his ranks and breaking his will to fight. Certainly there are many that qualify, all of which deserve the distinction. Who can deny that title to the famed Douglas A-1 Skyraider, which not only could carry its own weight in ordnance, but which, at one time or another, carried nearly every type of ordnance available? And who would argue the punch that could be delivered by the Navy's Lockheed AP-2H Neptune, or the sting of North American's OV-10A Bronco? Then there's the tough Fairchild A-10 Thunderbolt II that made quick work of Iraqi armor. The list goes on, but the distinction between attack and gunship aircraft has long been ill defined. Often, it boiled down to nothing more than an official designation, to which few aircraft truly remained committed.

For the purpose of this book, attention is focused on U.S. Air Force cargo aircraft converted to gunships since the early days of the Vietnam War. Coverage includes projects that contributed directly to the development of these flying battleships. Not overlooked are peripheral projects for Southeast Asian allies that involved side-firing light aircraft labeled gunships. Important also is the lesser known, yet serious, consideration given armed light aircraft during programs that intermeshed with Air Force development of the *big guns*. The pioneers who devised and nurtured the various gunship models faced stiff opposition and suffered setbacks, but they persevered, becoming the grandfathers of sophisticated machines that served, and continue to serve, in world trouble spots. Whether defending outposts, obliterating enemy supply lines, or supporting troops trading blows with the enemy, these awesome aircraft and their systems, in the hands of skilled and dedicated crew members, have become the most striking element of aerial warfare.

Easily qualifying as a gunship, despite its official attack designation, the A-26K Counter Invader assumed the interdiction role, at one time replacing AC-119 models in the intense anti-aircraft environment in Laos. Having served as a star performer during the Korean conflict, the Air Force contracted On Mark Engineering to upgrade the A-26 with improved engines, tip tanks, eight wing ordnance stations, radio package, new brakes, and spar caps to solve the problem of wings being shed on attack runs. Although the aircraft's original upper and lower gun turrets were removed, the eight .50-cal. nose guns were retained, giving it incredible punch. (U.S. Air Force)

CHAPTER ONE

BEGINNINGS OF THE BIG GUNS

The C-131B, S/N 53-7820, flew the first cargo-type aircraft lateral-sighting and firing tests for the 7.62mm minigun, which became the mainstay of gunships. It arrived with the sight at the Air Proving Ground Center on 26 August 1964. The success achieved in six firing missions over an Eglin AFB water range led to the development of a multi-gun system for the C-47 or C-123. The Convair Samaritan is seen here with the 4950th Training Wing at Wright-Patterson AFB in 1970. (via Stephen Miller)

Much like famous inventors Edison, Marconi, Galileo, Goddard, and the Wright brothers, Ron Terry had an idea; a simple, yet ingenious, idea that he cultivated with perseverance and ambition. Although the concept upon which Terry based his idea was not new, his plan was to refine the side-firing pylon turn method, shaping it into a revolutionary form of aerial warfare. The power of Terry's idea did not become clear until a number of dedicated people who shared his conviction ushered the concept along its unstable course.

Firing weapons from the side of an aircraft dates back to World War I. However, firing them while the aircraft executed a pylon turn was a radical departure from the standard firing pass. Firing weapons during this maneuver was first recorded in 1926 when U.S. Army Air Corps instructor Lt. Frederick Nelson mounted a stationary .30-cal. machine gun on a de Havilland DH-4. With one wing dipped during a pylon turn, and peering through a strut-mounted sight, Nelson was able to concentrate fire on a ground target. The French gave it a try in 1932 by mounting a fixed side-firing Schneider P.D. 12 75mm cannon to a four-engine Bordelaise A.B. 22 bomber. Ironically, the A.B. 22 was slated for use in France's colonial territories including Vietnam—then called Indochina. In 1939, Capt. Carl Crane proposed the tactic in an Army Air Corps Tactical School research paper, but the idea garnered little interest.

In April 1942, 1st Lt. Gilmour C. McDonald of the 95th Coast Artillery (AA) proposed fitting light aircraft with a side-firing machine gun to give Civil Air Patrol pilots an edge when they hunted submarines off the U.S. coastline. McDonald reasoned that a side-firing aircraft in a pylon turn could keep a surfaced sub under fire, not only preventing the vessel's crew from manning their guns, but eliminating the loss of precious time by repositioning for another strafing pass. McDonald persisted, and three years later wrote the Research and Development Service Sub-Office proposing the installation of a side-firing bazooka in light aircraft. Again, nothing came of the idea.

Never having lost confidence, years later McDonald saw President Kennedy's 1961 counterinsurgency directive as an opportunity to re-submit his idea. In September 1961, he sent his proposal entitled "Transverse Firing of Rockets and Guns," to the Air Force Systems Command limited war program. Since the limited war panel was actively soliciting ideas, McDonald's follow-up submission explaining the advantages of flying a banked circle while firing guns spurred a short test program with a liaison aircraft at Eglin AFB, Florida. Although the project fizzled, McDonald's enthusiasm did not.

Later that year, at Eglin, McDonald met Ralph E. Flexman, an assistant chief engineer with Bell Aerosystems. Flexman closely monitored limited war projects with which his company was becoming involved. He took special interest in South American missionary Nate Saint's air delivery of mail and supplies to remote villages. While flying a tight pylon turn, Saint lowered a rope with a weighted pouch, which remained over a point on the ground. Flexman imagined that a stream of fire from a banked aircraft's stationary gun would mimic the straight line of a rope. Hearing of McDonald's proposal for side-firing aircraft was all the encouragement Flexman needed to enlighten his colleagues at Bell.

In late December 1962, Flexman sent a letter to Dr. Gordon A. Eckstrand of the Behavioral Sciences Laboratory, Wright-Patterson AFB, Ohio, explaining the combat effectiveness of a side-firing aircraft in a pylon turn. Flexman then passed the letter to his friend, Air Force Capt. John C. Simons. Enthused by the concept, Simons in April 1963 forwarded Flexman's outline to the Aerospace Medical Research Laboratory (AMRL) at Wright-Patterson. Familiar with limited war studies, but assuming its stance of critical analysis, AMRL officials questioned the dispersion of projectiles, the ability of a pilot to keep the target under fire, and the time required to execute the pylon turn when a target appeared. Such were fair questions that Flexman had already considered. When Simon's supervisors presented the idea to weapon and ballistics experts of the Aeronautical Systems Division (ASD), they rejected it as unsound, explaining that bullet drop would result in an inaccurate firing pattern. In response, Flexman cited a published report by Bell Engineer Dr. W.H.T. Loh, which outlined computer-produced equations proving the feasibility of bullet trajectory from an aircraft flying a pylon turn. Simons, meanwhile, firm in his conviction, asked the Army Ballistics Lab to study the dispersal pattern of side-firing guns. Simons' independent course of action did not sit well with his supervisors, and he was told not to get involved with weapons.

Undaunted and encouraged by his boss, Dr. Julian Christensen, along with ASD pilots Captains J.D. Boren and J.A. Birt, Simons asked ASD officials for a nine-month study, using a T-28 aircraft to personally test all aspects of the concept. Although the Air Force denied Simons' request, they named the study *Project Tailchaser*, an obvious expression of their view of the futility of the endeavor. Dismissing the insincere moniker, one of Simons' supportive supervisors gave Simons a T-28 to fly sighting tests, which he masked by flying other test flights.

In June 1963, Capt. John C. Simons flew sighting missions in North American T-28As to test the side-firing concept later adopted for all fixed-wing gunships. This T-28A, S/N 49-1495, wears the emblem of the Air Force Systems Command to which it was assigned in 1963. (Duane Kasulka via Stephen Miller)

In June 1963, with test pilot Capt. Harley Johnson in the rear seat of his T-28, Simons flew sighting missions from Wright-Patterson AFB. Using only a grease pencil mark on his canopy, Simons found that he could easily keep his target in a fixed point as he flew a pylon turn. Air Force officials kept their distance, allowing Simons free reign, even giving him a Convair C-131 to test lateral sighting from a cargo-type aircraft. His first flight, with Capt. Boren as copilot, convinced Simon that cargo aircraft could indeed keep a target in the crosshairs and saturate it with fire. He was also convinced, along with ballistics experts, that the bullet drop problem could be solved by using high velocity guns no smaller than .30-cal. Next, SSgt. Estell P. Bunch, of the medical research laboratory, worked with Simons to create a frame for holding gun sight components.

The momentum continued. Next, a fixed sight and three cameras were installed in a C-131B. A camera in the cockpit filmed the pilot's sight picture; another simulated a gun position in the cargo area; a third showed a test instrument panel. A follow-up camera installation recorded the pilot's line of sight and three guns, but the test summary was given a low priority and shelved. During the following seven months, only two check flights were made. Hundreds of planned test hours slipped away, and some of the project members, including Simons, were called back to their original assignments. Simons selected 1st Lt. Edwin Sasaki to fill in, and project pilot Capt. Edwin J. Hatzenbuehler was replaced by Maj. Richard M. Gough. The *Tailchaser* team remained confident, knowing that the concept's acceptance hinged on live-fire tests.

And so it went until Capt. Ronald W. Terry showed up. Terry had been a fighter pilot and equally important was his ability to work the bureaucratic system, steering around those who would say no. He was a perfect fit for the project, having a common-sense approach and brimming with ambition.

Ralph D. Kimberlin, then a 2nd Lt. with the Air Force Systems Command Laboratory, Research Technology Division at Eglin, picks up the story:

Vice President Hubert H. Humphrey is briefed on the minigun system by Test Project Officer 1st Lt. Ralph Kimberlin. Humphrey made a surprise visit to Eglin's sprawling facility on 31 October 1966. (U.S. Air Force/Ralph Kimberlin Collection)

The weathered condition of this Douglas AC-47D belies its capability as an effective gunship. Like a number of AC-47Ds, this aircraft would be lost to enemy ground fire during the war in Southeast Asia. Most Spookies wore the last three numbers of their serial number on the oil cooler scoop below the engine accessory section. This FC-47D's full serial number is 43-48356. The "FC" designation itself would be short-lived. (U.S. Air Force/Charles Boatwright Collection)

At the Air Proving Ground Center at Eglin AFB, an F-100D, S/N 55-3706, was used for testing the original SUU-11/A minigun pod. Here, in 1964, it undergoes static firing using a jack stand to stabilize the Super Saber. Engineering Test and Development of the first minigun included high-G test and functional tests on the F-100D. John F. Harvell, who nurtured the weapon through its development, flew the F-100D, firing the gun at 6 gs. (U.S. Air Force/John F. Harvell Collection)

"Not being a fighter pilot, Project Officer Lt. Sasaki enlisted Capt. Terry of the Cargo Test Branch at Wright-Patterson—at that time the Air Force maintained Fighter, Cargo, and Bomber test branches at Wright-Patterson, as well as at Edwards AFB. Capt. Terry had recently returned from an AFSC fact-finding trip to Vietnam. He immediately recognized the value of the concept for applying fire on a ground target from a circling aircraft, which could remain at high enough altitude to be above the effective range of any ground fire from small arms."

Kimberlin describes what followed as the birth of the real *Terry and the Pirates*:

"On a Friday afternoon about 3:00 pm, Terry and a crew of people from Wright-Patterson arrived at Eglin unannounced wanting to install a gun on the C-131 and fire it at some targets. I was one of the few test project engineers who had a gun in test at the time. It was the prototype SUU-11/A 7.62mm Minigun Pod which was intended for under-wing carriage on counterinsurgency aircraft. However, it was in ground test on Eglin's Range 22, mounted in a welded angle-iron stand, which held a bomb rack that supported the gun for ground firing. After considerable hand wringing and a miniscule amount of paperwork, it was decided that we could mount the gun in the C-131 by bolting the angle-iron stand to a cargo pallet and insert this in the cargo door.

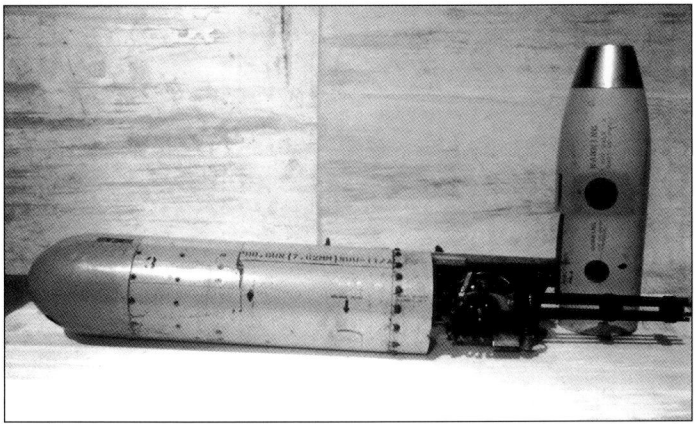

The 7.62mm minigun pod. A removable forward fairing, which provided access to the unit's GAU-2 gun, was left off the pod for the lateral firing installation. This early unit is marked as an SUU-11/A, which later became SUU-11A/A. (Ralph Kimberlin)

One of the prototype miniguns pallet-mounted in the C-131B at Eglin AFB. A standard trash can strapped to the gun's frame was first used to catch spent shell casings. The large upward-opening door would be removed for the flight test. (Ralph Kimberlin)

Aboard the C-131B, the minigun was attached to its original ground test frame with a standard 14-inch bomb rack. The frame was of welded steel construction. (Ralph Kimberlin)

When C-47s went through Air International in Miami, Florida, for conversion to gunships, standard Mk 20 Mod 4 gunsights were installed. A camera is mounted behind the pilot's seat in this AC-47D. (U.S. Air Force)

"However, land range time at Eglin was hard to get and after much argument we were able to arrange for a water range with a square raft as a target. After working through most of the weekend, we were able to put together a firing mission over the water. The missions were a resounding success.

"Ron Terry had been a general's aide and knew the commanding general at Eglin. The general was driving near Range 22 and saw Ron walking and stopped to pick him up. Ron, who missed his calling as an Evangelist preacher or a used car salesman, proceeded to tell the general about the project, and before we knew it, several high-ranking officers from the 1st Combat Applications Group (a tenant organization involved with counterinsurgency) were flying with us on the firing missions. One was Lt. Col. O'Brien. He was quite impressed and asked if a side-firing system could be installed in a C-47 or a C-123, as these were the only aircraft that were then allowed in Vietnam under the rules of engagement. This was all Terry needed. He immediately organized a return to Wright-Patterson, with me in tow, to fashion systems for C-47s and C-123s.

"Back at Wright-Patterson, again with much hand-wringing and little paperwork, a C-47 was set up behind screens (for secrecy)

The first C-47 used by Ron Terry and his team at Eglin AFB in 1964. First used for lateral sighting tests, serial number 43-48462 became the first minigun-armed AC-47. It would later serve the 4th Air Commando Squadron in Vietnam, where it was lost on 23 March 1967. (via Larry Davis)

Capt. Ron Terry and his team was named "Terry and the Pirates." Shortly after he began sighting tests with number 462, the nickname was applied to the aircraft. The lateral sight mount is visible in the pilot's window opening. Above the doorway, through which air conditioning is being pumped, is the emblem of the Air Force Systems Command. (Jack Morris via Larry Davis)

The prototype FC-47 in Vietnam, S/N 44-76558, which flew the first minigun missions in combat. Like all aircraft of the 1st ACS at Bien Hoa AB, Vietnamese Air Force insignia was worn to give the impression that U.S. forces served only in a training capacity. The practice ceased in August 1965 when the U.S. Air Force assumed a more active combat role. (Ralph Kimberlin)

in the hangar that now serves as the Air Force Museum Annex. The modification shops were charged with designing and fabricating the mounts for three miniguns that were going to be installed in the C-47—no C-123s were available at Wright-Patterson for the modification. The mounts that were fashioned were essentially the same as the welded angle-iron mount used in the original test, except these were fashioned from aluminum, which was riveted together. The sight for this prototype remained the camera viewfinder used in the original tests.

"Once the C-47 installation was complete, the aircraft and test crew returned to Eglin AFB for firing tests. The returning crew was not as large as the original crew on the C-131. It included Capt. Terry, Lt. Sasaki, me, T.Sgt. Thomas Ritter, our aerial photographer, and S.Sgt. Bunch. Upon arrival at Eglin, the team was joined by A1C James H. Schmeisser and A3C Alan W. Sims, armorers who had been working on the SUU-11/A test program.

"Since the guns required initial harmonizing with the gun sight, Kenneth Cobb of the Ballistics Group of ASD's Detachment 4 made the calculations and the guns were harmonized with the sight at Range 22. Firing missions were then conducted at Eglin Range 5 using mannequin and truck targets that were being used for fixed-wing minigun tests. In addition, mannequins that simulated a Viet Cong squad were placed in a wooded area and firing runs were made against them. Test results showed that a three-second burst from the three miniguns placed one 7.62mm round in every 2 square feet over an area several hundred square feet."

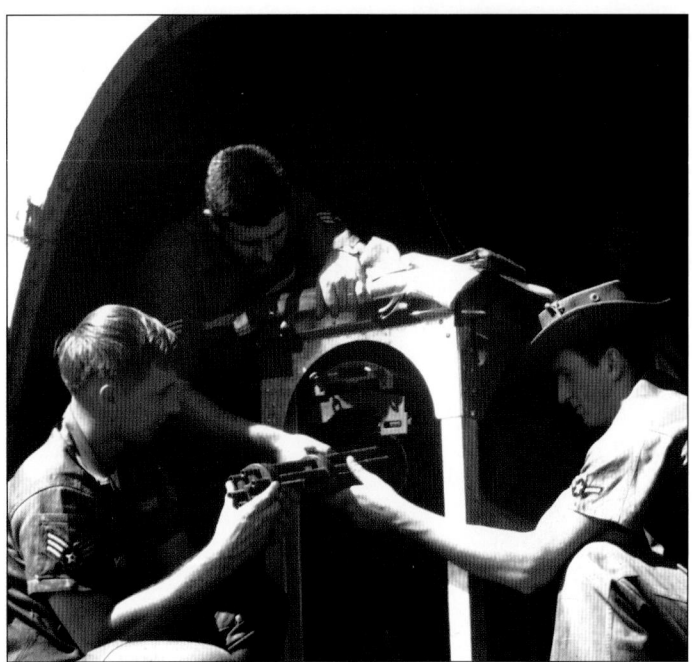

From left to right, A1C Ron Snyder, A1C James Schmeisser, and A3C Allan Sims work with a minigun in FC-47D serial number 43-48471 at Tan Son Nhut Air Base. The minigun is secured into the first mount used for combat evaluation. (U.S. Air Force via Larry Davis)

The original AC-47D test team, known as "Terry's Pirates." Left to right are SSgt. Bunch, A3C Sims, Capt. Terry, TSgt. Ritter, Lt. Sasaki, A1C Schmeisser, and Lt. Kimberlin. While in Vietnam, the team drew upon the 1st Air Commando Squadron (ACS) for aircraft and support. (Ralph Kimberlin)

Capt. Ron Terry and TSgt. Ritter share a light moment amid crates of Mk 6 flares at Bien Hoa Air Base. The FC-47 in the background was serial number 43-48472 of the 1st Air Commando Squadron in Vietnam. (Ralph Kimberlin)

The original gunsight for the C-47 was fashioned from a camera viewfinder. This sight was used on the prototype aircraft and the first three gunships in Vietnam. (U.S. Air Force)

This simplified riveted-aluminum minigun mount served as the standard for FC/AC-47Ds. The mount was installed in the first batch of gunships converted by Air International. (U.S. Air Force via Larry Davis)

Staff officers are shown the minigun's loading mechanism aboard an FC-47. Ammunition is being fed from containers acquired from the U.S. Navy. (U.S. Air Force)

The SUU-11A/A minigun units were 8 feet long, leaving little room for crew movement in the AC-47D's cabin. Ammunition containers are secured to the center floor area, and 24 flares are visible near the aft bulkhead. Ballistic curtains were used liberally along the aircraft's left side since the gun side was more often exposed to ground fire. (U.S. Air Force)

Early minigun mounts were not adjustable to depress the weapon. Later mounts featured level front sections, while their rear sections were adjustable and used spacer blocks for gun depression. An empty ammunition container was secured in front of the gun to collect spent cartridges. Belted ammunition was stored in cans secured to the gun mount. (U.S. Air Force)

The tests at Eglin, which the ASD's Limited War Office had assigned a FAST COIN priority, involved both the C-131 and a C-47, the latter having three SUU-11/A guns installed. Twelve missions were flown, six per aircraft, with a total of 47,000 rounds fired. With successful testing of the C-47 gunship complete, the unapproved project entered a hold status—it had never been officially approved by the Air Force.

Kimberlin continues:

"Shortly after completion of the tests, the Air Force came under criticism for its lack of counterinsurgency efforts—remember that we had just emerged from the policy of massive retaliation, where the Strategic Air Command had been preeminent. Air Force Systems Command was casting for new ideas to present to the Air Staff, so the commanding general of the ASD scheduled Ron Terry, Ed Sasaski, and Tom Ritter to brief the Air Staff on the side-firing project.

"The briefing of Air Force Chief of Staff Gen. Curtis LeMay occurred on 2 November 1964, the morning after the first Viet Cong mortar attack on Bien Hoa Air Base, which killed four U.S. soldiers and destroyed nine aircraft. Gen. LeMay was livid about the attack. He was so hot he was eating his famous cigars. When Ron Terry finished his briefing, during which he prudently emphasized base defense, the general asked how many miniguns existed. At the time there were nine pre-production prototypes. When LeMay heard this, his response was, 'Send three C-47s.' And we were off! Shortly thereafter, I, along with A1C Schmeisser and A3C Sims received teletype orders signed by the Chief of Staff to report to Travis AFB, California, within three days for transport to the Republic of Vietnam for a combat evaluation of the side-firing concept. We now had an Air

Force–approved project. The tests were successful and Terry now had all his pirates.

"At Travis we were joined by Capt. Ron Terry, Lt. Sasaki, TSgt. Riter, and SSgt. Bunch. Six miniguns, nine mounts, and 200,000 rounds of 7.62mm ammunition followed on two C-124s. Three miniguns were already in Vietnam being tested on the A-37A by the 1st Combat Applications Group."

The Gooney

The Douglas DC-3/C-47 needs no introduction, having become the most prominent and influential aircraft in the history of aviation. Durability, ruggedness, and versatility are but a few of the accolades bestowed upon the airplane throughout its long life. Conceived as a result of competition in the airline industry during the 1930s, the DC-3 became the catalyst that revolutionized that industry and allowed it to prosper.

The C-47, military version of the DC-3, began earning high marks as early as 1938 during the Spanish Civil War. From then on it would serve in every theatre of war during the twentieth century, and it continues to serve in trouble spots across the globe today. Known as the Skytrain—and the Dakota outside of the U.S.—during World War II the airplane was affectionately dubbed the "Gooney Bird," the meaning of which is anyone's guess.

The DC-3 began life as the DC-1 to satisfy a specification submitted to Douglas by Trans Continental & Western Airlines. Competing with Boeing's Model 247, Douglas flew its DC-1 for the first time on 1 July 1933, five months after Boeing's maiden flight. Douglas soon offered an improved version called the DC-2 and orders began coming in from air carriers, with the first military variant, the R2D-1, going to the U.S. Navy in 1934. Although the DC-2

The first FC-47Ds that saw service in Vietnam retained their original color schemes prior to the introduction of camouflage. Number 43-48471 is seen here at Bien Hoa AB in 1965 armed with the ad hoc M-2 .30-cal. gun package. (U.S. Air Force)

To accommodate the ten-gun .30-cal. package, holes were simply cut in the rear section of the C-47's cargo door for four of the weapons. In the container behind the guns are spare parts for in-flight repair. (U.S. Air Force)

enjoyed the lion's share of airline operation, it had shortcomings, which sent Douglas designers back to their drawing boards. The result was the larger, faster, longer-range DC-3, which first flew on 17 December 1935. Barely able to keep up with orders, Douglas opened several new plants. More than 400 were ordered by the big names in U.S. air travel, and in September 1940, the U.S. Army Air Corps placed its first order for 545 Skytrains, the first example of which rolled off the production line in January 1942. Soon military variants fell under an encyclopedic array of designations in conjunction with their myriad functions. The C-47 was also built under license in Japan, and the USSR produced more than 2,000 of its own version called the Li-2.

When the U.S. Air Force came into being in September 1947, the list of sub-types grew even longer. A Super DC-3 was introduced in 1950. With improved aerodynamic features and more powerful engines, Douglas hoped that airline companies would upgrade their DC-3s with the new design. But the airlines sought newer and larger aircraft, and only 100 Super DC-3s were built for the U.S. Navy as R4D-8s, later called C-117Ds. Although the designation AC-47D is typically associated with Vietnam War–era gunships, it was first used beginning in the late 1940s to identify C-47s modified by Hayes for airways checks. Assigned to the Airways and Air Communication Service of the Military Air Transport Service (MATS), AC-47Ds were distinguished by a nose radome and other communications equipment. They were later re-designated EC-47Ds, with the AC-47D designation given to the gunship version. That designation, which stands for "Attack, Cargo," remains probably the most contrasting and unusual aircraft designation used by the Air Force.

Generally, the C-47 was powered by a pair of Pratt & Whitney R-1830 Twin Wasp, 14-cylinder radial engines. Their 1,200 horsepower (each) gave the aircraft a maximum speed of 224 mph; cruise speed was 160 mph. The C-47's maximum takeoff weight was 31,000 pounds, and it had a range of 1,600 miles. Its service ceiling was 26,400 feet. Having a payload of 6,000 pounds, normally a crew of three and 28 troops could be carried. The DC-3's long admired features are its robust airframe and ease of maintenance. Although the exact number of DC-3s and C-47s built probably will never be determined, the most accurate published total exceeds 10,600 airframes, with production ending in 1946. Even more impressive, perhaps, is that several hundred of these aircraft are still flying today, still earning a profit for their operators more than 70 years after its inception.

The Gun

Although the C-47 aircraft and its adaptation as a gunship have, deservedly, received ample coverage in print, published material recounting the development of the gun system itself is limited.

When Richard J. Gatling patented his multi-barrel, rapid-firing gun in 1862, he couldn't possibly have imagined the impact his invention would have on future weapons development and airpower. Since Gatling's gun was long before its time, only rudimentary adaptations would follow. The concept finally came to fruition many years later. In 1960 the conglomerate General Electric (GE) began studies of Gatling's design, and by 1962 had designed, tested, and built a basic electric-powered weapon. U.S. Air Force officials were interested enough to award GE a contract for prototypes. The success of the

Makeshift mounts and ammunition feed systems were used to complete the .30-cal. gun installation. The vintage Brownings proved troublesome and crews were happy to have them replaced with miniguns. (U.S. Air Force)

The window installation of the interim .30-cal. gun system. The gun feed tray covers are in the open position, and cooling vents, which were found to be ineffective, are visible in the window openings near the barrels. (U.S. Air Force)

first live-firing of the gun in December 1962 provided the impetus for increased research and development that resulted in a wide range of weapons. Concurrent testing was done by Army and Air Force weapons labs whose directorates envisioned aerial applications of Gatling-type guns.

Every subject seems to have a master, and for the Gatling gun that is John F. Harvell. Having flown jet interceptors following graduation from the Naval Academy, Harvell continued his education at the Air Force Institute of Technology and M.I.T. After graduation, he worked on the GAM-87 Skybolt program before being assigned to conduct the Engineering Development Tests on the new 7.62mm gun pod intended for use on counterinsurgency aircraft. The pod was the SUU-11/A incorporating the GAU-2 Gatling gun. Harvell conducted not only the Engineering Development Test, but the Prototype Tests and Production First Article Tests for the SUU-11/A.

With a perspective that could come only from someone with first-hand experience, Harvell provides insight into his involvement with the gun:

"In the early 1960s, since the great powers could not afford direct confrontation, they chose, instead, to conduct proxy wars of insurgency and counterinsurgency. Conventional munitions development had been starved for funding during the mid to late '50s as the nation sought to build up their nuclear arsenals and the means to deliver nuclear weapons. As counterinsurgency began to receive renewed emphasis in the early '60s, there was a flurry of new developments for conventional weapons to be used on both U.S. and Allied COIN aircraft, such as the T-28D, the B-26, and later, the AT-37.

"Detachment 2 of Aeronautical Systems Division was a tenant at Eglin AFB and was the development agency for conventional weapons to be used on USAF aircraft. The Air Proving Ground Center (APGC) was the owning agency for Eglin AFB and its land and water test ranges. The mission of APGC was conventional munitions testing.

"Bill Aumen, a civil servant, was the Program Manager at Det 2 for the development of the SUU-11/A gun pod. This was conceived as an under-wing store for any aircraft with a 14-inch bomb rack, 28-volt dc power, and a trigger signal. This encompassed all U.S.-derived aircraft used for counterinsurgency, and most European-derived aircraft. The weapon used in the SUU-11/A was the GAU-2, a high-performance machine gun using the NATO-standard 7.62mm cartridge, later to be known as the minigun.

"After the demise of the GAM-87 program in early 1963 I was assigned to the Munitions Test Directorate of APGC, initially to participate in the competitive tests of the SUU-16A and the Mark 4 20mm gun pods. When those were concluded in late 1963 or early 1964, I was reassigned to become the Test Project Engineer for the SUU-11/A. Test Project Engineers were responsible for defining, securing and scheduling all of the assets needed for their projects as well as actually conducting the tests. This included test item instrumentation, aircraft instrumentation, and range instrumentation, any needed aircraft modifications, data reduction support, and test report writing. Of course, most of this was available cafeteria-style from APGC assets, but it still required a great deal of day-to-day effort to keep everything moving smoothly, as well as a substantial amount of insight into

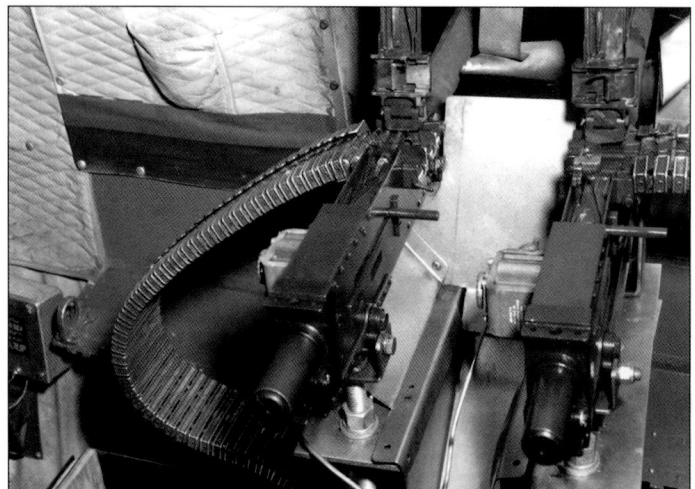

Interior view of the breech assemblies of window-mounted M-2s. Initially, flexible ammunition feed belts, like those used on U.S. Army Huey helicopters, were tried, but with less-than-favorable results. Army aviation experts were often consulted, in view of their extensive involvement with helicopter gunships. (U.S. Air Force)

Various types of wind spoilers were tried to direct gun smoke and gasses away from window openings. These experimental units had ports that directed wind blast through flexible tubes to cool the guns. Although the product of sound engineering, they did little to prevent the guns from overheating. (U.S. Air Force)

the inter-relationships of the various functions at APGC. I can honestly say that was the most fun I had in my Air Force career. I was largely my own boss, I got to do a lot of flying, I was able to do a good job, and nobody argued that I had to change anything for political reasons.

"The SUU-11/A was composed of, from front to back, an aerodynamic fairing containing the gun, a feed system alongside and behind the gun, an ammunition drum containing 1,500 rounds, which was also part of the feed system, and a Ni-Cad battery and associated charging and control circuitry. The pod was essentially a high-speed ammunition-processing machine. It did not care whether a round fired or not; it would keep on pumping rounds through the system as long as the trigger was depressed. Operating power was provided by a three-horsepower dc electric motor about the size of a small motorcycle starter. Overall the pod was about 12 inches in diameter, 8 feet long, and weighed about 200 pounds empty and 800 pounds fully loaded. It was designed to survive 8 gs and to function at 6 gs. I flew the initial high-G tests in the F-100 and it did, indeed, fire at 6 gs, although it slowed down above 4 gs.

"The GAU-2 can best be thought of as six bolt-action rifles back-to-back in a single assembly. The bolts each had a ball bearing cam follower riding in a cam machined into the housing, which operated the bolt. At the most forward position the bolt head stopped and a cam on the bolt caused the head to rotate and lock for firing. A firing pin within the bolt was cocked and released by a tang on the firing pin at the appropriate places in the cycle. A removable section of the housing contained the firing portions of the main cam and could be removed to safe the gun.

"The nominal firing rate was 6,000 rounds per minute, and the entire system was supposed to reach that rate within the first second. Realize that this meant that it was necessary to accelerate not only the gun, but also all of the elements of the feed system, and up to 600 pounds of ammunition to that feed rate within one second! It was a mechanical engineering tour-de-force. You can only fire as fast as you can feed and control the ammunition. One of the nice things about the minigun was the recoil adapters. These were basically tuned shock absorbers, so that when the gun was firing it just sat back against the recoil adapters and dithered. The effect was just to provide a pretty steady push rather than a cyclic recoil that could rattle your teeth.

"The Engineering Test Unit (ETU) was the first Minigun and the first pod. Bill Aumen had wanted to develop a system that was driven by gun gasses bled off the barrels and avoid the battery and electric motor, but that idea foundered on problems with fouling from the combustion products. For that reason the ETU was perceived as a fallback unit intended to demonstrate a concept rather than a final configuration. In the end, the gun gas drive never could be made to work reliably and the ETU was actually fairly representative of the first production units. GE, Burlington, Vermont, was the contractor that developed the SUU-11/A, and of course all of the M-61 20mm applications.

"The Engineering Development Tests included a fair amount of static firing from a ground stand, and a small number of functional tests on the F-100. We also did an air-to-ground demonstration with the F-100 which didn't really prove much. Most of the testing was static performance and reliability testing at Range 22. This did establish that the pod actually worked pretty well.

This FC-47D, S/N 43-48491, was one of three armed with ten .30-cal. guns due to a minigun shortage. This early *Spooky* was assigned to the 1st ACS at Bien Hoa AB in 1965. Visible above the wing leading edge is a locally fabricated wind baffle at the gun window. Incorporated in 491's nose art are the words, "Git Em Bullit." (U.S. Air Force)

The early minigun installation in an FC-47 in 1965. Void of markings, this aircraft appears to have been prepared for fresh paint. The rear cargo door section remained operable since it was the only means of boarding and loading the aircraft. (U.S. Air Force)

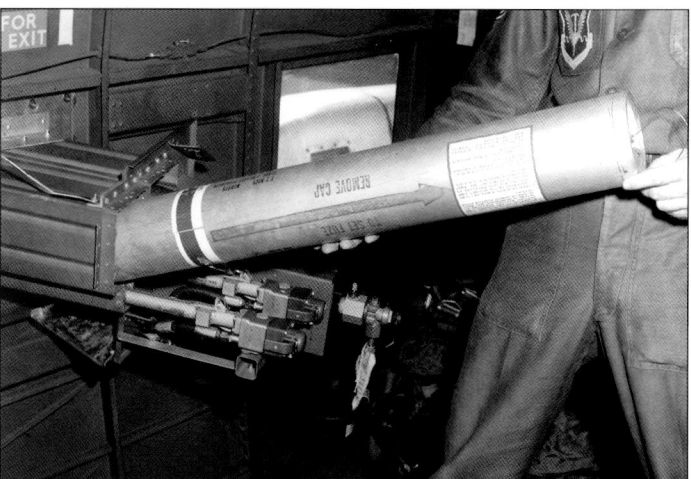

This view of an early gunship shows the extent to which the flare launcher protruded from a forward window position. The modification was short-lived since flares launched with this device often struck the horizontal stabilizer. The launcher was relocated to the wing root area; however, both designs were soon abandoned. Crews found it easier to stand in the cargo doorway and throw the flares with their arming lanyards attached to the aircraft. The Gooney's drab paint scheme was reminiscent of its use in two previous wars. (U.S. Air Force)

A flare-launch capability for the C-47 was developed concurrently with the gun systems. The Gary Corporation was contracted to produce this launcher, which used an actuator mechanism obtained from U.S. Navy stocks. The actuator, called a Pogo Stick, fired the flares too fast and often prematurely. The device, which was first installed in 1965, was removed following an incident in which a flare deployed as soon as it was launched, catching on the horizontal stabilizer. The AC-47 landed at a commercial airport dragging the flare. (U.S. Air Force/Doug Blair Collection)

When the window-mounted flare launcher proved unsuccessful, it was relocated to the aircraft's wing root as seen here. Arrows point to the three minigun pods. Seldom were the cargo door sections seen here installed with a minigun mounted in the doorway. (U.S. Air Force via John F. Harvell)

This interior view of the flare launcher's wing root installation shows the flare-loading port near floor level. Although this modification eliminated the hazard of flares striking tail surfaces, crewmen found it difficult to load the bulky flare canisters at this level. A modification that moved the doorway mounted minigun farther forward cleared the cargo doorway from which flares were thrown by the loadmaster. (U.S. Air Force via John F. Harvell)

Fabricated in unit shops, spoilers helped direct wind away from window openings, thereby preventing gun smoke and gasses from being blown into the cabin. (U.S. Air Force)

All of the test requirements were pretty well verified and the reliability was better that virtually any machine gun system in that caliber range.

"By the time the Prototype Tests came around, Bill Aumen had pretty well accepted the idea that the gun gas drive was not feasible and the prototype units had a production electrical package that was substantially more robust than the ETU. The rest of the pod was very much like the ETU. We subjected the prototypes to environmental testing like sand and dust, salt spray, and low and high temperature testing in the Armament Strato-Chamber. It passed most of these with flying colors, but the testing at 70 degrees below zero did a real number on the battery (as we expected) although it did fire, just very slowly. We found that if we energized the field of the motor from an external source (like aircraft power) it would fire more or less normally, but using the battery it was less than marginal. Eglin borrowed a T-33 from the Air Force Weapons School to use as a test platform and we subjected two prototype pods to higher gs than we could safely do with other aircraft, even the F-100. We also did some weapons effects testing against simulated personnel and light vehicles in an air-to-ground mode. We also greatly extended our reliability and maintainability testing on the ground stand.

"For the Production Acceptance Tests we had eight units to play with. We were able to work with the Air Commandos at Hurlburt to use the YAT-28 and the YAT-37 as test platforms, in

The original "Puff," FC-47D, S/N 43-48579, in late 1964. (Michael L. Custance)

addition to the T-33, since they were conducting tests of those air-frames as potential COIN vehicles at the same time. We greatly expanded our weapons effectiveness tests, firing up to six gun pods simultaneously against ground targets. A good time was had by all. Thirty-six thousand rounds per minute is very impressive, particularly with tracer ammunition. We also verified that the production pods worked as well as the prototype units in environmental testing and further expanded our reliability and maintainability database.

"Through all of the testing, Bill Aumen was very interested in having as many people exposed to his baby as possible, so any time someone was looking for a weapon to fire from some type of air vehicle we ended up doing at least a fit check of the pod on their airframe. In addition, we had a firing demonstration on the Army's OV-1 Mohawk out over the water, and a more extensive test series on the Canadian CL-41G, including some air-to-ground work. Interestingly, the Canadians concluded that the firing pattern of the two pods on the CL-41G was too tight. Bill also took a pod to hang on an Army helicopter. And, of course, we got called when some crazy captain from ASD wanted something to shoot out the side of a C-131.

"Ron Terry was a project manager in the multi-engine branch at ASD. He had managed to convince someone there to let him conduct some lateral sighting tests with one of their air-

Later versions of the MXU-470/A minigun module had their flexible-casing ejection chutes attached to the left side of the drum cover. Visible on the gun in the foreground, minus its control box, are jack screws attaching the gun to its stand. The adjustable screws allowed boresighting adjustments of plus-3 degrees in azimuth, and plus-3 to plus-18 degrees in elevation. (Robert Stein)

planes. He installed a gun sight with a camera adjacent to the pilot's seat of a C-131 and rigged a trigger to operate the gun camera. He then flew a couple of missions to evaluate his ability to track a ground target by flying a pylon turn around that point and recorded the results on the gun camera film. He used that film and a pretty good song-and-dance routine to promote the next phase of testing, which involved actually shooting at something out the side of the airplane. He was even able to get a pretty high priority so that it cut through some of the bureaucratic delays that normally accompany any test project.

"The test setup was pretty simple. We used our ground test stand, which was just a welded angle iron assembly with a 14-inch bomb rack bolted to it to support and stabilize the pod. None of the ground stand components aligned with the floor beams so we had to fasten the ground stand to an aluminum cargo pallet, and then fasten the pallet to the floor beams so the gun could fire out through the bailout door at the rear of the passenger compartment. Then we had to wire the airplane to provide 28 volts at 15 amps to charge the pod battery, and to provide a trigger circuit.

"Because of Ron's priority we were able to compress a review process that normally took about three months to around two weeks. We had to get mechanical and electrical drawings made of the installation, get the Class 2 Mod engineers to buy off on the structural and safety aspects of the mod, get the Class 2 mod shop to actually modify the airplane and test rig, conduct ground firing tests for function and boresight geometry, get the test plan approved by all and sundry including Range Safety, and find something to shoot at. Since no one had any confidence in where the rounds might actually go, it was decided to conduct the test on one of the water ranges where the only ones we could hurt would be ourselves. There was an old barge moored in one of the water ranges that was ideal for the purpose, so we used that.

"The Air Force was kind of funny about letting people fly as crew members. None of our munitions maintenance people were on flying status, so that's how I became the first lateral-firing gun mechanic. It also helped that I flew with Test Ops and was familiar with all of the procedures to check in with Mission Control and get cleared on and off the ranges.

"It was a typical gorgeous Florida day when we flew the tests, not even a significant haze. It was so bright that we couldn't see the tracers against the water. On the other hand we could see the splashes very well. They really stood out against the blue-green of the Gulf. Ron wanted to try two basic tactics. The first was to fly low alongside the target and just walk the firing pattern along the target. The second was the pylon turn tactic which was done from a higher altitude and concentrated the fire in a relatively small area. Ron was able to hit the barge with no difficulty using either tactic, but the fly-by technique would have been considerably more hazardous and harder to execute in the hills and jungles of Vietnam. I think we flew only the one mission during that phase, but that was enough to get Ron off and running."

Eventually, the podded minigun came in three versions; the SUU-11A/A was capable of firing only at a rate of 6,000 rounds per minute, while the SUU-11B/A had a variable firing rate of 3,000 or 6,000 rounds per minute. Since the Army did not appreciate the rate at which the minigun ate up ammunition, its system, labeled XM-18, had a lower adjustable rate of 2,000 or 4,000 rounds per minute. All of these pods used the GAU-2B/A gun, which was an improvement over the prototype by having an improved motor and heavy-duty barrels. The muzzle velocity of the 7.62mm projectile is 2,850 feet per second, and it has a maximum effective slant range of 7,000 feet.

Reflecting on some of the sidelights of his involvement with the gun, John Harvell notes:

"Bill Aumen never missed a chance to market his product so he would hang them on anything where it would physically fit. The pods were fairly light and two or three guys could hang them on anything they could reach. Bill often had the local GE rep throw a couple of pods in the back of his station wagon and hare off somewhere to show them off. Now, Homeland Security and BATF would have a cow!

"Another sidelight; because my gun pods were both spectacular and completely unclassified, I was often called upon to brief visiting firemen. Two of these stand out in my mind. Barry Goldwater and Jimmy Stewart were both USAF Reserve generals and they both had their two weeks of annual active duty at Eglin while I was there, so I got to brief them both. I briefed General Goldwater in the command conference room. General Stewart came down to Range 22 while we were conducting extended parts life testing on the production pods. I gave him the dollar tour and offered to let him fire out the pod, but he demurred so I went ahead and hosed-off about a 1,000-round burst to empty the pod. I'm not sure he realized that we were just trying to get as many rounds fired as we could for parts life testing instead of putting on a show, especially for the brass. He gave exactly the same impression that he does in the movies; quiet, earnest, slow-talking."

Harvell continues about the follow-on work with the minigun:

"After the C-131 test was completed, we didn't hear much from Ron for a while. Then one day he showed up with a C-47 rigged up with a lateral sight and ten .30-cal. machine guns set up to fire out the windows on the left side of the aircraft. These were set up in three grouped mounts. He flew some tests over the land ranges this time but his testing was limited because of the fire hazard on the ranges that year; it had been very dry. The guns did not work out terribly well. They required a lot of personnel support in flight because they didn't have anything but a standard belt feed and they couldn't put too many segments on a belt without causing problems with belt whip, which causes jams.

"We were part way through our production acceptance tests at the time, so we had a total of eight pods at Eglin. Ron decided

to have miniguns, so we ended up losing three of our production pods and some spare parts to him. This created another problem, however, because the SUU-11/A was not yet in the active inventory, and there was not any training for munitions maintenance technicians in its care and feeding. There were certain things the system demanded that were outside the usual 'gun plumbers' experience. That was when Ralph Kimberlin saved the day by volunteering to go along for the TDY tests in Vietnam to provide technical support in flight.

"The SUU-11/A provided unprecedented firepower for lateral firing, although it was not designed for that, being an underwing store. For one thing it was designed to dump the spent brass and cleared rounds overboard as they were fired. Three pods dumping 6,000 rounds per minute of spent brass on the floor of an airplane while people were trying to work around them was not a very good idea. They solved that problem using regular office trash cans positioned below the guns, as an interim solution. That worked, but they could get a buildup of gun gas in the trash cans from the spent casings, and they filled up quickly. We had a hand-crank reloader, which worked pretty well on an aircraft parking ramp between missions. Reloading the SUU-11/A in flight was a lot of work when you're expending more than 20,000 rounds on

For acceptance tests of the first MXU-470/A minigun modules conducted from February through May 1966, a window was added forward of the cabin doorway. Since the AC-47D had two floor planes, with their junction just forward of the cargo door, the modification placed the rear gun on the same plane as the other two. This simplified ground harmonization of the depressed guns. The change brought the added advantage of clearing the cabin doorway. Crewmen were grateful for the extra room for loading ammunition and for throwing flares. (U.S. Air Force)

The original installation of the MXU-470/A minigun modules in the AC-47D. The unit was 43 inches high and 34 inches long, including barrels. Its major components were a GAU-2B/A minigun, a MAU-81/A link-less feed system, a control box with control panel, and drum. The drum held 2,000 rounds, which were fed upward through spiraling feed trays. For module acceptance tests, the rear gun was moved forward with its barrels protruding through a newly cut window. (U.S. Air Force)

Although FC-47Ds became widely known as Puff, the Magic Dragon, shortly after their introduction into Vietnam, S/N 43-48579 was the only aircraft to wear the name. A more elaborate dragon appeared on Puff, seen here at Bien Hoa AB in February 1966. Gunship pilot Dick Noble adds, "Only one aircraft had the dragon painted on it. I recall a real brouhaha when the original Puff was handed over to the 14th ACS as a replacement aircraft, and the dragon was painted over with the camouflage design. Somehow, overnight the dragon reappeared on the nose. I believe it was allowed to stay." When Ron Terry selected this aircraft from the inventory of the 1st ACS for the minigun installation, it had been flying cargo runs from Nha Trang Air Base. (David W. Menard)

This AC-47D, S/N 44-77263, served as a training aircraft of the 4412th Combat Crew Training Squadron from 1967 to 1970. As such, it differed from combat aircraft, having troop seats in the cabin, what appears to be a leaflet chute on its lower right fuselage, and no FM homing antenna on the nose. In the forward window opening is a push-out smoke-clearing intake. On its fresh day-camouflage scheme, it wears the IG tail code of the 4412th CCTS, 1st Special Operations Wing at England AFB, Louisiana. In July 1969, the 4412th came under the 4410th Combat Crew Training Wing. (David W. Menard)

During the war in Southeast Asia, famed cartoonist Corky Trinidad documented in Stars and Stripes *the trials and tribulations of Spooky operations from both the Allied and enemy point of view.* (Corky Trinidad)

GUNSHIPS: THE STORY OF SPOOKY, SHADOW, STINGER AND SPECTRE

a mission. The SUU-11/A holds only 15 seconds worth of ammunition, which is pretty good for a forward-firing weapon, but when you're hosing down some bad guys with a near-continuous burst you use it up in a hurry. This meant a lot of reloading exercises while you were milling around in the dark, with a lot of smoke, and a lot of noise. Another problem was that the pod was 8 feet long. Even though we removed the fairing and stuck the barrels out the window, it still didn't leave much room to get around the pod in flight in the narrow confines of a C-47 cabin.

"All of these things got fed back to GE [General Electric], who whipped up a new feed system and mount expressly for the AC-47. Where the ammunition drum for the SUU-11/A was behind the gun and oriented along the length of the pod, the new system was 'folded' so that the ammunition drum was oriented vertically and situated below the gun. GE had to come up with a mounting scheme to react the firing loads without flexing, and carrying those loads down into the floor of the aircraft. They didn't have to operate at 6 gs, or survive at 8 gs, so the support structure could be lighter. The battery and electronics were mounted at floor level, and they came up with a ventilated hopper to catch the spent brass. Best of all, the space was such that they could load 2,000 rounds in the drum instead of 1,500, and they came up with a device for power-loading."

The new gun system that Harvell describes was the MXU-470/A, which satisfied the requirement for an improved lateral-firing system for Air Force cargo aircraft. The ASD negotiated with GE's Missile and Armament Division, which resulted in contract AF 33(657)-15450. With guidance from the Air Force Armament Laboratory, GE engineers developed three MXU-470/A machine gun modules for the GAU-2B/A minigun. Originally designated the A/A 37B/8 fire control system, the module underwent three phases of testing aboard an AC-47D of the Air Force Special Air Warfare Center (SAWC) at Eglin.

For production acceptance testing during early 1966, the guns were first boresighted to fire along the aircraft's lateral axis, and then were depressed 10, 12, and 14 degrees in an attempt to improve their effectiveness. The optimum gun depression angle for maximum accuracy was found to be 14 degrees. With the guns declined, the aircraft's angle of bank was more shallow, producing a more stable platform and reducing erratic motion of the pilot's sight pipper. The standard Mk 20 Mod 4 gun sight was used with the MXU-470/A, which, fully loaded with 2,000 rounds, weighed 380 pounds. The gun itself was mounted atop an aluminum ammunition drum. Attached to the backside of the drum was a control box, having a control panel attached to its side. Although the system could be loaded by hand, an MAU-82/A power loader was the easier option. This unique feature reversed the electric motor, thereby driving the entire system backward. Belted ammunition was fed into the loader, stripped of its links, and inserted into the drum. Links were then dumped through a chute into a container. A rounds counter recorded rounds fired and those remaining in the drum.

As in early gun pod tests, cameras were mounted behind the pilot's head and positioned to photograph the instrument panel. Three

of the 20 test flights with the gun modules were made over Eglin's water ranges and tests revealed that although the module had a floor-level roll-back feature for maintenance, it was easier in flight to swing out or remove a gun for replacement. Firing missions were usually flown at 3,000 feet between bank angles ranging from 37 to 70 degrees F. It was found that firing all the guns at their high rate of 6,000 rounds per minute actually created a recoil thrust that caused the aircraft to slip in a turn, requiring rudder compensation. The evaluation of the MXU-470/A was so successful that it was ordered into production. Meanwhile, Terry and his six pirates had arrived in Vietnam; the date was 2 December 1964.

Vietnam

One of Terry's team members, who served as the minigun test project officer, Ralph Kimberlin, recalls:

"Upon arrival in Saigon, we were assigned to the Air Force Test Unit, which was housed with the Army Concept Team in Vietnam. The three additional minigun pods that we needed to equip three C-47s were located in a warehouse in downtown Saigon. I was given the assignment of retrieving them. With a Vietnamese driver and a pickup truck, and unarmed, I retrieved the three gun pods and transported them to Bien Hoa on a highway that occasionally suffered Vietcong attacks.

"Once the remaining guns, mounts, and ammunition arrived at Bien Hoa by C-124, things got underway in earnest. However, we were not welcomed with open arms at Bien Hoa. The fighter pilots flying A-1Es were not too pleased with a bunch of cargo 'trash haulers' infringing on their territory. In fact, the vice commander of the A-1E fighter wing told Ron Terry, 'Captain, you are all going to get your asses killed!' Undaunted, the true believers, Terry and the Pirates, continued on. The first mission to train C-47 pilots of the 1st Air Commando Squadron (ACS), our hosts at Bien Hoa, in side-firing tactics occurred on 11 December 1964. It was during one of these training missions that we suffered the only hit from enemy ground fire.

"We were returning from a training mission over the South China Sea, where we had been firing at flares dropped in the water. The weather was bad so the pilots elected to go low. I controlled the gun safety switch on these missions and was seated in the flight engineer's position between the pilots. The flight was so low that we were pulling up to clear the hedgerows and then returning to the tops of the rice paddies. Airspeed was 180 knots. Suddenly, we cleared a hedgerow and saw a hut in which were two black-pajama-clad individuals with rifles. As soon as they saw us they rushed out of the hut, dropped to one knee and fired. One bullet, a tracer, passed just in front of the windscreen. I thought it had hit the pilot. The other bullet passed underneath the cockpit and struck the left propeller, making a terrible racket. Even though we knew that these were Viet Cong, the rules of engagement at the time did not allow us to fire unless we had a

This often publicized time-exposure photo captures the gunship's lethal "cone of fire," which earned it the name Dragon Ship. Although it was said that firing only tracer rounds melted gun barrels, not only was it done to study the prototype's pattern of fire, Ron Terry said, "We fired all-tracer in Vietnam at times, and it was a sight to behold. When we found out that the tracer ignites after it leaves the barrel, we fired the hell out of them." (U.S. Air Force)

Vietnamese observer along to verify that they were Viet Cong. We had no observer, so we rapidly pulled up and entered the traffic pattern for nearby Bien Hoa.

"While training flights were going on, Ron Terry was flying night combat missions with a 1st ACS copilot. We started with five training missions over the water, but the next 24 were all combat missions. Viet Cong activity was in the rice-rich Mekong Delta, where the enemy would attack the triangular forts to which the local populace retired for the night. It soon became our mission to position ourselves over the Delta and wait for an attack. We would then move in, drop magnesium flares and, after proper identification of Viet Cong by our Vietnamese Air Force observer, would attack. We soon became very popular with the Vietnamese. Since we were firing one-in-five tracers and the three guns were putting out a total of 300 rounds per second, the light show was fantastic. We began to get sent to phony attacks on forts just so the people in them could see us fire.

"Initially, Terry called the aircraft the FC-47, for Fighter, Cargo. This nomenclature was also picked up by the pilots of the 1st ACS, who wanted to rub it in to their fighter pilot colleagues that they were now in the fight.

"The longest single mission lasted more than 12 hours. All firing on combat missions was conducted at altitudes of 3,000 feet or above to minimize danger from ground fire. Daylight operations consisted of pre-assigned out-and-back missions, and airborne alert. On both types of missions we worked with Forward Air Controllers (FACs) in O-1Fs, who would mark our targets with smoke. From the airborne alert posture we also worked independently in an armed reconnaissance role in the many free-fire strike areas in the delta. Most targets during daylight were interdiction targets consisting of sampan traffic along the many rivers and canals, suspected supply dumps, training camps, and troop concentrations. The terrain in which these targets were located varied from the rugged mountains of central Vietnam to the

After Ron Terry arrived in Vietnam and began calling gunships FC-47s, for "Fighter/Cargo," the fighter community protested so loudly that the designation was changed to AC-47. This unofficial patch was designed during the short life of the unique designation. Gunship pilot Dick Noble said, "We took great pride in entering FC-47 in our logbooks." (Larry Davis Collection)

heavy jungles and flat rice paddies of the delta region. Although most day missions were interdiction, some were close air support, two of which produced post-strike reports from friendly forces. On one mission in support of an Army unit in a heavily wooded area, two Viet Cong bodies were found, and an unknown number of dead or wounded were seen being carried away. The other strike was a building where Viet Cong were known to be holed up, producing 13 bodies.

"A day-night mission flown after the end of the evaluation period produced the best results for the weapons system. An Army sergeant who had been captured and being used as a litter bearer was in both strikes. The VC outfit that had captured him was of battalion size or larger, and he reported that after the first strike he carried away 80 bodies. We hit the same area that night and the sergeant escaped. He reported that the second attack panicked the enemy and they ran, saying, 'It's that damn ray gun again. Let's get the hell out of here.' Friendly ground forces who later moved into the area found 70 bodies in trenches. Some

The designation AC-47D was first used during the late 1940s and into the 1950s to identify C-47s of the Air Force Communications Service. Modified with an extended nose and communications gear, they were used for airways checks. They were re-designated EC-47Ds to avoid confusion with attack AC-47Ds being developed during the early 1960s, and in keeping with the 1962 revised designation system, which used the A prefix for "Attack." (Stephen Miller)

captured Viet Cong soldiers called the aircraft 'a fire-breathing dragon,' so it picked up the nickname 'Puff, the Magic Dragon,' after a popular song by Peter, Paul, and Mary. The reports that come back from the control center at Can Tho in the delta were that we had the VC all screwed up. Before, they knew that they had at least 40 minutes of unmolested attack before the A-1s showed up to defend the forts at night. A flare ship could set up and drop flares all night and it wouldn't bother them. But then we appeared on the scene. We looked like any other flare ship and we dropped flares too. But after we dropped those flares we'd shoot the hell out of them.

"We could carry 35 flares and 20,000 rounds of ammunition and still be within gross weight limits. The AC-47 was found to be especially well suited for fort defense at night. By operating airborne alert, dropping our own flares, and reloading our guns in flight, we were able to successfully defend all forts that we were called to. Remaining airborne most of the night, we could move from one attack to the next. To assist their defending aircraft at night, forts marked their four corners with lights, and in their center had a fire arrow, which pointed in the direction of the enemy. All that remained was for us to find out the distance to the enemy. We did this by carrying our own Vietnamese navigator who could talk directly with the fort by FM radio. On one night mission, we fired 18,000 rounds of ammunition in a two-hour period.

"Missions continued at a fast pace and we soon began to have gun barrel problems. These barrels were designed for under-wing use where they would fire in two- to three-second bursts and have adequate cooling time. In this application the guns were reloaded many times in flight and this caused the gun barrels to rupture after long bursts. The problem was solved with new barrels, but the breakage of other parts due to high usage did not allow us to have three airplanes operational during the evaluation. Despite the problems with the guns, before the evaluation ended on 15 January 1965, Gen. Joseph Moore, 2nd Air Division commander, requested that a squadron of side-firing C-47s be modified and deployed as quickly as possible."

Testing of the nine minigun pods in Vietnam began on 11 December 1964, with the final mission, number 33, flown on 15 January 1965. Some of Terry's Pirates returned to the U.S. after completion of the evaluation, including Terry, who was to brief the Air Staff. With approval of a squadron of side-firing C-47s came the official aircraft designation AC-47D. The project was labeled *Gunship I*.

The push was on for more AC-47D gunships, but miniguns were in short supply since GE still had them in production. Ron Terry decided to fashion an interim gun system with Browning M-2 .30-cal. machine guns. Terry received approval from the commander of the Air Force Logistics Command to take a large number of M-2s from a warehouse at McClellan AFB, California. Ralph Kimberlin adds, "Solenoids for this system were hard to come by, so for the prototype we borrowed the gun solenoids from the B-24 bomber *Strawberry Bitch* displayed in the USAF Museum. It may still be missing them."

Doug Blair, who was one of the original "gun plumbers" at Hurlburt, returned there in November 1964 after a three-month assignment in the Congo working on three B-26Ks that were turned over to mercenary forces. Blair describes his involvement with the M-2 guns:

"On 16 July 1965, I and A1C Richard Haughaboo left for Wright-Patterson to assist in the first installation of the .30-cal. gun kit in a C-47. Less than ten days later, with Capt. Ron Terry at the controls, we left Wright-Pat with the modified aircraft. When we arrived at Hurlburt, a major came running out of base ops, very agitated and hollering at the top of his lungs. When he saw the ten .30-cal. barrels sticking out the side his anger turned to amazement. He said, 'What the hell is this?' Capt. Terry very politely explained that it was sort of a sensitive project and we moved the aircraft to a less visible location. We flew several missions over the Gulf shooting at Mk 6 smoke drifts and had a few interested parties. As soon as three more kits were finished, we got on a C-130 and headed to Clark AB in the Philippines. Capt. Terry had arranged for support from the Air Base Wing there and they did excellent work. We did the gun installation and they did the wiring and sheet metal work. Crews from Bien Hoa AB ferried aircraft to us to work on. Once we had them ready to fly, we did a couple flights to boresight the guns and be sure all were timed properly. Our target was a small island not far from Clark. When the last aircraft was finished, the rest of the team returned to the mainland and I tagged along to Bien Hoa to train crews on the guns. The first combat mission was flown on 16 August 1965 by the crews that had been flying the minigun-equipped AC-47. The pilots were used to holding the trigger down on the minis for five-second bursts and continued the practice with the .30s. This led to rounds cooking off in the chamber when they let the trigger up. They were not impressed with the .30-cal. guns. By the time the 4th ACS arrived from Forbes, the .30s were used up, as they had been old when we got them."

Four C-47s each had ten .30-cal. guns installed; two guns were mounted in the rear two cabin windows, two in the cargo doorway, and four poked through holes cut in the rear section of the cargo door. The ten guns firing at once put out only as many rounds as one minigun pod, but they did the job. Three aircraft were sent to Vietnam and one went to the 4th Air Commando Squadron at Forbes AFB, Kansas, for training Vietnam-bound gunship crews. Since the vintage guns and their ammunition proved mechanically troublesome, crews were happy to quickly replace them with miniguns as they became available.

The side-firing gun system had several advantages over other more conventional weapons. Installed in cargo aircraft, a large amount of ordnance and flares could be carried. The aircraft could maintain long airborne alerts and spend considerable time over the target. While maintaining a firing circle, the gunship could saturate a target with a high-density bullet pattern in a very short period of time. Single weapons could be reloaded, repaired, or replaced while other guns continued firing. Seldom were all three guns fired simultaneously, to conserve ammunition, and to have a backup gun in case another malfunctioned. These characteristics made the gunship ideal for attacking troops in the open, defending forts and hamlets, and escorting convoys.

The gunship, however, had its drawbacks. It was ineffective against reinforced structures, armor, and some vessels. Because of its size and slow speed, skeptics initially were concerned that the gunship was highly vulnerable to ground fire. This was proven unfounded since enemy forces attacking at night did not carry anti-aircraft–type weapons. Due to the use of flares, flying a pylon turn, and peering sideways through a sight, pilot vertigo was a common problem, making it vital that the copilot monitor instruments. When making vertical and horizontal sight corrections, pilots also had to consider slant range (the distance between the gun and the target), wind, airspeed, terrain, and enemy fire. Gravity drop of the bullet, which is also affected by drag, depended on the slant range and the gun angle. The gunship, typically, was boresighted for a slant range of 4,500 feet and a gun angle of 42 degrees.

Overall, the minigun was a success, and is best summarized by John Harvell:

"The minigun is a great little gun, but if you get in a peeing contest with a guy with a .50-cal. or a 12.7mm, all he has to do is stay back at extreme range and eat you up. Although it has pretty good dispersion, the minigun is really more comparable to a shotgun than a rifle. It's just what you need for relatively close quarters work, but not great for standoff ranges. The reason they worked so well in AC-47s is that they had the gravity gradient working for them, and against the bad guys; and their firing rate was such that they didn't have to be too terribly precise. Over the years the lateral firing standard changed to larger and newer equipment, but the fact remains that without 'that crazy captain from Wright-Pat' the gunships would probably never have come to be. Ron Terry deserves the credit for having had a vision and seeing it through."

The lore associated with gunship operations during the war in Southeast Asia was characterized not only by call signs, aircraft nicknames, and special patches, but by songs and cartoons. This cartoon illustrated the frustration of the enemy, whose intent to fire upon Allied aircraft was often met in merciless fashion by Spooky gunships. (Corky Trinidad)

CHAPTER TWO

SPOOKY GOES
TO WAR

Although Spooky crews were adept at forward air control, or FAC, they relied upon aircraft designed specifically for the job. The original FAC mount was Cessna's O-1 series Bird Dog. This O-1G, with a seasoned observer in the rear seat, carries rockets to mark targets for strike aircraft. (U.S. Air Force)

Acting on the request by Pacific Air Forces staff in mid 1965 that a 16-gunship squadron be made operational by November 1966, the Air Force Systems Command ordered that 20 C-47s be taken out of storage to be overhauled to form the squadron. Ralph Kimberlin, the minigun project test officer who had been assigned to the modification process, recalls, "Many of these aircraft had seen service during World War II and during the Berlin Airlift. Some still had 6 inches of coal dust under the floor boards."

As minigun units became available from General Electric, they, along with the C-47s, were sent to Air International in Miami, Florida, which had been contracted for gunship conversions. Engineers from the Warner Robins Air Material Area oversaw the conversion process. Complete with improved gun mounts, gun sights, VHF, UHF, and FM radios, as well as TACAN (tactical air navigation) and IFF (identification friend or foe) equipment, the AC-47Ds were coming on line. As some of these began arriving in Vietnam, the five FC-47s (two with miniguns and three with .30-cal. gun packages) were rotated from Vietnam to Clark AB, Philippines, for conversion and camouflage paint, bringing the total number of FC-47Ds to 26. Air International had concurrently modified at least two C-47s with the three .50-cal. gun kits for delivery to South America. Doug Blair, who was one of the original USAF Air Commando AC-47 gun mechanics, was sent to Air International to help design a boresight frame. He remembers, "Most of the guys there were Cubans, a fair percent of who were veterans of the Bay of Pigs."

Dick Noble, who served as an AC-47 navigator, describes the events taking place in Vietnam while the gunship was taking shape stateside:

> "I was assigned to the 1st Air Commando Squadron in October 1965 as a navigator. It was a composite squadron with A-1s, Bird Dogs, and armed and unarmed C-47s. The missions of

Typical of the remote outposts that Spookies were called upon to defend is this artillery base in South Vietnam in 1967. Dense vegetation in proximity to such positions required that Spooky's fire be extremely accurate. (Rodger D. Fetters)

Capt. Robert Stein, Spooky pilot of the 4th ACS in 1966, poses with gun number three. Since miniguns were used without their fairings, guns usually wore canvas covers to protect their intricate mechanisms while on the ground. Twenty-six mission marks are painted below the gun windows. (Robert Stein Collection)

the clean birds were psywar leaflet drops, and ferrying the U-2 photos to Tan Son Nhut AB after they had landed at Bien Hoa. We had one C-47 with three miniguns and three with .30-cal. guns. Each afternoon we would take off around three o'clock and fly to a staging base (Da Nang in I Corps and Pleiku in II Corps). The Bien Hoa alert bird would cover III Corps or fly down to Binh Thuy to cover IV Corps. If by midnight, we hadn't been scrambled, we would take off for airborne patrol, waiting for a fort to come under attack. Our call sign was Puff, followed by a number. When the 4th Air Commandos arrived in-country, we 1st ACS FC-47 crews were transferred from Bien Hoa to Tan Son Nhut and incorporated into the 4th ACS."

Preparations also had been under way at Forbes AFB, Kansas, where the newly activated 4th Air Commando Squadron trained for the gunship mission. Although the unit initially had no C-47s assigned, it soon received one of the four .30-cal.-armed FC-47s. Technically, the squadron had been activated under the 2nd Air Division at Tan Son Nhut AB, Vietnam on 2 August 1965 and attached to the 6250th Combat Support Group the same day. The 4th ACS deployed to Vietnam with its full complement of AC-47Ds (16 for combat, plus 4 for support and attrition), arriving at Tan Son Nhut AB on 14 November. The squadron's arrival could not have been better timed, in view of the dire situation in Vietnam. Then–Air Force Chief of Staff, Gen. John D. Ryan, explained, "In 1965 a takeover seemed inevitable. Communist forces controlled most of the country. South Vietnamese morale was low and the fall of the government was imminent unless the Vietnamese were given substantial assistance. Airpower was the only way of providing assistance quickly in amounts large enough to take the initiative and victory away from the Viet Cong."

Loadmasters and gun mechanics did not arrive in Vietnam until December and, again, there was a wait for miniguns. All of them had been removed at Forbes to reduce aircraft weight on the trans-Pacific journey. Fortunately, many of the squadron's pilots had combat experience from World War II and Korea, reducing the amount of time necessary to train new pilots. Formed concurrently with the 4th ACS was the 5th ACS, which also trained at Forbes. Flying C-47 and Helio U-10 aircraft, the 5th would fly psychological warfare (called "psywar") missions, delivering leaflets and loudspeaker messages to encourage the enemy to surrender, or "Chieu Hoi." Crews from both squadrons ferried their C-47s to Vietnam. Meanwhile, the AC-47D crews were kept busy flying courier, cargo, and flare missions, as well as familiarization flights. Losses suffered by the 4th ACS began early in its deployment. On a courier mission flown 17 December, an AC-47D and its crew of nine went missing on a flight from Tan Son Nhut to Phan Rang. When the wreckage of S/N 43-49492 with no survivors was found on the 23rd, it was obvious that the Spooky had been shot down. The first armed reconnaissance mission was flown on the 21st in the Foxtrot region of Eastern Laos. By late December enough miniguns had arrived for combat missions to be scheduled, although aircraft carried only one or two guns.

As was customary, changes in procedures often took time. Bob Stein, who flew gunships early in the war, provides this insight into the evolution of the bonding relationship between gunships and the grunts (ground troops):

"Upon their arrival in 1965, Spookies were totally unknown to the ground troops. They were, however, familiar with flare-dropping aircraft, usually C-47s, and they were used to calling for them when support was needed. A familiar scenario began to repeat itself in the night sky. The ground troops would call for support and Spooky would be dispatched. On arrival over the target area, Spooky would be asked to 'drop a flare here, a flare there.' Pilot Jack Haller was one of the first to complain to the 'gravel smashers' that 'we have guns up here.' The requests for flares continued. Frustrated, Jack then asked the ground controller to identify an empty rice paddy in the near vicinity. After confirming that no friendlies were in the area of the paddy, Haller fired all three guns into the paddy. The ground controller had his mike keyed and everyone heard him say, 'Oh my God!' After several such incidents, the Army began to request Spooky's guns as well as flares. Over time, Spooky was requested more and more frequently, and it required less and less time over the target to convince the VC to quit and go home."

When AC-47 gunship responsibilities shifted from the 1st Air Commando Squadron to the incoming 4th ACS, the move was not without the rivalry that typically existed between units. Dick Noble, a gunship navigator during that period, recalls this exchange:

"In November there was a meeting at Clark between Lt. Col. Rickelman, commander of the 1st ACS AC-47 element, and Lt. Col. Max Barker, commander of the 4th ACS. Rickelman expected to be the expert on the AC-47, on in-country tactics, and just about everything else. Barker stiffed him with, 'I've been in two wars. I don't need your advice.' One fallout of the meeting was Rickelman saying that Puff was his unit's call sign, and that the 4th should get their own. Headquarters bought it because the 1st would be flying missions for another six weeks. Then, at the end of December Rickelman took a couple of airplanes from Bien Hoa to Bangkok for unofficial R & R rather than fly them directly to Tan Son Nhut to turn them over to the 4th. I personally benefited from the rift."

The 4th ACS did acquire their own call sign. Speculation abounds as to how both the aircraft nickname and the call sign used throughout the war was derived, but in the end its origin seems lost to history. The most valid explanation given outside of the Officers' Club was this: When a 7th Air Force officer asked about the unit's call sign, a pilot's response included, "those damned spooky Gooney Birds." And "Spooky" it was. Another landmark decision concerning titles was made in December 1965; after the fighter community had had enough of gunships being called FC-47s, their designation officially was changed to AC-47 on 9 December.

Shortly after the 4th ACS set up shop at Tan Son Nhut AB, a detachment (A Flight) was sent to Da Nang AB to provide gun support in Laos and in the northern regions, often supporting U.S. Marines along the Demilitarized Zone (DMZ). Dick Noble comments on his involvement with the Da Nang detachment:

"When the 4th sent their detachment up to Da Nang, I met with their senior nav, Joe Christiano. I arranged for one of our experienced navs to fly along with their crew when they went into Laos, to help them update their maps and stay out of trouble. On December 24th, I was scheduled to fly with Christiano's crew. We briefed the night before, updating his maps. I met him at the airplane on the 24th and he told me I didn't have to go on that mission. I told him I felt I needed to as they were going into a sector where they hadn't been, and I had. He finally told me, 'You can't go.' The 4th's headquarters had no knowledge about the help we were providing and definitely didn't want any. They had ordered me off the crew. That was fine with me since it was the day before Christmas and all my mail was at Bien Hoa, and there was a bird leaving in an hour. I caught the airplane and was met by my commander as we exited the airplane. He wanted to be sure I had gotten on the airplane because Christiano's airplane didn't come back. I wondered if I had been there, maybe my knowledge might have saved the day, or I would have been one more MIA. I wore Joe's MIA bracelet for years."

Christiano and five other crew members had taken off on their daylight mission, using the call sign Spooky 21, to hunt for targets over southern Laos. A mayday call from the aircraft was heard by other aircraft in the area, but nothing further was heard from the gunship. No trace of the AC-47D, S/N 45-1120, or the crew was ever found. Unconfirmed reports suggest that Maj. Christiano and SSgt. Arden Hassenger escaped from the aircraft but were captured. Two Spookys and their crews had been lost within the first two weeks of operations—and they certainly wouldn't be the last.

The 1st Air Commandos with Puff in December 1965, prior to their assignment to the 4th ACS. (U.S. Air Force via Dick Noble)

The AC-47D (S/N 43-49516) of the 4th ACS, wearing the squadron's EN tail code. (John Bessette)

The AC-47D (S/N 44-77263) was assigned to the 4412th CCTS at Forbes AFB, Kansas from 1967 to 1970 for crew training. Wearing fresh paint, it is seen here at Webb AFB, Texas, in September 1967. Camouflage colors were Green No. 34079, Green No. 34102, and Tan No. 30219. Gloss Gray undersides were used on stateside aircraft, while Gloss Black was used in the combat theatre. When number 263 was given a fresh coat of paint in 1969, its serial number and squadron tail code were applied to the tail fin in white. (Stephen Miller)

In the training role, number 263 was armed with three SUU-11/A minigun pods. The hatch of the fifth cabin window, with gun number one, has been removed. (Stephen Miller)

The cargo compartment of the AC-47D was a busy place during firing missions. Crewmen toiled to maintain and load guns and handle flares, usually while the aircraft was in a 30-degree left bank. Visible are ballistic curtains, which helped protect against minigun shrapnel and small arms fire. Parachutes are stowed in the racks at right. (John Bessette)

With its camouflage showing the effects of many missions, AC-47D number 43-49421 of the 3rd SOS undergoes maintenance at Bien Hoa AB in 1968. Number 421 was shot down in September 1969, becoming the last Spooky lost during the war. (John Bessette)

The operations trailer of C Flight, 3rd ACS at Bien Hoa Air Base in 1968. (John Bessette)

Serial number 43-49274 was so badly damaged from a mid-air collision and crash landing that it was written off. (John Bessette)

As expected, Spookies quickly amassed impressive statistics. By the end of 1965, the 4th ACS had flown 1,441 hours during 277 missions, expending more than 137,000 rounds and 2,548 flares. They were credited with 105 enemy killed.

Meanwhile, the AC-47D pipeline for new crews had been established. Bob Stein describes his introduction to the gunship program:

"In November of 1965 I was ordered to Hurlburt Field, known as Eglin AFB, Auxiliary Number Nine. Along with several other crew members, I was taught by instructors who had recently returned from Vietnam, and they taught us the techniques they had used or learned during their time there. We pilots learned low-level navigation, assault landing techniques, the use of short, dirt fields and parachuting supplies to troops in the boondocks. I also had the opportunity to attend Survival School at Stead AFB outside of Reno, Nevada. Some of the information was useful, but winter in the Nevada mountains did not prepare one for the sultry weather of Vietnam. Of considerably more benefit

The loss of Spooky 73 of the 3rd SOS on 13 December 1968 underscored the hazard of a combat mission flown by multiple aircraft. A mission near Cu Chi was being controlled by an OV-10A Bronco when it was hit by ground fire and went out of control, striking the gunship. In a superior display of airmanship, Maj. Frank Reeder struggled to fly the badly damaged Spooky back to Bien Hoa. Both main landing gear sheared off on landing and the aircraft burst into flames. Thanks to the local base rescue HH-43 Pedro helicopter, the crew escaped with minor injuries. (U.S. Air Force via John Bessette)

was Jungle Survival School held in the vicinity of Clark AB in the Philippines. The week in the jungle was topped off by a 24-hour escape and evasion problem during which we were hunted by local natives. I then departed for Saigon's Tan Son Nhut Air Base. I got a rather large surprise when I checked in with the personnel office. I was told that the 1st Air Commando Squadron, where I was to be assigned, had been disbanded. One of the options presented to me was the 4th Air Commando Squadron that was flying AC-47s. I immediately volunteered and became the first crew replacement of this very new unit. The date was 25 February 1966. I subsequently received all of my gunship training via OJT [on-the-job-training] during regular combat missions."

A pilot transitioning into the AC-47D received 60 hours of flight training at the Special Air Warfare Center (SAWC) at Hurlburt. Once in Vietnam, he received additional training, which included flight with an instructor pilot. His indoctrination also included pre-planned *Night Owl* flights, in which he identified and illuminated targets for jet attack aircraft that visually dropped ordnance.

By early 1966 the Spooky squadron was flying with its full complement of miniguns. To provide ample coverage of the expanding war, detachments of the 4th ACS were established at Pleiku and Binh Thuy Air Bases. The Pleiku detachment, called B Flight, spent a great deal of time on missions defending Special Forces camps under attack. The Binh Thuy detachment was called E Flight. On 8 March the 14th Air Commando Wing (ACW) was organized at Nha Trang, becoming the parent command of the 4th ACS on that date. In May, the 4th's headquarters relocated to Nha Trang, from which C Flight flew flare missions only. In June, the D Flight detachment was established at Bien Hoa, which was tasked mainly with hamlet protection. Detachments were typically comprised of five aircraft, and the Spooky crews normally consisted of pilot, copilot, navigator, flight mechanic, loadmaster, and two gunners. A Vietnamese Air Force observer usually flew on each mission to translate radio communication from ground units.

Although air base perimeter and fort defense were its primary mission, as crews gained experience, missions were expanded to include close support of ground troops. Some pilots had fired within 50 meters of friendly forces without inflicting casualties. Soon, Spookies were flying reconnaissance sorties over roads and waterways, in addition to supporting search and rescue (SAR) missions, working by the light of their own flares. Night missions were flown along the Cambodian border to detect enemy units seeking sanctuary across the border. The escort of truck convoys supplying outposts became the norm. Spooky crews also became adept in the role of forward air control, and with an endurance of seven hours, far exceeding the range of other Fighting Air Command (FAC) aircraft, the FC-47 was a natural for assuming this role. Accordingly, pilots were given an abbreviated course in forward air controlling.

Often, Spooky crews found it necessary to fly below the established 3,000 feet minimums to prevent outposts from being overrun, and they would sometimes pay the price for their efforts with more

Spookies being lost to ground fire. At least two of the shoot-downs were the result of ground fire hitting unprotected flare containers, which eventually were wrapped in armor. Maj. Harley Jeans, operations officer of the 4th ACS, lamented, "I haven't felt safe since I carried my first flare, and I won't feel safe until I carry my last." Through trial and error, other field modifications were made. Dual radio headsets were installed on all aircraft for the South Vietnamese Air Force (VNAF) observer and navigator, and squadron gunners altered the minigun mounts for optimum depression. In addition, Spooky crews tested the night vision "Starlight Scope," as well as the .50-cal. gun package. Although the results of the .50-cal. gun tests were inconclusive, starlight scopes were found to be successful in locating the enemy. Before long, enemy gunners became reluctant to fire on the old Gooney Bird, never sure whether or not it was a fearsome fire-breathing dragon gunship.

With aircraft airborne around the clock, the 4th ACS averaged 25 sorties every 24-hour period, often with other aircraft, and flying several types of missions within that period. Nor was it unusual for multiple Spookies to participate in a large operation. Alfred "Ace" Bowman, who was an AC-47D navigator, comments, "There were never two identical missions. Other than a huge set of radios, installed and carry-on, we were not loaded down with techie toys. Our Mk 1 eyeballs, everybody aboard, were the number one combat support systems. Radar, FLIR [forward looking infrared radar], and heat seekers were not our bag."

When not actually flying strike missions, Spookies flew a patrol pattern. After a strike order came from the Tactical Air Command and Control Center at Tan Son Nhut AB, the gunship came under the direction of a Forward Air Controller. Flares were usually dropped first to identify the target, and then the pilot entered the firing circle, normally in a 30- to 33-degree bank, with the miniguns depressed 12 degrees. Some pilots, during their initial run, fired all three guns for shock effect and to check the guns. One orbit usually allowed the pilot three- to four-second bursts. Guns were fired one at a time, and in sequence as the gunners reloaded, preventing gaps in firing. This could continue until an alert aircraft was sent. Turnaround time for reloading back at the base averaged 30 minutes. Spooky tactics also differed according to the terrain over which detachments operated. The navigator usually found himself without much work over the Delta, since pilots had DME (distance measurement equipment) and VOR (VHF omnidirectional range) to navigate over flat regions. The VOR gave compass direction from a station, and DME gave the distance from that station. The navigator, on the other hand, was a critical appendage over mountainous northern regions.

Spooky pilots agreed that dropping flares was the most difficult tactic to master. They had to know when and where they should be dropped, how they should be pre-set for ignition in relation to altitude, and account for wind drift. Timing for release was vital to ensure the flare would not illuminate friendly troops. The loadmaster acted as the flare "kicker," on the pilot's command, manually pitching the 30-inch-long, 21-pound cylinders from the cabin doorway. The 2.5-million-candlepower flares had a 3-minute burn time. Until early 1965, the Mk 6 750,000-candlepower flare had been used until Mk 24 Mod 3 units were obtained from Navy stocks. A normal load was 45 flares; however, that was increased to 60 when Spookies began running out of them before their ammunition was expended. That brought the AC-47D's gross weight up to 29,000 pounds, requiring that the standard ammunition load of 21,000 rounds be reduced to 15,000 rounds. During 1967 the Mk 24 was augmented by the 5-million-candlepower, 5-minute-burn-duration Briteye flare, also a Navy development.

The AC-47D's capabilities did not go unnoticed by U.S. Ambassador to Laos William Sullivn, who in early 1966 asked that they join the interdiction effort against the Laotian portion of the Ho Chi Minh Trail. After his request was approved in late February, four AC-47Ds and five crews were sent to Udorn RTAFB to begin a six-month tour. In April, they were relocated to Ubon RTAFB when Udorn's ramp became overcrowded. Spooky's two-fold mission in Laos was armed reconnaissance over the trail, and serving as an airborne command post for strike aircraft in the *Tiger Hound* geographical area of Laos bordering South Vietnam. The gunships flew two six-hour reconnaissance sorties every night and Spooky crews soon became skilled truck killers, carrying a Lao observer who was given targets by clandestine Roadwatch teams hiding along the trail. The enemy countered this success by moving in heavy anti-aircraft defenses. The Spookies were outgunned and by the end of June, four had been lost to devastating ground fire, three of which went down in Laos. The use of AC-47Ds in the heavily defended Trail region necessitated a hard look at the aircraft's vulnerability. The gunship force was spread thin and they were needed in South Vietnam for hamlet defense, while C-123s in Vietnam that had been pressed into service as flareships in Spooky's absence were needed for airlift. The 4th ACS flew its last *Tiger Hound* mission on 20 July, and in August the gunships returned to Vietnam. Their replacements over the trail were Douglas A-26 Counter Invaders.

Ace Bowman, an AC-47D navigator, explained Spooky gunship operations:

"In the early spring of 1966, I was stationed at Los Angeles International Airport, where I was in charge of the Navigator Flight of the USAF Space Systems Division, Air Force Systems Command support group. I looked after about 100 navigators assigned to the division. Additionally, I flew as a crew or instructor navigator in the division commander's C-118, and in C-47 and T-39 aircraft. I really did not care for mission support flying. I needed to get a new job elsewhere. I had been talking to Maj. Ron Terry, who developed the gunship theory with the Gatling guns. I signed on and was sent to Hurlburt Field for training. The instructors in large measure were those I flew with in C-123s in Vietnam.

"Binh Thuy Air Base was located near Can Tho, deep in the Mekong River Delta. It was primarily a Vietnamese fighter base. There were no major U.S. or ARVN [Army of the Republic of Vietnam] units in the area. Virtually all ground combat units

The crew of 274 of the 3rd SOS at Bien Hoa AB the day after they survived a mid-air collision and crash landing, which destroyed the AC-47D. (John Bessette)

The cockpit area of number 43-49499 of the 3rd ACS was destroyed during a mortar attack on Binh Thuy AB on 29 September 1968. (Robert McGarry)

The AC-47D 43-49339 of the 3rd ACS. Spookies of the 3rd ACS wore tail code EL, while AC-47Ds of the 4th ACS were identified by tail code EN. Spookies armed with XMU-470/A minigun modules had all three guns forward of the cabin doorway, while those armed with earlier SUU-11/A minigun pods had the third gun mounted in the doorway. (John Bessette)

The AC-47D number 43-16065 was one of the oldest Spookies of the war. This view shows the standard AC-47D camouflage and markings of the 3rd ACS. (John Bessette)

The AC-47D number 43-16065 of the 3rd ACS at Bien Hoa AB is surrounded by ground support equipment, including a power unit pumping cold air into the Spooky's cockpit. (John Bessette)

An AC-47D (S/N 44-76207) of the 4th ACS in 1967, prior to application of the unit's tail code. The last three numbers of its serial number are repeated below the pilot's window. The space taken up by the third minigun hampered movement through the cabin doorway. Miniguns wore protective covers when the aircraft was parked. When this aircraft was shot down on 5 May 1968, five of its crew and passengers were saved by Sgt. Nacey Kent, earning him the Air Force Cross. (Tom Hansen)

were Vietnamese Regional or local forces. The USAF units were small flights, like us, E Flight of the 4th ACS. We usually had assigned five aircraft and five crews. Usually, a VNAF observer flew on each mission to translate radio calls from the ground units we were supporting. He sat at or near the nav table. Between the navigator and the observer was a note pad. As the observer received information from the ground, he would write it out in English, after which the navigator relayed it to the rest of the crew. Unfortunately, it wasn't a perfect system. Sometimes the observer's English was less than proficient, and often the ground operator was totally ignorant of the tactical situation, knowing only that he was deep in a bunker and being mortared. In the FAC role it would get busy handling all the radio traffic, leading to periods of communication saturation. With the pilot on UHF with fighters, the copilot on VHF with choppers, the navigator on FM and HF with artillery and TACC, and the observer on FM with the ground, the loadmaster would decide it was an opportune time for an intercom announcement of the arrival of a .50-cal. slug in the cargo compartment. One night I talked to 'Charlie' on FM. The enemy was apparently monitoring our frequency while the observer talked to the outpost we were defending. A voice came up in Pidgin English, 'Spooky, you go home and we stop attack, okay?' I answered, 'We stay and you stop attack anyway, okay?' We stayed and the outpost wasn't bothered again that night. When the duties up front got slow, the front people were more than welcome to help load the miniguns or carry and arm flares for the loadmaster.

"When beginning work, at 1600 hours, the four duty crews reported to the base theatre for an intelligence briefing. Much of that was crap; Department of Defense-driven McNamara numbers about KIA [killed in action], Chieu Hois, and other made-up and meaningless blather. Then our local intelligence officer made his presentatio n, and that was usually both well presented and useful. He actually went afield almost every day; out to the villages, over to the river patrol units, a check-in with the Army helicopters at Can Tho, and other meaningful activity. After a little time on station, one's instincts and senses developed as well. For instance, if the quarter's maids and other female Vietnamese labor didn't show up for work, that was a real hint that the base was slated for an attack.

"We rounded up our survival gear and personal equipment, which included M-16 rifles and an M-60 machine gun. This used the same ammo as our miniguns and could be used in the event we were shot down. We carried the same weapon each time, the same weapon we took to the firing range. Ditto the portable radio, an Army FM type we hand-carried onto the aircraft. Superstition abounded. Virtually everyone always wore the same headgear on every mission. If such got lost, the aggravation could be extreme. At 1830 hours, the aircraft was loaded with equipment. At 1900 hours, the first Combat Air Patrol (CAP) was airborne and on station over the base. Binh Thuy itself was the biggest target in the heart of the Mekong Delta. Until directed to do otherwise, the CAP provided base defense. There actually were a few nights when the Viet Cong stood down and the first

FAC pilot Maj. William Dorrh (left) presents an AK-47 to Capt. Charles Boatwright for his and his crew's defense of a Special Forces camp in November 1966. Looking on is Maj. Harley Jeans, operations officer of Det 3, 4th ACS. Among Boatwright's 214 Spooky missions was his position as aircraft commander of serial number 43-48356 when it was shot down shortly after takeoff from Bien Hoa AB on 23 March 1967. (U.S. Air Force/Charles Boatwright Collection)

Although the seven crewmen of number 356 survived the shoot-down and crash landing, three were injured, including AC Capt. Charles Boatwright. Boatwright crash-landed 356 next to a minefield. Standing upright at left is the aircraft's left horizontal stabilizer, the only portion of the aircraft that remained intact. (U.S. Air Force/Charles Boatwright Collection)

CAP flew five hours over the flagpole. The second CAP relieved the first at midnight, and repeated the boredom until full daylight. Meanwhile, the other alert crews, joined by first CAP, continued playing cards in the alert trailers. Gambling was not too popular because when the alert phone sounded, there was no time for counting or squaring accounts.

"When a target was announced by Paddy Control as the CAP got airborne, the navigator gave a rough heading to the pilot for the target. A refined radial and distance from the base TACAN was then provided to the pilot, and appropriate terrain maps with the target coordinates were sent up front. Firing clearance was rarely provided at initial contact. Nonetheless, flares were readied and the guns brought fully on line. Once the friendlies were identified and the enemy location determined, work began in earnest. Usually a flare or two was tossed out, which illuminated the area for the friendlies and for us, gave us a good wind indicator for developing our attack pattern, and made it difficult for the evil guys to pinpoint our location. Every now and then, Charlie got lucky and scored a few hits. And there were a few widely dispersed really good gunners down there that we learned to avoid. Any target, any time in Kien Hoa Province, for instance, was a great time to be cautious. Defending the base was its own category. No waiting for clearances and other niceties; just get the guns on the mortars. We didn't bother with flares for these. These attacks were personal and intense. There was one instance where the aircraft descended to less than 50 feet and

In May 1968, AC-47D S/N 45-0919 of the 3rd SOS suffered a landing mishap when it ground looped, causing extensive damage. It was repaired and transferred to the VNAF in June 1969. Following its conversion to an FC-47D, number 919 had served the 1st ACW at Hurlburt, the 2nd Air Division at Tan Son Nhut AB, the 377th Combat Support Group, and the 22nd Tactical Air Support Squadron before assignment to the 14th ACW. (U.S. Air Force via John Bessette)

fired full force, point blank into a mortar position. The next day's BDA [bomb damage assessment] patrol announced that no bodies could be counted, but parts were plentiful. There was no standard target, or a case of 'always' or 'never.' Such would be self defeating and perhaps suicidal. The first-alert bird [call sign Spooky 51] inevitably became the busiest bird on busy nights.

"The 16th and 17th of February were memorable. We were barely airborne for First CAP when we received our first target, an enemy attack on a large Military Assistance and Advisory Group compound. As we arrived, we could see recoilless rifle and mortar flashes for miles in all directions. We went in firing and expended about half of our ammunition before we got formal clearance to fire from Paddy. We informed them of the situation. In just a few more minutes, we were expended and Spooky 52 was inbound. And so it went for everyone that night, a precursor to Tet 1968. At 7 am, as we finished our day and looked forward to Miller Time, we had flown four sorties and fired 85,000 rounds.

"More often than not, there were extra people on-board for a variety of reasons; training, checking out new personnel, or upgrading systems. Sometimes the flight surgeon was observing the crew. Media folks came from time to time; if they got a hot mission, few volunteered for seconds. Rarely was a target more than 15 to 20 minutes away. When Paddy finally gave the clearance to fire, the pilot rolled into a 30-degree bank to put the pipper on the target. When he pulled the trigger, what happened next in the aircraft cannot be truly described. There is no sound and there is no color on earth that can match it. The shrieking of 300 rounds per second can neither be described nor fully recorded. The light from the barrels of each gun illuminated the compartment, but it was unlike any other light anywhere else. A pale green sometimes, but just plain ugly. Earplugs were not much help. The path of the red stream was easy to track as 70 of those 300 rounds were tracers. In many cases, the first burst ended the world for some, and that part of the evening for us. Maybe a few more flares, a close look at the area, an initial BDA guess, and we were ready to go home and reload, or go to another target."

As the Spooky's reputation became widely known, and more ground units learned to rely on its firepower, AC-47D crews increased their tally of enemy kills. The following are the recollections of Robert K. Stein, Jr., a Spooky pilot with E Flight:

"At 1800 hours on 23 April 1966, we took off from Binh Thuy in Spooky 51 and were called to a target almost immediately after takeoff. We learned that an ARVN force had trapped a large group of VC along a riverbank. Illumination from flares prevented the VC from escaping across the river. When we arrived we were given permission to fire into the riverbank area at will. Our standard load was 40 flares and 23,000 rounds of ammunition. We almost always used the miniguns one at a time so our ammunition would last longer. Our crew flew four missions on that target over the next 12 hours, and, as the sole armed

As enemy air defenses increased, O-1 and O-2 aircraft were replaced by more powerful and more heavily armed North American OV-10A Broncos. A Bronco collided with an AC-47D after its cockpit area was hit by anti-aircraft fire in December 1968. (U.S. Air Force)

An AC-47D, S/N 43-48499 of the 4th SOS during the late 1960s. Spookies armed with minigun modules had all three units mounted forward of the cabin doorway. This arrangement not only kept the guns on the same mounting plane, it gave the loadmaster, called a "flare kicker," ample room to launch the large Mk 24 flare. (U.S. Air Force)

C-47s of the 5th SOS, and later the 9th SOS as well, were modified with loudspeakers for broadcasting to the enemy the option to surrender. These psywar platforms often flew low and slow to drop leaflets or to broadcast. Spookies normally accompanied the "Bullshit Bombers," although at a distance, attacking when the psywar aircraft were fired upon. (U.S. Air Force)

Spooky gunship pilot Capt. Joh Bessette of the 3rd ACS in 1968. Visible in the cabin doorway of number 43-16065 is a metal flare container and a ballistic curtain. A vent attached to the gun window's forward edge helped direct gun smoke into the slipstream. (John Bessette Collection)

Spooky crewmen of the 3rd SOS load Mk 24 flares in September 1968. Flares endangered friendly ground forces and villages since their casing split and fell free prior to parachute deployment. Parachute malfunctions could cause flares to hit the ground while still burning. Being self sustaining and burning with intense heat, magnesium flares could melt steel and could not be extinguished. (John Bessette)

aircraft in the area, received credit for more than 300 KBA [kills by air].

"The end of the night was also memorable but more embarrassing than exciting. It was 0600 and just about dawn when we returned from the fourth sortie. I happened to be in the left seat and making the landing. As I rounded out, I let the airspeed get a little low and the C-47 veered off into the tall elephant grass alongside the runway. After applying full power, I was able to fly (at about 6 inches of altitude) back to the runway and complete the landing. I figured the crew would be tight-lipped about it,

but as we exited the plane I heard the ground crew laughing as they approached. My relief turned to embarrassment as I turned to see the main gear covered with elephant grass. So much for graceful entrances."

In his narrative, Stein omitted the formidable anti-aircraft defenses and poor visibility mentioned in his citation for the Distinguished Flying Cross, which he was awarded for that mission.

A similar engagement that typified Spooky's accomplishments during 1966 occurred on 15 April, when a ground unit trapped an

The more powerful Cessna O-2 replaced the O-1 during the late 1960s. Air Force FAC aircraft were dispersed among five Tactical Air Support Squadrons (TASS), all of which were based in Vietnam, except the 23rd TASS at Nakhon Phanom Royal Thai Air Force Base. This O-2A, seen at Phu Cat AB in 1970, wears a Raven zap, representing the covert FACs that operated "across the fence." (Roger Besecker)

The AC-47D number 43-49517 being prepared for a mission at Nha Trang AB in 1967. Near the Spooky's cargo doorway, ready for loading, are flares and 7.62mm ammunition containers. Ballistic curtains, which were included in the modification order, are visible in the rear cargo area, and in forward windows. As their name implied, these curtains were an anti-ballistic measure to protect crewmen from misfired gun projectiles and exploding gun barrels. (S. Alexander via Larry Davis)

GUNSHIPS: THE STORY OF SPOOKY, SHADOW, STINGER AND SPECTRE

estimated battalion-size enemy force near a river at Tan An. While Army helicopter gunships prevented the enemy's escape across the river, the 4th ACS flew six sorties, attacking until their ammunition was expended. After-action reports counted 470 enemy dead. The AC-47 displayed its versatility by helping a U.S. Coast Guard cutter capture an enemy supply ship moving along the coastline. The Spooky fired on the ship to silence a machine gun, and then attacked an enemy force on the shoreline. When Coast Guard personnel boarded the steel-hulled vessel, they found 7,000 weapons aboard.

To bolster its counterinsurgency forces in Thailand and Laos, the Air Force in 1966 decided to assign eight AC-47Ds to the composite 606th ACS at Nakhon Phanom (NKP) RTAFB (Royal Thai Air Force Base). More orders went to Air International and by year's end the eight aircraft, along with more than 200 personnel, had begun operations. Although Spookies operating from Vietnam and Ubon RTAFB were successful in the Tiger Hound region of Laos in 1966, having claimed 204 trucks destroyed or damaged, losses were high. Losses occurred in the months of March, May, June, and December, with 4 aircraft and 28 crewmen lost.

On its weathered exterior, the crew of 010 kept a scoreboard indicating successful attacks in Laos against troops, anti-aircraft batteries, and trucks. The window added immediately forward of the cabin doorway indicates that minigun modules are used. Seldom seen on Spookies is the armament placard, normally required to indicate armament loads. (Larry Davis Collection)

The AC-47D S/N 44-76722 of the 4th ACS in 1967. Numerous antennas corresponded to Spooky's wide variety of communications and navigation gear. Protruding from the nose is the glide path antenna, while FM command homing antennas were mounted to both sides of the nose. Visible atop the fuselage is a localizer-omni antenna, and an FM whip antenna. (Robert C. Mikesh)

A Spooky of the 3rd SOS shares ramp space with the prototype AC-130A at Bien Hoa AB. The AC-130A was on its second evaluation tour in Southeast Asia, which lasted from February to November 1968. (U.S. Air Force via John Bessette)

Named Mac's Marauders, S/N 44-76625, of the 4th SOS became part of the 432nd Spooky Operations Unit in Thailand in 1969. (Larry Davis Collection)

Serial number 43-49010 was one of three AC-47Ds assigned to the Spooky Operations Unit of the 432nd TRW at Udorn Royal Thai Air Force Base in late 1969. After successfully defending Lima Sites in Laos, and serving as airborne command posts, the three aircraft were transferred to the Royal Laotian Air Force. Spookies of the 432nd used the tail code OS. (Larry Davis Collection)

Serial number 45-1117 of the 3rd SOS, named Sweet Pee. (John Bessette)

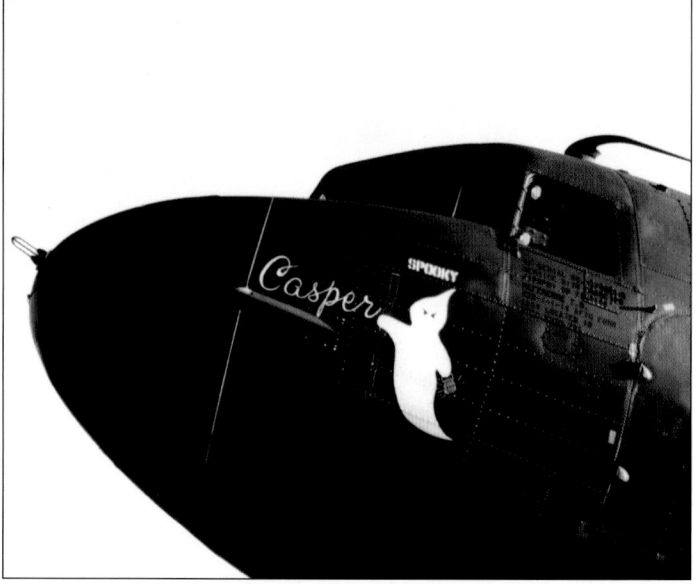

Serial number 43-49211 of D Flight, 3rd SOS at Binh Thuy. (Larry Davis Collection)

Delta Queen *was AC-47D 44-76717, which, earlier, wore the name* Annette. *Like most* Spookies, *it was passed to the Vietnamese Air Force.*
(U.S. Air Force)

As Spooky's operational success carried over into 1967, the 4th ACS saw a number of changes to keep pace with the expanding war. The flareships of Nha Trang's C Flight were replaced by four AC-47Ds from the 606th ACS in Thailand. Also in January, MXU-470/A minigun modules arrived; however, their mounts were found to be unsatisfactory, requiring continued use of the SUU-11/A. After mount alterations, minigun modules were not installed until mid-year, and then only in two aircraft due to gun shortages. To the relief of air crews, armored flare boxes were also introduced. In March, E Flight broke all previous records for a single month's operations by flying 188 combat sorties, expending 4,431 flares and firing 1,627,050 rounds of ammunition. These statistics translated to the defense of 55 outposts, 9 villages, and 7 ground units. In May, A Flight was relocated from Da Nang to Phu Cat AB. Sorties flown by E Flight's Spookies on the night of 27/28 June to repel a major attack against an outpost in Phong Dinh Province marked the 1,000th outpost defended by Spooky crews.

Throughout 1967, devastating enemy rocket attacks on American air bases necessitated an increase in AC-47Ds for perimeter defense. Thus began rounds of deliberation among various commands, with proposals ranging from converting C-7 Caribou aircraft into gunships, to modifying C-47s drawn from a VNAF transport squadron. Hesitation to add AC-47Ds was the result of the Air Staff's quest for a better gunship. A great deal of attention was given the prototype C-130 gunship, which arrived at Nha Trang on 21 September to begin combat evaluation. In the end, the Secretary of Defense authorized an additional ten AC-47Ds. This would bring the total to 32 aircraft to

be divided between the 4th ACS and a new gunship squadron. The Air Staff ordered an additional eight gunships, with the 18 aircraft drawn from units flying C-47B, VC-47D, and TC-47D models. The new Spooky unit, the 14th Air Commando Squadron, was slated for activation on 25 October 1967. The year 1967 would end with Spooky rightfully maintaining their claim that they had not lost an outpost while they were overhead. Besides defending 1,596 outposts, Spooky crews were credited with 3,650 confirmed kills, with nearly as many considered probable. The loss of five aircraft and many crewmen during 1967 tempered the squadron's victories, however.

The 14th ACS, which officially had been activated on 25 October 1967, became operational on 15 January 1968, with its 14 AC-47Ds immediately put to work for the Tet Offensive. The squadron's headquarters was established at Nha Trang, and detachments were sent to Phan Rang (B Flight), Bien Hoa (C Flight), and Binh Thuy (D Flight). An operating location (OL) was also established at Da Nang. The squadron's only combat loss occurred early in operations on the night of 14 February when AC-47D S/N 43-49859 was shot down near Phan Rang, killing all eight aboard. Non-combat mishaps also took their toll on the squadron's aircraft; S/N 43-49274 was ground-looped on 14 January, and on 11 February an AC-47D was started with the brakes unlocked and no chocks, causing it to roll 200 feet before crashing into and destroying an already battle-damaged F-4 Phantom. The 4th ACS, meanwhile, scored a major victory on 1 March when two of its gunships teamed with U.S. and Vietnamese gunboats to attack a 700-ton munitions trawler attempting to deliver arms and ammunition to Han Hoc Peninsula.

AC-47D loadmaster A1C John L. Levitow of the 3rd SOS received the Medal of Honor for saving his crew when the Spooky was rocked by a mortar blast during a mission in February 1969. (U.S. Air Force)

This AC-47D, S/N 44-76534, wore a number of "zaps," which were emblems of other units mischievously applied when the aircraft was unattended. The kangaroo came from an Australian unit, while a lion appears over a cabin window. Farther forward is the spook character associated with the F-4 Phantom community. (Tom Hansen)

After firing nearly 40,000 rounds, the ship ran aground and exploded, sending a fireball 1,000 feet into the air.

During late March 1968, John Bessette, after flying as a navigator on KB-50s and C-130s, was assigned to the 4412th Combat Crew Training Squadron at England AFB, Louisiana. The 4412th CCTS had been activated under the 1st Air Commando Wing in October 1967 for training C-47 and AC-47D aircrew. During March and April, Bessette's training included three basic C-47 navigation flights over the Gulf of Mexico, followed by three VFR night low-level navigation missions to targets. These were flown in a mix of C-47D, VC-47D, and TC-47D aircraft, using the call sign Mutt. This was topped off by a day of firing mission in an AC-47D at Fort Polk's Peason Range. He noted, "The noise was horrendous." In Vietnam, Bessette was assigned to the 14th Air Commando Squadron's C Flight at Bien Hoa AB. He added, "There were six crews and we had four crews and aircraft on alert. We launched two aircraft at sunset (*Spooky 71* and *Spooky 73*), while two others stood alert (*Spooky 72* and *Spooky 74*)."

On 1 May the 14th ACS was re-designated the 3rd ACS, and on 1 August the Air Commando titles of the 14th ACW, 3rd ACS, and 4th ACS were changed to Special Operations. On the night of 4/5 May, the 4th ACS suffered the loss of two gunships launched from Phu Cat to attack enemy forces firing rockets and mortars at the Pleiku AB. Both were shot down within minutes of each other. Both pilots and the navigator aboard S/N 43-76207 were killed, while six crewmen were killed aboard S/N 43-16159. The flight engineer of 207, Sgt. Nacey Kent, was awarded the Air Force Cross for re-entering the wreckage to save fellow crewmen and passengers despite his injuries.

The year 1968 would prove to be the busiest year for Spooky gunships. Boosting the statistics for that year was action at Duc Lap, a Special Forces camp that came under attack by a 4,000-man force

During their frequent low-level work, Spookies often encountered ground fire. Serial number 44-76717 of the 4th SOS was met by fire fighters with lots of foam after it was hit in the left engine and landed at Da Nang AB. (U.S. Air Force)

beginning on 23 August. For the next several nights, Spookies remained overhead dodging heavy anti-aircraft fire while dropping flares and laying down sheets of suppressive fire. The camp was saved but not before the Spookies dropped more than 1,000 flares and fired 761,000 rounds from their miniguns. The year also saw a number of experiments to improve gunship operations. In September, an AC-47D was teamed with a Marine UH-1E Huey helicopter gunship equipped with a night observation device. Called "Night Hawk," the hunter-killer concept had the helicopter crew locating and marking targets at night, then clearing the area for Spooky's lethal dose of minigun fire.

Although results were negligible, they pointed out the need for night observation devices in gunships. Other experiments included armored jettisonable flare boxes, semiautomatic flare launchers, smoke-clearing systems, and air-dropped sensors to be used in conjunction with gunship sensor monitors. Some AC-47Ds would have these innovations installed, but all of them became standard equipment on Spooky's replacements. Back in the U.S., the development of those replacements gained momentum. John Bessette commented, "In January 1969, a pilot and I were sent to Tan Son Nhut, where the 71st SOS [Special Operations Squadron], which had newly arrived in Vietnam with AC-119G Shadows, was establishing a flight. We flew several missions aboard Shadow, helping the crews familiarize themselves with the III Corps area. That was an education, as we Spooky types used the Mark One Eyeball for our target area work, while Shadow had the night observation system. Very interesting."

As both Spooky squadrons in Vietnam amassed missions, one became noteworthy, which highlighted the mettle of Spooky crews. On the night of 24 February, *Spooky 71* of the 3rd SOS was into its fifth hour of combat air patrol near Saigon when it was directed to an attack on Long Binh Army Base. As the pilot, Maj. Kenneth Carpenter, lined up for a second firing pass, his loadmaster, A1C John L. Levitow, handed a flare to gunner Sgt. Ellis Owen. Ellis had his finger through the flare's safety ring when the aircraft was rocked by a tremendous blast. A mortar round had exploded in the right wing. Crewmen in the back were thrown violently about and injured as shrapnel tore through the aircraft, which fell into a steep right turn. Severely injured by shrapnel, Levitow crawled to the doorway to drag to safety a man who was close to going out the opening. He then spotted the armed flare rolling amid ammunition cans. Trying vainly to grab the skidding flare as the aircraft was still banking, he finally grabbed it and dragged it while crawling to the doorway. As seconds ticked by, he pushed it out of the opening just as it ignited in a lethal 4,000-degree blaze. Levitow then lapsed into unconsciousness. Carpenter regained control of the badly damaged aircraft, landing at Bien Hoa with five injured crewmen, two of them seriously, including Levitow. After recovering in a hospital in Japan, Levitow returned to add 20 missions to top the 200 mark before returning to the U.S. On 14 May 1970 (Armed Force Day), Levitow was honored at the White House where President Nixon awarded him the Medal of Honor.

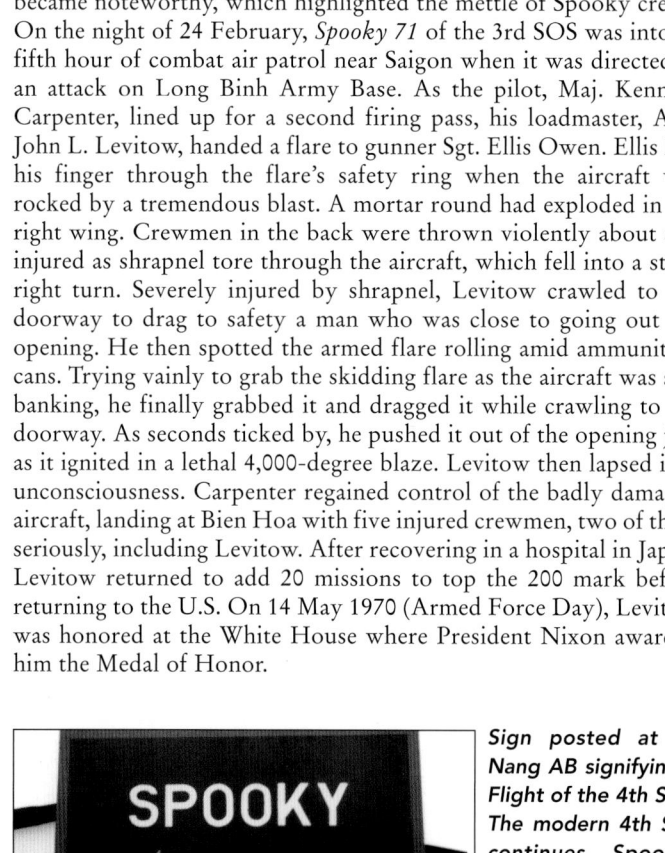

This sign marked the confines of D Flight, 3rd SOS at Binh Thuy AB. The ghost theme was apparent in patches and AC-47D nose art. (Larry Davis Collection)

Sign posted at Da Nang AB signifying A Flight of the 4th SOS. The modern 4th SOS continues Spooky's proud tradition, calling itself "Ghost Riders." (Larry Davis Collection)

An ongoing concern of 7th Air Force officials was that AC-47Ds often were without ample protection from ground attacks at air bases. These 4th ACS Spookies, numbers 274, 591, and 117, share ramp space in early 1967. (Terry Love)

AC-47D S/N 43-48916 was taken out of storage during August 1965 for conversion to gunship. After serving with the 3rd ACS in Vietnam, the aircraft became a stateside trainer assigned to the 4412th Combat Crew Training Squadron of the Tactical Air Command at England AFB, Louisiana. The 4412th was established in October 1967 under the 1st Special Operations Wing for C-47 training. Aircraft assigned wore the squadron's IG tail code and color red on the tail fin tip. (Clyde Gerdes via Stephen Miller)

U.S. Air Force AC-47Ds

43-15510	display at Eglin AFB marked as 43010
43-15584	3rd SOS
43-16065	3rd SOS, hit by .50-cal. fire in both wings on 15 January 1968; 4th SOS; later to VNAF
43-16133	3rd SOS; 432nd TRW; to Royal Laotian Air Force in 1969
43-16140	from storage to VNAF
43-16159	4th ACS, shot down in South Vietnam 5 May 1965, seven KIA
43-16368	4th SOS, flew last 4th SOS mission on 1 December 1969 as *Spooky 41*; later to VNAF
43-16379	605th SOS Super Puff Howard AFB, Canal Zone 1969
43-16605	3rd SOS
43-48263	606th ACS; later to VNAF; then to Khmer or Royal Laotian Air Force
43-48330	4th SOS
43-48356	FC-47, 4th ACS, shot down and crash landed near Bien Hoa on 23 March 1967
43-48462	early tests at Eglin AFB in 1964, first armed C-47
43-48466	
43-48471	1st ACS, first armed with SUU-11/A
43-48491	FC-47 *Git Em Bullit* 1st ACS; later to VNAF
43-48499	1st ACS; 4th ACS; 605th SOS
43-48501	1st ACS; 4th ACS; later to VNAF; then to Royal Thai Air Force
43-48579	Puff 1st ACS; 3rd SOS, base aircraft with no guns, call sign Orbit; to storage 24 November 1969
43-48591	606th ACS; 4th SOS, lost in South Vietnam 2 October 1967 *Raven 50* seven KIA
43-48686	606th ACS; later to VNAF
43-48701	3rd SOS; later to VNAF
43-48801	1st ACS; 3rd SOS; 4th SOS; later to VNAF
43-48916	3rd SOS; 4412th CCTS; 4th SOS
43-48921	606th ACS; 4th SOS, on 26 April 1967 crashed into sea near Cam Ranh Bay after mechanical failure of elevator system, seven killed
43-48925	4th ACS, shot down in Laos on 3 June 1966, six MIA
43-48929	4th ACS; 3rd SOS; later to VNAF
43-48941	
43-49010	3rd SOS; 4th SOS; 432nd TRW; Khmer Air Force; to Royal Laotian Air Force in 1969; to Royal Thai Air Force in 1975
43-49021	606th ACS; 3rd SOS; 4th SOS, shot down in South Vietnam on 1 September 1969 *Spooky 42*, eight KIA, last Spooky loss of the war
43-49124	4th ACS, lost in South Vietnam on 9 January 1967, seven KIA
43-49211	3rd SOS *Casper*; 4th SOS; later to VNAF
43-49268	4th ACS, lost South Vietnam on 13 March 1966 *Spooky 73*, seven MIA (also reported as having been shot down in Laos)
43-49274	1st ACS; 3rd TFW at Bien Hoa; 4th SOS; 3rd SOS, mid-air over South Vietnam with OV-10A on 13 December 1968, crash landed at Bien Hoa AB and written off, both OV-10A crewmen killed
43-49330	3rd SOS, destroyed in ground attack at Binh Thuy AB on 16 March 1968
43-49339	3rd SOS; later to VNAF
43-49354	4th SOS
43-49421	3rd SOS; 4th SOS, written off northeast of Bien Hoa after shot down at Long Khanh on 1 September 1969, last Spooky lost during the war
43-49423	3rd SOS
43-49492	4th ACS, shot down on transport mission from Tan Son Nhut to Phan Rang AB on 17 December 1965, nine KIA, first Spooky loss
43-49495	1st ACS; later to VNAF; then to Philippine Air Force
43-49499	4th SOS; 3rd SOS, destroyed in ground attack at Binh Thuy AB on 29 September 1968
43-49503	4th ACS; 3rd SOS, damaged by mortar fire at Bien Hoa AB on 16 June 1968
43-49516	3rd SOS; later to VNAF; then to Khmer Air Force
43-49517	606th ACS; 3rd SOS; 4th SOS; later to VNAF; then to Colombian Air Force
43-49524	later to VNAF
43-49546	4th ACS, shot down in Laos on 15 May 1966 *Spooky 10*, ten KIA (eight U.S. and two Vietnamese)
43-49770	damaged in flight by mortar round on 24 February 1969 *Spooky 71*, Levitow Medal of Honor; later to VNAF
43-49852	converted to AC-47D 1966; display at Bishops Museum, Honolulu, Hawaii
43-49859	4th SOS, 14th ACS, shot down near Phan Rang on 14 February 1968, eight KIA
43-49955	
44-76207	606th ACS; 4th SOS, shot down in South Vietnam on 5 May 1968, three KIA, Kent Air Force Cross
44-76290	4th ACS, crashed during mission in South Vietnam on 9 March 1966, one KIA, two MIA *Spooky 70*, Collins saved crewman
44-76354	3rd SOS; later to VNAF; then to Royal Laotian Air Force
44-76370	3rd SOS; 4th SOS; later to Royal Laotian Air Force
44-76394	later to VNAF; then to Philippine Air Force
44-76457	1st ACW
44-76534	4th ACS, shot down in South Vietnam on 29 March 1967 *Spooky 44* seven KIA

U.S. Air Force AC-47Ds CONTINUED

44-76542	4th ACS, destroyed in landing accident at Binh Thuy on 18 February 1967
44-76558	FC-47 test of first SUU-11/A; later to Philippine Air Force, derelict at Nichols AB in 1980, later at Villamor AB, Philippines
44-76593	1st ACS; 4th ACS; 3rd SOS
44-76606	later to VNAF
44-76625	4th ACS *Mac's Marauders*; 432nd TRW; later to Royal Laotian Air Force
44-76626	
44-76657	Khmer Air Force in 1972
44-76701	4th SOS
44-76717	4th SOS *Annette, Delta Queen*; later to VNAF
44-76722	1st ACS; 4th ACS
44-77263	4412th CCTS from 1967 to 1970
45-0916	1st ACS
45-0919	1st ACS; 22nd TASS; 3rd SOS; 4th SOS, ground looped at Binh Thuy AB in April 1968; to VNAF in 1969
45-0927	317th ACS, England AFB from June 1966 to April 1968; 4th SOS; later to VNAF
45-0934	
45-1047	3rd SOS; later to VNAF; then to Royal Laotian Air Force
45-1057	3rd SOS; later to VNAF
45-1065	4th SOS
45-1117	3rd SOS; *Sweet Pee*; 4th SOS; later to Royal Laotian Air Force
45-1120	4th ACS, shot down in Laos on 24 December 1965 *Spooky 21* six MIA, second Spooky loss
45-1121	later to VNA

This 4th ACS Spooky crew is being congratulated by Lt. Col. Trusty Whitehead (third from left), squadron operations officer, on 1 December 1966 for firing 80,000 rounds of ammunition at the enemy in a single night, a record for one crew. Crewmen, from left to right, are TSgt. Henry Eaton, TSgt. Grover Farmer, Maj. Sam Watson, Capt. Kurt Wehrle, Capt. Ace Bowman, Lt. Col. John Vastine, A1C Billy Vanschaick, and A1C Bruce Brown. (U.S. Air Force/Ace Bowman Collection)

An AC-47D of the 4th ACS is parked next to an EC-47N of the 360th Tactical Electronic Warfare Squadron in 1966. The Electric Gooneys of the 360th TEWS, which were easily identified by their elongated nose sections, detected enemy radio traffic, providing targets for Spookies. The narrow window above and forward of the cabin windows is the navigator's window. (Terry Love)

Patch worn by members of the 4th ACS prior to mid-1968, when all Air Commando Squadrons were re-designated Special Operations Squadrons. (Author's Collection)

Patch worn by Spooky crewmen in Vietnam. Such emblems side-stepped official guidelines for unit emblems. (Author's Collection)

Serial number 43-49770 of the 3rd SOS after the mission on 24 February 1969 when it was hit by a mortar round, which exploded in the right wing. Five crewmen were injured, including Levitow, who managed to throw out an armed flare seconds before it detonated. (John Bessette)

Although 1969 would mark the end of Spooky operations in Southeast Asia, AC-47D crews not only built on their enviable record in South Vietnam, but returned to Thailand. John H. Lamb, an AC-47D pilot with the 3rd Special Operations Squadron, provides this perspective:

"*In the spring of 1969, a classified program for USAF flight operations in Laos was developed by Colonel William H. Ginn, Deputy Commander for Operations of the 14th Special Operations Wing. His concept was to provide AC-47 gunship aircraft and crews to protect Laotian Lima Sites, similar to the way in which nighttime support was given to U.S. and Allied outposts and forward operating locations in South Vietnam. Since there was no basing of American aircraft and personnel in Laos, the crews operated from Udorn RTAFB in northern Thailand.*

"*Lima Site 50 and 50/A were two of many strategic outposts located on adjoining mountaintops near important lines of transportation and communications near the Plain of Jars (Plaines des Jares) in north-central Laos. Members of the Hmong tribesmen, who were supporting the American effort in the war, occupied the sites. The Hmong, led by General Vang Pao, were also attempting to prevent communist takeover of Laos by the Pathet Lao groups who were supported by the North Vietnamese Army. The Hmong always had their families with them. Any military battle involv-*

ing the Lima Sites inherently involved women and children. The Lima Sites were also used to pre-position American search and rescue assets for missions in North Vietnam, or to provide safe bailout areas for U.S. aircrews coming back from North Vietnam air strikes. Some, such as Lima Site 85, were critical sites where

An early version of a patch worn by the 14th ACS, which became the 3rd ACS. (Larry Davis Collection)

semi-permanent navigational radios had been set up for U.S. air-craft. The Pathet Lao had overrun Lima Site 85 the year before in March 1968 in a historic battle.

"In the secret meeting between General Vang Pao and Colonel Ginn to finalize planning and coordination for the oper-ation, Ginn looked Vang Pao in the eyes, shook his hand and said, 'Sir, you will not lose another Lima Site.'"

The 7th Air Force ordered four AC-47Ds to Udorn from the 4th SOS, which arrived in March 1969. Four crews were to serve 30-day rotations until November. Just three days after their arrival, Spooky crews went into action defending an outpost, and so it went, with Colonel Ginn making good on his promise to Vang Pao.

John Lamb offers this assessment of Spooky missions over Laos:

"Each mission was a highly challenging, perilous naviga-tional journey in itself. Missions were always during the hours of darkness. The old and slow AC-47 had to climb to 13,000 feet to get over the mountain range along the Laotian/Thai border, and then navigate to the target area by dead-reckoning, as there were a very limited number of navigational aids in Laos, and extremely rugged karst formations made the range of reception for any navigational device very limited. The crews had to fly through intense thunderstorms that hovered over the moun-tains. Once committed to altitudes for working the targets, if an engine failed, it would have been virtually impossible to get back to Thailand. Missions were flown in darkness because the enemy preferred to attack at night. The crews were under strict orders not to be seen in daylight hours over Laos in airplanes with USAF markings and, more importantly, they were at great risk from large anti-aircraft artillery weapons. Each member of the crew knew that being shot down and captured in Laos was a death sentence."

Lamb recounts this memorable mission on 7 April 1969 in sup-port of an intense firefight at Lima Site 50/50A in the Barrel Roll area of northern Laos:

"After penetrating the weather along the Thai/Laotian border, the crew of Spooky 03 navigated to the target area via a non-direc-tional beacon [NDB] near Long Tien, which was headquarters for General Vang Pao. To find the target, the crew had to fly off a bear-ing from the NDB until they could get within range of the ground troops on FM radio. The navigator located the target area quickly by being able to interpret the limited English spoken by the Hmong ground controller whose call sign was Lulu. When we arrived at the Lima Site, there was an intense firefight between the Hmong defenders and the Pathet Lao. The enemy was so close and the noise level was so high that Lulu was under great duress. We launched a flare and got Lulu to provide heading and distance to his location. When he knew that we were overhead, Lulu marked his position with a ground flare. Our navigator talked with Lulu throughout

the battle, giving us direction of the enemy where firepower was needed, and the status of the friendly troops.

"The crew commander, Capt. George W. Thompson, told his crew to help sort out the situation on the ground and locate the exact position of the Hmong outpost. Visibility in the area was obstructed by ground fog typical in the pre-dawn mountainous jungles, and there was a great deal of smoke and dust from explosions, mortar flares, and burning ground flares. Although the Laotian mission was significantly more challenging than any Thompson had flown in Vietnam, his rapid risk assessment, with input from crew mem-bers, plus my directing our firepower, saved the lives of the besieged fighters. Thompson put his life and career on the line and showed great courage in committing the crew of Spooky 03 to remain in the fight after sunrise, turning the tide of the battle in favor of the Hmongs. Ground troops reported many casualties and evidence of an estimated 60 to 75 bodies dragged off."

Monsoon rains limited air operations to the extent that two AC-47Ds were returned to Vietnam; however, their success in Laos gave rise to a plan not only to provide the Laotians with gunships, but to establish USAF gunship operations on a more permanent basis. Such a request in October by the Air Attache in Laos was passed to the Air Force Chief of Staff. Upon his approval, three AC-47Ds (serial numbers 44-76625, 43-16133, and 43-49010) were assigned to the 432nd Tactical Reconnaissance Wing at Udorn RTAFB. Officially called the 432nd Spooky Operations Unit, the trio became responsible for nighttime defense of Lima Sites, with a secondary responsibility of serving as radio relay between friendly sites under attack and an airborne command post, beginning 1 December. The 7th Airborne Command and Control Squadron maintained four orbits of C-130s, called Airborne Battlefield Command and Control Center (ABCCC); Cricket and Alleycat over northern Laos, and Hillsboro and Moonbeam over the south. The Wing itself was unique in that it was the only coordinated reconnaissance/strike unit in the Air Force. On 29 December, the AC-47D unit was phased out and its three aircraft transferred to the Royal Laotian Air Force (RLAF).

On 1 September 1969, a 4th SOS Spooky on night patrol was directed to assist troops who were under attack about 20 miles east of Bien Hoa. When *Spooky 42* arrived and began firing, it was hit in the right wing by ground fire and crashed in Long Khanh Province, killing its crew of eight. This was the last USAF Spooky lost during the war. The 3rd SOS was deactivated on this date and its aircraft passed on to the Vietnamese Air Force. The 5th SOS, which began sharing its psywar mission with the 9th SOS in 1967, and which also suffered losses, was also disbanded in 1969. Spookies also worked with EC-47Ns, a modification of the C-47 for electronic warfare. Assigned to the 360th and 432nd Tactical Electronic Warfare Squadrons (TEWS), the "Electric Gooneys" detected enemy radio traffic, and then called Spookies to finish the job.

Lt. Col. Adam W. Swigler, commander of the 4th SOS, flew the unit's last Spooky mission, taking off from Phan Rang AB on

30 November 1969 and landing on 1 December. Two weeks later, the squadron was inactivated. During more than four years of service, the accomplishments of the 4th SOS included nearly 4,000 outposts successfully defended, and crews were credited with 5,300 of the enemy killed. It had fired 97 million rounds of ammunition and dropped nearly 270,000 flares. And it had suffered the loss of 15 AC-47Ds and numerous crewmen. Of the squadron's 14 AC-47Ds, three were transferred to the VNAF, eight were ferried to Thailand for subsequent transfer to the RLAF, and three were assigned to the 432nd TRW at Udorn RTAFB. Since the deactivation of the 4th SOS signaled the end of AC-47D operations, military leaders in Thailand, along with the U.S. Ambassador to Thailand, lobbied strongly for continued gunship support. This cleared the way for the transfer of these aircraft, five crews, and support personnel to provide support until the RLAF was prepared to assume the gunship role. The AC-119K had been considered to support Lima Sites; however, the AC-47D not only required less maintenance support, it was thought to have a better chance of survival over the forbidding mountainous terrain.

There was a saying among soldiers in Vietnam: "The night belongs to Charlie." However true that may have been at the war's onset, it held no merit after Spooky gunships flew the unfriendly skies of Southeast Asia. For Spooky crews, nothing instilled a sense of accomplishment more than hearing from the occupants of the forts they had defended, "Thanks, Spooky. We wouldn't be here now if you hadn't come."

Although it has been commonly written that a total of 53 C-47s were converted to AC-47D gunships, 74 are known to have been converted, and possibly as many as 79. The five additional airframes likely became lost in the shuffle of AC-47s passed to foreign air arms. Although, as with production of the famed DC-3/C-47 itself, the exact number of gunship conversions may never be known, photographs, personal logbooks, and available documentation substantiate this larger number.

Besides the gaping hole in 770's wing, more than 3,500 holes were counted in the aircraft. It was never determined which side had fired the mortar round during the attack at Long Binh Army Base, which Spooky 71 was defending. (U.S. Air Force via John Bessette)

CHAPTER THREE

LITTLE BROTHER

Built by American Electric, the Piranha was the only singular-built private entry in the counterinsurgency light aircraft trials in 1965. Truly a mini-gunship, the tough, high-performance Piranha could carry seven tube-rocket launchers on its wing tips, and a 500-pound bomb on a belly centerline station. Pulled prematurely from the evaluations, the Piranha was stored for seven years before it was acquired by private owners and overhauled. The Piranha's designers likened its fuselage construction to the rugged tubular framework of the Lockheed F-104 Starfighter. (U.S. Air Force)

Spooky's immediate successor, the AC-119 Shadow, was often called Big Dumb Brother. That dubious endearment likely was derived from a lesser known gunship program called *Project Little Brother*. Like most Air Force research and development programs aimed at bolstering its counterinsurgency (COIN) force, *Project Little Brother* was based at the sprawling Eglin facility.

Prior to giving the *Gunship II* and *Gunship III* programs their full attention, Air Force planners also considered light, yet heavily armed, ground-attack aircraft. It was hoped that such aircraft would provide close support of counterinsurgency ground forces, especially U.S. Army commando teams, surpassing the accuracy of Army artillery. It was also hoped that small, yet heavily armed aircraft would give the South Vietnamese a gunship within the scope of their operating parameters. Based on proposals of a Limited War Study Group and an Air Force Systems Command task force, *Project Little Brother* had officials gathering Cessna, Beechcraft, and Piper aircraft at Eglin AFB. Cessna models 337 and Model 206, a Beechcraft Model

S35, and a Piper Cherokee 6 were leased from their manufacturers, while Cessna O-1E Bird Dog and O-2A Mixmaster were culled from Air Force training units based at Eglin. The first five O-1 Bird Dogs for the Air Force had arrived at Eglin for FAC tests in 1963. A small, dynamic, one-of-a-kind aircraft, called the Piranha, would also join this unusual mix. Despite the wide variety of propeller-driven aircraft gathered at Eglin, this group of light airplanes in civilian markings raised more questions than the Air Force was willing to answer.

Experiments with the seven light aircraft, which also contributed to ongoing evaluations for FAC platforms, got under way in 1965, with the models leased from manufacturers undergoing extensive modification for *Little Brother*. Cessna's Model 337 Super Skymaster was favored in view of its high-wing design, twin-engine power and safety, and 2,000-pound payload.

During late 1966, evaluators presented to Cessna officials a proposal for a tandem-seat, side-firing version of the Model 337. The exotic conversion would be called the O-2C, which would feature

This Cessna Model 337, in civilian paint and wearing registration number N6309F, was a Cessna test bed, which, in 1968, was extensively modified in response to an Air Force proposal for evaluation of a tandem-seat, turbine-powered O-2. The 337's minigun pictured here was but one of many under-wing stores evaluated at Eglin's ranges. (U.S. Air Force)

more powerful engines, armor plating, self-sealing fuel tanks, a laser range finder, and external microphones for detecting the location of ground fire. An automatic pilot would ease pilot workload, and night-flying instruments would ensure the cover of darkness. In keeping with the pylon concept proven by Spooky, large side-firing weapons were considered, including multiple .50-cal. machine guns and 20mm cannon. Planners settled on the MXU-470/A minigun module, citing its availability, weight, and minimal recoil. The O-2C's crew was to consist of a pilot and gunner.

The most amazing entry in the COIN light aircraft trials was the Piranha, which was conceived by Milt Blair and Richard Ennis in 1962. After buying-out Ennis' interest, Blair convinced American Electric to build the airplane. A mere 18 feet in length, with a 20-foot wingspan, the Piranha was built for military use. Rumored to have been fabricated from a C-130 external fuel tank, its fuselage was, in fact, patterned by its designers after the strong cylindrical airframe of Lockheed's F-104 interceptor. Combining both durability and high performance through superior design and craftsmanship, this unique craft boasted a gross weight of 2,000 pounds, and was able to get off the ground in only 800 feet. Blair's death while flying another aircraft caused the Piranha to be pulled from the evaluations, much to the dismay of those anxious to put the mini-gunship through its paces.

Little Brother aircraft are known to have been tested at Eglin's vast ranges with minigun pods, fire bombs, general purpose bombs, droppable re-supply containers, flares, and various types of rocket launchers. Dummies were even thrown from the Model 337 to test the feasibility of bailing out should the aircraft become disabled. Were it not for the fire-control system tested aboard *Little Brother* aircraft, the AC-119 and AC-130 would not have had so much success with their refined computerized fire-control systems. The Air Force Avionics Laboratory (AFAL) was responsible for development of this system, the design of which is credited to Royal Air Force Wing Commander Thomas C. Pinkerton, who was assigned to the AFAL. Several flights with the system aboard *Little Brother* aircraft were so promising that work began immediately on an enhanced version for the AC-130. Coordinating guns and sensors, improved fire-control equipment allowed heavy gunship crews to precisely acquire and engage targets, on day and night missions.

Especially interesting among *Little Brother* aircraft was the Beechcraft Model S35 Bonanza. After being fit with a conventional tail and having its wings strengthened for six hard-points—its outboard stations stressed for 300 pounds and inboards for 600 pounds—it was re-designated the Model D33. Although the *Little Brother* program lost momentum due to funds and hardware devoted to heavy

The seriousness of Air Force leaders about using light aircraft as gunships prior to completion of the AC-119 is evidenced by the miniguns and 250-pound bombs carried by this Cessna Model 206. The Super Skywagon was built in 1965 and leased by Cessna to the Air Force for the Little Brother project. Aircraft leased from manufacturers for the project retained their civilian livery and markings. (U.S. Air Force)

gunship development, it was kept alive with continued interest in the Model D33. Evaluation of the Beechcraft continued to the extent it was further modified with a more powerful 350-hp Continental G10-520 engine, driving a three-bladed propeller. Complete with an Air Force Southeast Asia camouflage scheme, the aircraft became the Model PD-249 but, although it showed promise, its evaluation came to an end during the early 1970s.

Despite the O-2's success in FAC and psywar roles plus Cessna's expanded research of the O-2, the closest it would come to the gunship role was marking targets with an AN/AVQ-12 PAVE SPOT laser illuminator.

Although the end of *Project Little Brother* shifted the focus back to heavy gunships, it would not close the chapter on Air Force involvement with light gunships. Late in the war, during the 1970s, when Southeast Asian governments were in a dynamic state of flux, the Air Force would again raise the issue of light fixed-wing gunships, this time, for Allied nations to continue the fight. Collaborating with the Fairchild and Helio companies, both of whom offered single-engine, short takeoff and landing (STOL) air-

craft easily converted to gunships, the Air Force oversaw the development of Fairchild's AU-23A and Helio's AU-24A. Under *Project Credible Chase*, Fairchild's AU-23A emerged as the gunship version of the Pilatus Turbo-Porter, while Helio's U-10A Courier gunship conversion became the AU-24A. Mounted in their left cargo doorway was a GE XM-197 20mm Gatling gun, which could be substituted for an MXU-470 minigun module.

Of the 17 AU-23As built, 15 were sold to the Royal Thai Air Force for counterinsurgency work, while 15 of the 17 AU-24As produced went to the Cambodian Air Force. Both aircraft types featured under-wing hard-points to accommodate a variety of stores, in addition to a fuselage centerline hard-point.

Despite the deserved attention and credit given the family of heavy gunships, the mighty midgets of *Project Little Brother* wrote a most unusual chapter in Air Force history. In what may be a comeback of light COIN aircraft in early 2007, the Aeronautical Systems Group at Wright-Patterson AFB conducted a market survey of potential sources to provide a light, yet heavily armed COIN aircraft for the government of Iraq.

Modified MA4A bomb shackles allowed the Cessna 206 to carry miniguns and bombs during tests at Eglin AFB. Although proven successful aboard large gunships, the SUU-11/A system was designed as an under-wing store, with spent cartridges and gun gases ejected through ports in the pod's casing. The MA4A was rated for a 350-pound maximum load, easily accommodating the SUU-11/A unit. (U.S. Air Force)

As part of Project Little Brother, this Beechcraft Model S35 Debonair, registered N5847K, was given a conventional tail, along with six wing hard-points for ordnance. Such major modifications resulted in a designation change to Model D33, seen here mounting a BLU-10 fire bomb outboard, flanked by a LAU-10A Zuni rocket launcher, and a seven-tube LAU-32 rocket launcher. (U.S. Air Force)

The proven Cessna O-1 Bird Dog, which entered the Air Force in 1963 at Eglin AFB, was included in Project Little Brother. Destined to become the Air Force's first pure FAC platform in Southeast Asia, its performance was adversely affected by the addition of bulky underwing armament. (U.S. Air Force)

The minigun pod mounted to the O-1 during the trial at Eglin was unlike those used aboard heavy gunships. It's likely that this unit featured a slower feed system for rates of fire between 2,000 and 4,000 rounds per minute, versus the 6,000 used on heavy gunships. The slower rate was standard for the Army's minigun system, called the XM-18, since helicopters carried ammunition only in the pod. All versions of the pod held 1,500 rounds of ammunition. (U.S. Air Force)

Piper's contribution to Little Brother was this Cherokee Six evaluated as a gun platform, seen here in this low-quality but extremely rare photograph, flying over an Eglin range with a pair of SUU-11/A minigun pods. The Piper's low-wing configuration blocked the pilot's downward view and proved to be a drawback for close support missions. (U.S. Air Force)

After Project Little Brother, Air Force planners remained optimistic about heavily armed light aircraft, renewing their quest for light gunships during the early 1970s. Their search resulted in Helio Courier's AU-24A and Fairchild's AU-23A. The latter is seen here with four under-wing stations. A three-barrel 20mm XM-197 Gatling gun is mounted in the left cargo doorway, keeping alive the proven side-firing concept. Peacemaker was one of 15 AU-23As delivered to the Royal Thai Air Force. (U.S. Air Force)

CHAPTER FOUR

SHADOW:
SPOOKY'S BIG DUMB BROTHER

This C-119C, S/N 51-2571, shows the distinctive features that earned it the name Flying Boxcar. The C-119 was sometimes called the "Pregnant P-38" since it drew upon the famous fighter's basic design of twin tail booms that incorporated the engines. Separating the fuselage from the tail unit allowed rear fuselage truck-bed loading through clam shell doors. The liberal use of glass gave the C-119's crew excellent visibility from the cockpit. (Fairchild Aircraft)

Once the concept of large, multi-engine aircraft concentrating massive amounts of ordnance on targets had been accepted, the door was open for advancing the gunship design. Total air superiority—over South Vietnam, at least—not only encouraged Air Force leaders to develop, test, produce, and commit to combat heavy gunships, it brought them closer to their goal of possessing the ultimate aerial gun platform. Such refinement would be found in the Lockheed family of AC-130s.

Although the AC-130 *Gunship II* program was well under way, the Fairchild C-119 Flying Boxcar was chosen as the AC-47D's immediate successor. This was due mainly to its quicker availability in large numbers. But it wasn't that simple, as a sufficient number of C-130s could not be spared due to worldwide airlift commitments, especially in Southeast Asia. Nor was the conversion of a large number of them to gunships cost effective. Air Force leaders prudently agreed that the C-119K, with jet augmentation providing additional power and subsequent safety, should be the basis for such a conversion. The Air Staff was dismayed when they learned that Air Force Secretary Harold Brown instead selected the C-119G in June 1967. Brown cited K model modification costs and deployment delays as the basis for his decision; AC-119K conversions would cost nearly five times more than AC-119Gs.

Gen. John P. McConnell, Chief of Staff, held firm his stance on the AC-130 in view of its search-and-destroy capability, survivability, and effectiveness over jet aircraft in the close-support role. Such opposition at the command level led to the development of the three major types of gunships. Following an Air Force Logistics Command cost-and-feasibility study of modifying C-119Gs into gunships, the Air Staff's hopes for rapid deployment of 12 AC-119Gs diminished when funding problems again loomed, and when Secretary of Defense McNamara hedged on his approval of the transfer of 46 Air Force Reserve C-119Gs to the active Air Force. Finally, on 20 October 1967, the order was given to begin conversion of a prototype.

The Dollar-Nineteen

Until the advent of the *Gunship III* program, the C-119 Flying Boxcar with its distinctive profile was remembered as a reliable workhorse of the Korean War. Spawned from Chase Aircraft's, and later Fairchild's, late–World War II C-82 Packet, the C-119 was first flown in November 1947, with delivery of C-119B production models beginning in 1949. Minor changes resulted in the production of 303 C-119Cs, which was surpassed by a total of 480 C-119Gs. Before production ended in 1955, nearly 1,200 Flying Boxcars would be delivered, primarily to the Air Force with the remainder placed in service with the U.S. Navy and Marine Corps, and foreign air arms. Fairchild acquired the Hiller Aircraft Company in 1964 and Republic Aviation Corporation in 1965, going through a number of corporate changes before its existence ended in 2002.

Nicknamed the "Dollar-Nineteen," the C-119 was a rather ungainly looking aircraft. Sacrificing beauty for function, the 119 featured a massive boxy fuselage with shoulder-mounted wings, necessitating the use of long, sturdy main landing gear located immediately aft of the engines. Adding to the 119's awkward appearance were upswept twin tail booms joined at the rear by a single horizontal section. From such features, however, came practicality. The Dollar-Nineteen was one of the first aircraft to offer truck-bed-height loading, along with large rear cargo doors allowing loading straight into the fuselage. This unique design also enabled paratroopers to jump without fear of striking any part of the aircraft.

Following the end of hostilities in Korea, C-119s served the active Air Force until 1957, when they filled the inventories of Reserve and Air National Guard airlift units. The C-119G model would become the most produced Dollar-Nineteen, and it would serve as the basis for the gunship conversion. This G model, S/N 51-8059 of the 939th Tactical Airlift Group, rotates on takeoff from Portland, Oregon, in 1968. (U.S. Air Force/Ron Olsen Collection)

The C-119 could carry 62 fully equipped troops or 30,000 pounds of cargo. It weighed 40,000 pounds empty, and its maximum takeoff weight was 74,000 pounds. The Flying Boxcar cruised at 250 mph, and it had a range of 2,000 miles with a service ceiling of 31,800 feet. Normally it flew with a crew of five. Wright R-3350-85 Duplex Cyclone and Pratt & Whitney R-4360-20 Wasp Major engines, both rated at 3,500hp, were used to power C-119s. Both powerplants were used throughout C-119 production; however, since the Strategic Air Command (SAC) operated the aircraft during the 1950s, Gen. Curtis LeMay insisted that SAC's C-119s, B-36s, B-50s, and KC-97s all use the same engine, the R-4360, which was standard on most SAC aircraft.

The R-4360 was a 28-cylinder, four-row radial, air-cooled engine. Featuring turbosuperchargers, the Wasp Major was considered the most proven and technically advanced reciprocating powerplant (recip). Aircrews were not fond of the four-blade Aeroproducts propellers, however, as they required constant attention, periodically going into over-speed conditions. Later the switch was made on AC-119Ks to more reliable three-blade Hamilton Standard props, which did not over-speed but provided less thrust, a condition for which the K model's podded jet engines compensated. Flying Boxcars were built at Fairchild's Hagerstown, Maryland, factory, although about 80 were built under contract by the Kaiser-Frazer automotive works at Romulus, Michigan.

The C-119 was an early participant in the Korean War, flying troops and equipment between Japan and Korea. Its high-tail, twin-boom design proved ideal for airdropping paratroopers and equipment. The bare metal finish, sultry nose art, and dazzling red-and-white trim of this C-119C speaks volumes about the consideration given camouflage during the Korean conflict, especially in comparison to cargo aircraft that would serve a decade later in Southeast Asia. (Nick Williams)

Gloss white over bare metal or light gray was the standard finish of C-119s until they ended their career in camouflage. Typical was this C-119C, S/N 2605, of the California Air National Guard's 129th Air Commando Squadron in 1968. (Author's Collection)

A few weeks after North Korea invaded the south in June 1950, the Air Force Tactical Air Command's 314th Troop Carrier Group brought C-119s into the conflict. Assigned to Troop Carrier Squadrons during the war, the C-119 would prove its value as a troop and equipment transport, flying missions between Japan and Korea, and air-dropping supplies and paratroopers. The C-119 had its equivalent in the U.S. Navy and Marine Corps as the R4Q-1 and -2, which replaced the R4D (C-47) as a tactical assault transport. The R4Q-1, of which 41 were built, matched the USAF C-119C. An improved version, the R4Q-2, like its USAF C-119F counterpart, was powered by R-3350-36W engines. Marine ground forces in Korea came to rely on R4Qs, with many of the 58 R4Q-2s built remaining in service until the early 1970s.

Another War

The C-119 first saw service in Vietnam as early as 1954 in the hands of French forces but were usually flown by Civil Air Transport (CIA-sponsored) pilots. These Boxcars were key participants in the siege at Dien Bien Phu, flying supplies to beleaguered French forces while under intense enemy fire. After their retirement from active duty in 1957, many USAF C-119s served Reserve and Air National Guard units into the early 1970s.

Even more controversial than the selection of the C-119 for use as a gunship was the dramatic difference in performance between the C-119G and C-119K, which translated to safety. From the time the type was first considered as the replacement for the AC-47D, Air Force planners were well aware and justifiably concerned that the G's performance at combat gross weight was only marginal. Those upgraded to K models with the addition of two wing-mounted

General Electric J85 jet engines could climb at 500 feet-per-minute with one piston engine out. The C-119G's single-engine ability, on the other hand, was so poor at combat gross weight that 7th Air Force leaders in Southeast Asia in 1968 openly questioned whether the underpowered G model should even be allowed to fly combat missions. Despite this drawback, skilled and dedicated combat aircrews would maximize the G's performance. In February 1968 Secretary Brown relented somewhat by approving the conversion of both C-119Gs and -Ks to gunships. The plan called for a total of 52 gunships. The first 26 were to be AC-119Gs, followed by 26 AC-119Ks.

Since the first AC-119Gs were due in Southeast Asia in June 1968, there was little time to waste. All agencies responsible for the conversion had to be keyed in, and the process begun. An organizational structure was quickly established, with the Air Force Logistics Command selecting the Warner Robins Air Material Area (WRAMA), Robins AFB, Georgia, to oversee the project. WRAMA officials, in turn, agreed that the C-119's manufacturer, Fairchild Hiller, could best do the conversion. Accordingly, on 17 February 1968, WRAMA awarded a contract to the firm for the completion and follow-on service of 51 AC-119Gs, excluding the prototype. Four days later, the AC-119G/K conversion program was officially labeled *Combat Hornet*, although it was more commonly known as *Gunship III*. Once operational, it was best known as Shadow. The agencies involved were reminded that C-119 conversion would contribute to the Phase II AC-119K project, and the AC-130 program as well.

WRAMA officials recommended that the aircraft be drawn from one or two airlift units of the Continental Air Command so that these units could turn over their entire C-119 support inventory. To form the initial cadre of *Gunship III*, Secretary Brown decided to use not only the C-119s of the 930th Tactical Airlift Group and the 71st

The small number of C-119Gs that entered the shadowy world of special operations were painted overall flat black, such as this C-119G, S/N 53-8087. (Nick Williams)

Tactical Airlift Squadron (TAS) at Bakalar Air Reserve Base, Indiana, but their crews as well. Brown reasoned that the unit's activity level and experience shortened the workload and the time necessary to transition a unit into the AC-119 program. The units received their activation notice on 11 April 1968, and were then reorganized into the 71st Air Commando Squadron and moved to Lockbourne AFB, Ohio. The squadron's C-119Gs were gradually sent to Fairchild Hiller's Aircraft Service Division in St. Augustine, Florida, for conversion to the AC-119G. Some of the unit's aircraft went to other squadrons to replace C-119s that had been committed to the modification program. Prior to delivery in St. Augustine, the aircraft were assigned to the Tactical Air Command's Special Air Warfare offices. On 8 July 1968, the squadron was re-designated 71st Special Operations Squadron of the 1st Special Operations Wing at England AFB, Louisiana.

Initial plans to convert C-119s to gunships included this design proposing an Emerson rotating turret with a Gatling type weapon in the aircraft's belly. Given the C-119's cargo capacity, planners were enthused about the huge amount of ammunition that could be carried for the weapon, although this deviated dramatically from the side-firing concept. (U.S. Air Force)

The AC-119's four minigun installation. Depressing the guns decreased the aircraft's bank angle during firing runs, giving the pilot more control, while easing the workload on gunners. It was difficult enough for them to work in the dark, amid the noise, while the aircraft was flown in a left bank. Interior lights that were used, typically, had red lenses. (U.S. Air Force)

The Marine Corps version of the C-119 was designated R4Q. Since two powerplants were used interchangeably, R4Q-1s were powered by 4360 engines, while R4Q-2s used 3350 engines. This R4Q-2 of VMR-234 Minneapolis Reserve, like some Marine variants, had a nose radome housing AN/APN-59 radar. (Jim Burridge)

A single YC-119H, which was a highly modified C-119C, S/N 51-2585, was built to compete with the C-130 as the follow-on for an advanced gunship. Nicknamed the "Skyvan," the YC-119H featured a modified tail group, extended wing span, and under-wing fuel tanks. The H model was powered by R-3350-85 engines. (U.S. Air Force)

Shadow's Hardware

Powerplants for the C-119s would be two Wright R-3350-89B air-cooled, 18-cylinder, two-row radial engines, each of which produced 3,500 horsepower at takeoff. Since the R-3350 was considered easier to maintain than the R-4360, it was intended that any C-119s earmarked for the K conversion be retrofitted if they were not equipped with this engine. Much of the equipment slated for installation in the AC-119Gs was common to both G and K models. These items consisted of the four miniguns, gunsight, fire control system, flare launcher, illuminator and night observation system, gas turbine power unit, armor, and communications and navigation gear.

Replacing the 8-foot-long minigun pods with MXU-470/A modules gave crewmen more room to work during attack missions. Located at the top of the gun's control box was a tube through which ejected shell casings were directed into empty ammunition containers strapped to the gun mounts. (David Galvan)

Wind spoilers were attached to the forward edge of gun ports to help prevent gun smoke and gasses from being blown into the cabin. Above each port was an air scoop that directed outside air onto the gun barrels to aid in cooling. The aircraft's black finish was semi-gloss. (David E. O'Mara)

The AC-119G (S/N 53-3136) at Bien Hoa Air Base in July 1969. The crew doorway with boarding ladder was part of the modification package for AC-119G and K gunships. Visible at the mid-fuselage is the exhaust for the gas-turbine-power unit used to power much of the Shadow's equipment. (William Draeger)

The Shadow's powerful 20kw illuminator unit was mounted in the left rear doorway. The safety strap across the top of the opening was later replaced by a metal bar. Normally, the illuminator lens was covered during ground operations. (Larry Mersek)

The LAU-74/A flare launcher mounted in the right rear clam shell doorway used either pressurized air or nitrogen. Underscoring the danger of flares, which burned at 4,000 degrees F, was the unit's temperature sensors that triggered an eject mechanism, causing the unit to be ejected from the aircraft in an emergency. (David E. O'Mara)

Compared to the AC-47D, the AC-119's slab-sided fuselage gave the night observation sight operator ample room to work. Here, Navigator Maj. Robert N. Beaty of the 71st SOS checks the sight prior to a mission. On the AC-119K, an armor panel was added to the lower portion of the opening. (U.S. Air Force)

The operator's position for the night observation sight (NOS), which was also called the night observation device (NOD), occupied what had been the crew doorway. The smoke ejector scoops, which were located on both sides of the aircraft, are in the open position. (via Stephen Miller)

Working with a minimal amount of light, Shadow navigator 1st Lt. William C. Dawson peers through the night observation sight during a mission in 1969. Mounted atop the NOS was a three-power day sight. Based on what he saw through the scope, the NOS operator directed the Shadow's firepower. (U.S. Air Force)

At the heart of the system were four 7.62 miniguns familiar to the AC-47D. Firing out the left side of the fuselage, each gun had a rate of fire of 3,000 or 6,000 rounds per minute. Sighted and controlled by the pilot, they could be fired individually or in any combination, and each gun held 2,000 rounds and could be loaded in flight. Although ball and tracer ammunition was standard, aircrews favored armor-piercing incendiary (API) since it dramatically enhanced Shadow's effectiveness. A limited amount of API was obtained from the U.S. Army for use on a trial basis in AC-119Gs. The selling feature of API was its brilliant sparkle on impact, which enabled the pilot to see precisely where the bullets were hitting, further enabling him to adjust fire for pinpoint accuracy. Equally impressive was API's effectiveness against hard targets such as trucks, vessels, and structures.

A marked improvement over the AC-47D was a fire control system, tested during the *Little Brother* project, and made operational in the AC-119G. This intricate system, which was produced by General Precision Systems, Inc., vastly improved the gunship's ability to identify and hit targets in complete darkness. This system was comprised of an analog computer, sensors, safety CRT-type display panel, optical gunsight, sight amplifier, sight control panel, and boresight unit. Other interface units were integrated into the system.

Target identification was accomplished with a night observation sight (NOS). When aimed at the target, the NOS sent to the computer data on angular line of sight in relation to the aircraft's lateral axis. The computer added this data to the airplane's magnetic heading and altitude to give the aircraft-target association, or coincidence, and to position a moving reticle, representing the target, on the pilot's display. The computer corrected for wind, altitude, and aircraft heading and roll.

Three modes of firing were available to the pilot, two of which—automatic and semi-automatic—involved the full system, requiring

A navigator of the 17th SOS works at the illuminator's service module and control panel. Behind him, in the opposite doorway, is the 24-flare LAU-74/A launcher. (David Galvan)

Although the initial design of the NOS included a seat, operators found it easier to stand and brace themselves while sighting through the scope. (David Galvan)

that the pilot align the moving and fixed reticles on his gunsight combining glass. The two modes differed only in that in automatic mode the guns were fired only when both reticles were in perfect alignment. In semi-automatic mode, the NOS operator had to see, track, and confirm the target, signaling through lights on the pilot's display when the target was acquired, and when it was safe to fire. Built by TRW Systems, the display ensured that weapons were not trained on friendly troops. Remaining was the manual mode, in which the pilot had to see the target, and involved only the gunsight and fixed reticle. This mode also required that the aircraft fly at the altitude for which the guns were boresighted, and be in a 30-degree left bank.

From Electro-Optical Systems came Shadow's "eyes," the AN/AVQ-8 airborne illuminator and night observation sight. Mounted on the left-forward side of the aircraft in the crew doorway, the NOS swiveled on a yoke assembly, allowing 180-degree lateral travel, 70 degrees downward and 30 degrees upward. For night viewing, the NOS amplified available light, typically moonlight and starlight, thousands of times, giving the operator a relatively clear image of the target, although in a pale green hue. Mounted atop the NOS housing was a standard three-power day sight.

The illuminator system produced high-intensity light in either the visual or infrared spectrum. At its full power of 20 kilowatts (kw), the illuminator's beam was rated at 425,000 lumens, with a beam spread adjustable from 20 to 40 degrees. It was said that if the Shadow was overhead at 5,000 feet with its illuminator at full power, one could read a newspaper on the darkest night. With the beam spread to its 40-degree maximum, your friend a half-mile away could also read his. When in infrared mode, the illuminator could be used in conjunction with the NOS. The illuminator's lamp unit was pallet-mounted in the

The newly converted AC-119G, S/N 53-3170, was delivered to the 71st SOS at Nha Trang amid much fanfare in December 1968. Shortly thereafter, the crew door would be removed and mission equipment, including the miniguns, was installed. (U.S. Air Force)

left clamshell doorway, while its large desk-size service module and control panel was immediately forward of the doorway.

Filling the opposite clamshell doorway was a Stratus Western LAU 74/A flare launcher. The four-tube, semi-automatic launcher was pneumatically operated, launching flares singly in a starboard aft direction. The launcher held 24 Mk 24 MOD magnesium flares, rated at two-million candlepower each.

Shadow's communication and navigation equipment comprised UHF, VHF, FM, and liaison radios, with speech encryption and direction-finding capability. Power for the wide variety of special equipment, especially the illuminator, came from a Garrett 60-kVA power unit similar to those used in the Boeing 727 and Douglas DC-9 airliners. The unit was housed in a fireproof container located in the right forward fuselage.

Since incapacitating toxic smoke, along with searing heat and blindness, would result from the ignition of a flare inside the aircraft, a smoke-removal system similar to that used in the AC-47D was installed. Air Force specifications called for a system that had to clear the smoke in ten seconds. Fairchild Hiller complied by installing air scoops that could be opened on both sides of the forward fuselage. Smoke spoilers were attached to both sides of the rear fuselage, forward of the clamshell doors, forcing smoke out into the slipstream.

Completing the AC-119G's equipment package was the installation of Goodyear alumina ceramic armor plate in the cockpit area and cargo compartment. Although the first AC-119G was delivered to the Air Force in the tri-tone and light gray camouflage scheme familiar to aircraft in Southeast Asia, all 26 aircraft would receive a liberal application of black paint, with only the upper surfaces being camouflaged.

Crew Training and Duties

Shortly after AC-119G conversion began, the Tactical Air Command planned crew training, which was divided into two phases. Phase I training, which included simulator and field exercises plus checkout, became the responsibility of the 302nd Combat Crew Training Squadron at Clinton County AFB, Ohio. The C-119s came from the 302nd Buckeye Tactical Airlift Wing, with training conducted by Reserve personnel who had become old hands at flying and maintaining C-119s; the 302nd had received C-119s as replacements for their C-46s in 1957. On 1 July 1968, the 302nd was re-designated the 1st Tactical Airlift Training Squadron (TATS). It was also known as the 1st Combat Crew Training Squadron (CCTS). Before the unit closed its doors in 1972, ending C-119 training, it would graduate 457 pilots, 264 navigators, 202 flight mechanics, and 1,573 maintenance personnel, along with 242 aircrew and maintenance personnel from Ethiopia, Morocco, Jordan, and South Vietnam. During its five-year existence, the unit logged more than 13,000 accident-free flying hours.

Phase I graduates then received orders to report to the 4413th CCTS at Lockbourne AFB, Ohio. The 4413th had been established by Tactical Air Command on 1 March 1968. While at Lockbourne, aircrews received combat aircrew training and flew mainly dry fire missions. Other missions were flown including airborne support at

Pope AFB, North Carolina, combat cover missions at Eglin, and parachute tests at Wright-Patterson AFB, Ohio. Aircrew also completed the Basic Survival School at Fairchild AFB, Washington. In June 1971, the 4413th was relocated from Lockbourne to Hurlburt Field. At the time of transfer, the squadron had eight AC-119Ks and six AC-130As assigned.

The Shadow flew with a combat crew of eight men. David E. O'Mara, who served as an AC-119G pilot with the 17th SOS, best explains their duties:

"The aircraft commander, or AC, was responsible for everything on the aircraft during flight, and for his assigned crewmen when on the ground. He flew the aircraft into position using the ILS Course and Glideslope Indicator and side-mounted gunsight. He fired the guns with a yoke-mounted button under his right thumb. The copilot was second in command, assisting in every way he could, monitoring radios, check lists, fuel, engine instruments, aircraft attitude, crew coordination, and map reading. While in the firing circle, he was responsible for aircraft pitch control. Being a copilot was an extremely frustrating job, since pilots were taught only how to be an aircraft commander.

"The table navigator, or nav, was responsible for getting the aircraft safely to and from targets and landing fields. He was responsible for the master gun switch, a red, guarded switch located directly in front of him on the bulkhead above his nav table. He was also responsible for setting the coincidence ring. When the gunsight was in automatic mode, and the coincidence set at zero and the pilot's trigger depressed, the guns would fire only when the sights were perfectly aligned. The nav would use the master

switch if anyone called 'cease fire.' It was also his responsibility, using the FM radio, to check for artillery and tell the pilots how to navigate around such fire zones. This was usually accomplished using TACAN radials and arcs to fly courses around hot areas. He was an additional link in the chain of ensuring adequate fuel supply by monitoring the length of time airborne. This was much more critical on combat missions, when the crew was focused on the fight.

"The night observation sight operator, also a fully qualified table navigator, after freeing the sight from its cruise mountings, ran the gimbals through their range of motion. His primary duty was finding and aiming at targets the pilot could not see, giving him the awesome responsibility of directing the aircraft's firepower. The nav and NOS operator usually switched positions from mission to mission.

"The flight engineer, often called the FE or flight mech, sat between the pilots, monitoring the engines and mechanical systems. A rich fuel mixture caused the R-3350 to leave an exhaust signature, so to prevent advertising the aircraft's arrival in the target area, the FE worked with the copilot adjusting power in the firing circle to maintain proper airspeed and fuel mixture.

"The illuminator operator, or IO, operated the light, using a filter to change from white light to infra-red. He also manually armed and fired flares from the launcher. The IO, along with the FE, was responsible for the gas turbine power unit. Both were mechanically qualified and shared the same specialty code. There was enough work for two gunners, who were supervised by the IO, who often helped with their work. The gunners not only maintained, loaded, and cleared the miniguns, they adjusted the

Shadow pilot Capt. David O'Mara poses atop an AC-119G's forward fuselage, where numerous antennas were located. The horseshoe-shaped antenna is the VOR, while the wire antenna behind him corresponded to the LORAN. In the foreground is the radio compass wire antenna. The astrodome above the flight deck, at far right, is open. (David E. O'Mara Collection)

Connected to a power cart, AC-119G S/N 53-3136 of the 17th SOS goes through a pre-mission run-up in 1970. Unusual is the straight demarcation line, often called the "cheat Line," separating the Shadow's upper camouflage from black undersurfaces. Lower cockpit windows on some aircraft were painted over. (David E. O'Mara)

aiming angle for each of the four firing altitudes. Since the AC-119G was loaded to maximum gross weight for every combat mission, the gunners loaded 35,000 rounds of linked ammo. This was hot, dirty, and often dangerous work, since barrels periodically exploded. Keeping up with four miniguns in a blacked-out, maneuvering aircraft was demanding.

"It is a little known fact that all AC-119G aircrews were FAC qualified. Unlike our fighter jock brethren, the crew was on its own to navigate to and identify targets, coordinating every factor of combat missions. The ground commander became the director of the gunship's power, yet the AC and his crew were responsible for every round fired. During a Troops in Contact (TIC) mission was when the entire combat ready AC-119G crew was at peak performance. All crewmembers were involved in every aspect of the flight. We looked after each other but, foremost, we were mission oriented."

Growing Pains

As crews honed their skills with training flights and live-fire missions over ranges at Lake Erie and Camp Atterbury, Indiana, the modification process ran into snags. The AC-119G was overweight. The problem stemmed from engineers and technicians cramming a great deal of equipment into the AC-119G, much of which proved

The AC-119G S/N 52-5927 shows off the Shadow's color scheme. The upper camouflage pattern was applied to the tailplane. The scheme used a minimum of markings, comprising only small national insignia on the wings and fuselage, along with the serial number in red on the tail fin. (U.S. Air Force)

heavier than expected. The result was an unhealthy negative climb rate should an aircraft lose an engine during takeoff. As engineers advanced through the modification steps and set their goals, they were unaware that Pacific Air Forces staff was drawing up AC-119G performance standards more stringent than they'd expected. So the program continued, albeit headed for trouble, for lack of inter-agency communication and coordination.

Gas turbine engines and electronic components were on high-priority lists, which increased costs, but flexibility for time delays had not been figured into the conversion program. The 7th Air Force impatiently awaited their much-needed gunships, and anyone who was in any way involved with getting the aircraft to Southeast Asia was mindful that time was of the essence. From the onset, miniguns were in short supply, and this ultimately led to the cancellation of a parallel program in which 39 miniguns were earmarked for installation in VNAF AC-47s. Since USAF AC-47Ds had new gun modules, their gun pods, destined for the VNAF, were instead diverted to the AC-119G program. In March 1968 the Army agreed to provide a sufficient number of guns to fill the gap, and the Air Force Logistics Command (AFLC) hastened procurement of MXU-470 modules from General Electric.

To regain perspective of AC-119G modification and to keep it on track, a conference with all agencies involved was held during late April. Besides addressing problems, the attendees worked out a revised production schedule which called for the delivery of all 26 AC-119Gs from 21 May through 22 October 1968, and all AC-119Ks from 14 October through 31 March 1969.

Complying with the target date, Fairchild Hiller delivered the first AC-119G, S/N 53-8069, to the Air Force on 19 May 1968 at Warner Robins AFB. Number 069 went to the Tactical Air Command on 9 June and immediately was scheduled for limited flight testing concurrent with instructor pilot training. Within one week, four

instructor pilots had been qualified, enabling the 4413th CCTS to schedule its first class of Vietnam-bound AC-119G crewmen.

Evaluators of the 1st Combat Applications Group at Hurlburt put the AC-119G through its paces, flying 25 test sorties throughout June. Except for a problem with the fire-control system, all new systems checked out; the aircraft itself did not. As expected, evaluators quickly discovered that the AC-119G was too heavy to meet the engine-out standard of sustaining a 200-feet-per-minute rate-of-climb during hot weather at a gross weight of 62,000 pounds; the AC-119G's combat configuration would exceed that weight, requiring a smaller fuel load and, subsequently, less loiter time. In response to WRAMA staff's proposal to reduce the engine-out rate-of-climb requirement to 100 feet per minute, 7th Air Force staff cried "unacceptable," and responded, "It is necessary to maintain the specified 200-feet-per-minute rate-of-climb capability at 103 degrees F, 80 percent humidity." Equally unsurprising was the final test report's recommendation that the AC-119G's weight be reduced. The program's deployment goals seemed more distant than ever.

A conference held on 26 July and successive talks about reducing aircraft weight accomplished little more than producing a laundry list of removable items—from a heavy ammunition storage rack to access covers—and debating the reduction of performance requirements. Pilots experienced in the C-119 knew that in an emergency, a 100-foot-per-minute rate-of-climb on one engine was shaving it too close. Finally, on 24 August, WRAMA officials decided that Fairchild Hiller should do the weight reduction. The *Gunship III* program was becoming even more expensive. Such problems caused some Air Force staff members to re-focus on the reliable AC-47Ds, even suggesting that they not be too hasty to replace them all. The pall over the AC-119G's performance also caused the Air Staff's attention to shift toward the AC-119K, which would have auxiliary jet engines and more firepower. The only two factors preventing the conversion of all

Hooked up to a power cart, Shadow S/N 53-3136 stands alert at Bien Hoa AB in July 1969. (William Draeger)

C-119s into jet-equipped K models were an even longer deployment delay, and a shortage of J-85 jet engines, which were also being used to modify C-123s needed in Southeast Asia.

Although the last of the AC-119Gs was delivered to the Air Force on 11 October 1968, not all had been put through the weight reduction program. After much debate about gunship, and subsequent manpower, requirements in Southeast Asia, Deputy Defense Secretary Paul Nitze approved on 27 November 1968 the deployment of the 71st SOS. In conjunction with the order, Nitze ordered a study of the need for both AC-47D squadrons in Vietnam, proposing also the acceleration of the turnover of AC-47Ds to the VNAF. On 25 September Gen. Nazzaro, Commander in Chief, Pacific Air Forces, notified Gen. McConnel that the enemy's stepped-up attacks on populated areas and military installations proved the need for two AC-119G squadrons. Since AC-47D Spooky crews had written the book on gunship operations, it fell upon the next generation of specially trained crewmen flying vintage airplanes to write the chapter devoted to the AC-119 gunship.

Combat

The 71st SOS was to ferry 18 AC-119Gs to South Vietnam, with stops at McClellan AFB, California; McChord AFB, Washington; Elmendorf AFB, Alaska; Adak, Midway, Wake, Guam, and Clark AB, Philippines. The miniguns and their mounts were removed to accommodate a 500-gallon bladder-type fuel tank. Each aircraft carried a crew of five, while all other unit personnel and equipment made the trip in three C-141s. The first two AC-119Gs departed Lockbourne on 5 December 1968, while others left as they completed weight reduction at St. Augustine. The first two arrived at Nha Trang, South Vietnam, on 27 December, with four aircraft on hand by year's end. The unit's full complement of 18 AC-119Gs had arrived by February 1969. During the 9,800-mile trip, two aircraft required engine changes, which were accomplished at Tinker AFB, Oklahoma and Wake Island. As crews arrived, they were first sent to the Jungle Survival School, popularly called "Snake School," at Clark AB, Philippines, and then put through combat check-outs with their aircraft.

The 71st was assigned to the 14th Special Operations Wing (SOW) at Nha Trang AB. The 14th SOW was considered the most versatile in Southeast Asia with five combat squadrons flying seven different aircraft types from nine locations in Vietnam and Thailand. The wing boasted the only AC-119 gunship units in theatre, plus the only psychological warfare squadron, and the only Air Force UH-1 Huey helicopter combat squadron. Nha Trang would become the main support base for the 71st SOS. Shortly after the 71st arrived, 7th Air Force officials assigned it the call sign Creep. This accomplished nothing more than providing personnel of the 71st an early opportunity to show Air Force officials the ferociousness and determination they would display in combat. The call sign was quickly changed to Shadow.

The first AC-119G combat mission was flown on 5 January with squadron commander Donald F. Beyl at the controls of number 52-5907. During the four-and-a-half-hour mission 1,300 rounds were fired. The AC-119G would be scrutinized in its combat role until 8 March. On 7 March, aircraft number 52-5927 became the first to be hit by enemy fire. During May five more were hit, with one damaged by multiple 12.7mm hits resulting in injuries to a gunner. Less debilitating for crewmen, although having an adverse effect on crew workload, were flu-like illnesses caused by the Shadow's numerous door and window openings. Baffles added to the rear cabin reduced the cold winds experienced at higher altitudes, thereby reducing the number of grounded aircrew.

Shadow operated under the same gunship attack philosophy as its predecessor, Spooky—that being to fly a left pylon turn around the target with the pilot looking through a sight, maneuvering to keep the enemy under continuous fire. The aircraft's circular path, called "the firing circle," completely surrounded the enemy, permitting no recovery. As the Shadow's potential and availability became known to ground commanders, the following Air Force guidelines were distributed to maximize their use of heavy gunships:

"Controlling the Shadow and Stinger: When you have been assigned a Shadow or Stinger for support, there are some things that you can do to get the aircraft on target quickly.

"When contacted by the gunship crew, give them your exact position in UTM grid coordinates, if possible. Describe any prominent land features. If you can do so, mark your position with a strobe or some light and tell the aircrew how far your perimeter extends around it.

"All gunship work is done out of the left side of the aircraft. Since the aircrew cannot see straight down, direct the gunship into a counterclockwise orbit around your position.

"When requesting firepower or flare light from the gunship, give the aircrew the location of the target in magnetic direction and distance in meters from your position. If possible, mark the target with smoke or tracers. The gunship will fire a short marking burst of tracers or launch a flare on the designated target. You can adjust the fire or flares for greater accuracy by having the gunship move it in any direction the required number of meters.

"The gunship will probably work with no visible light, relying on the night observation sight and the illuminator in the infraredmode. Stinger may work with its infraredsensor (FLIR) being used for targeting.

"The gunship will work over the target until you and the aircrew feel that the area has been adequately covered. You can move the firepower to any area you desire by giving the aircrew the range and bearing from the last target. Constantly keep the gunship crew advised of the location of all friendly units in the immediate vicinity of the targets. It is absolutely necessary that the gunship crew be familiar with friendly locations to avoid short rounds.

"By following these procedures you will have the Shadow and Stinger giving you maximum close support. The free exchange of all helpful information will make a potent air-ground team to accomplish the mission of keeping Charlie reeling under constant pressure."

The Charlotte Representative *identified number 53-7848 of the 17th SOS in 1970.* (David E. O'Mara)

Shadow pilot Capt. David O'Mara jokingly adds to the aircraft's firepower. His .38-cal. revolver was standard issue for gunship crewmen; larger weapons were also carried in the event of they were shot down. After some hard lessons with AC-47Ds lost earlier in the war during ground attacks, high-wall revetments protected the aircraft at air bases. (David E. O'Mara Collection)

Nose art incorporating the name "Charlie Chasers" was worn by two Shadows of the 17th SOS during 1970. Survival vests and sidearms were worn by Shadow crews on all missions in Southeast Asia. (David E. O'Mara Collection)

This image, in which Capt. O'Mara tries to hand turn the aircraft's huge prop, shows the C-119's massive main landing gear, which often proved troublesome, requiring expert use of the controls on landing. (David E. O'Mara Collection)

This crewman's shirt advertises the use of Shadows over the Ho Chi Minh Trail, although limited. Missions "across the fence" were more often flown over Cambodia, where a more permissive environment allowed even daylight missions. (Larry Mersek)

Crews at all locations flew three missions each night with the first takeoff at dusk, followed by two more at two- to three-hour intervals. Missions usually lasted four hours or longer. During the combat evaluation period, emphasis was placed on Shadow's close air support of *Troops in Contact* and the protection of base camps and hamlets. The AC-119G also flew armed reconnaissance and interdiction, as well as forward air control missions. In the interdiction role, Shadow could detect and destroy enemy road and river traffic, along with enemy strong-points, and received high marks except in the FAC role, due to its slow speed, lack of maneuverability, and vulnerability to ground fire. The AC-119G's lack of all-weather systems hampered its use in fog and haze. While being evaluated, Shadow crews found nearly 600 targets, more than half of which were encountered during interdiction sorties in assigned patrol areas. During this period, the 71st SOS maintained an aircraft operational readiness rate of 79 percent, and was credited with destroying five large gun positions and 31 trucks, along with storage areas and base camps. Although 86 instances of ground fire were reported, only one aircraft was hit by small arms fire.

As more aircraft and aircrew arrived and a sufficient number of crews became combat ready, the 71st was dispersed to forward operating locations (FOLs) to adequately provide gunship support throughout the war zone. The first FOL was established at Tan Son Nhut AB in mid January with five AC-119Gs, called Flight C. Flight B began operating at Phan Rang AB by mid February with six AC-119Gs. Five of these aircraft remained at Nha Trang AB as Flight A, along with two spares. If an aircraft had to go to Nha Trang for heavy maintenance or inspection, one of the spares was sent to the FOL in its place. During March, AC-119G assets were further divided with Flight A operating from Tuy Hoa AB. Da Nang and Phu Cat Air Bases would also serve as launch sites for Shadow missions. Flight B was tasked primarily with providing support for *Troops in Contact,* mainly in Military Region II, and with training VNAF aircrews. Flight C had the three-fold mission of supporting *Troops in Contact,* convoy escort, and armed reconnaissance in Cambodia. It was not unusual for Shadows to perform all three missions during one sortie. To prepare Flight C aircrews for missions over the Ho Chi Minh Trail in Cambodia, they were sent to Nakhon Phanom RTAFB to fly missions with C-123 Candlestick flare aircraft. To familiarize crewmen with the FAC mission, an F-100 Fast FAC pilot was on board. After a few humbling missions over the heavily defended trail, Shadow crewmen returned to Tan Son Nhut and flew their first mission on 28 January 1969.

As enemy forces took greater control of Cambodia, a dramatic increase in operations in the beleaguered region included 24-hour interdiction of enemy supply routes. The country's relatively small size enabled the AC-119Gs to react quickly to enemy movements. Since forward air controllers constantly monitored enemy gun positions, Shadows flew daytime missions avoiding high-threat areas. As AC-119K gunships were deployed, they augmented Shadow operations in Cambodia during periods of peak activity. Trucks and sampans became the Shadow's primary targets, but the enemy learned quickly to protect vessels with armor. Although Shadow crews earned a reputation as truck killers, the AC-119K's larger guns would prove more effective against such hardened targets. Nevertheless, U.S. air support in Cambodia brought the AC-119G to center stage and its vigil over Allied river and road traffic brought relief to the critical petroleum shortage in the nation's capitol, Phnom Penh. Convoy cover by Shadows became a 24-hour affair, flying orbits over convoys at 3,500 feet. During daylight, convoys were monitored by FACs flying at 2,500 feet, and a U.S. Army light fire team, consisting of a command and control UH-1 Huey, two Cobra gunships, and two light observation helicopters, flying at 1,500 feet. Backing up the AC-119Gs at night were two U.S. Navy Huey helicopters and two OV-10 Broncos. This tri-service air cover package was controlled by 7th Air Force.

With ground radar as a backup, Shadow crews navigated to and within their assigned patrol area, called a "box," by TACAN, which gave the pilots constant distance and bearing data emitted from short-range UHF radio sites. Airfields were identified by their TACAN radio channels. Shadow pilot Jack Chandler wrote in his narrative, *Deny Him the Dark*:

> "Lights out. We turned the anti-collision beacon off. The wing and tail lights were already off. We never used the running lights except in the traffic pattern at Phu Cat. The aircraft carried no defensive systems at all; only the darkness protected us from ground fire. The night and our weaponry were effective. The worst thing about flying the old birds was that it took so long to get to the strike area. With troops in the wire, such as our friends in Laos had, the friendlies could all die before we could creep into their vicinity. It was a trade-off; the fighters could get there in minutes, but they couldn't hit a football field without wiping out the stands and the parking lot in the process. It took us longer to get there, but we usually delivered ordnance where it needed to be—and nowhere else."

When close to the mission area, the crew went through final preparations for firing. The copilot and the navigator verified the aircraft's position and the altimeter setting for B altitude of 3,500 feet (A altitude was 1,500 feet). The IO prepared the illuminator and flare launcher. He started the gas-turbine-power unit. Gunners loaded ammunition into the minigun canisters. Although they held 2,000 rounds each, only 1,500 were loaded since that was the amount stored in ammunition containers; every fifth round was a tracer. The gunners then shifted 100-pound ammunition cans into place beside the loaded guns, ready to reload as the guns emptied. Wrestling with the heavy cans made heavier by g forces, gunners struggled to maintain their balance during maneuvering. Maintaining 500 feet clearance from terrain, Shadow crews searched for targets.

When a target was detected and identified, and the location of friendly forces verified, crewmen plotted the coordinates and radioed for clearance to fire. This entailed a rapid but vital exchange between the aircraft commander, navigator, FAC, the ground commander, and the 7th Air Force Tactical Air Control Center. When the AC lined up the target and pressed the firing trigger, the aircraft interior was filled with a deafening roar as the brilliance of gun-muzzle flash eerily lit the aircraft interior. Jack Chandler adds, "An angry Shadow could put 400 rounds per second into a target with all four guns on line at high rate. We didn't usually fire more than one gun at a time because it took too much time to reload them all. Sometimes I shot two, but I preferred to stretch out our time on target. It kept their heads down longer. I walked my fire along the line of attackers with the rudder pedals. It was easier to move the fire around with the rudders than it was to offset the firing circle a few feet with each circuit, and I got them a lot quicker too."

Shadow gunner David Galvan recalls, "I've seen the six barrels of each gun turn cherry red, then white at the front third of the length, before running out of ammo. We once dumped 33,000 rounds on bad guys about to overrun at Siem Reap, Cambodia. It took roughly only 15 minutes. In our haste to keep up with [the] pilot's trigger finger, we were tossing the cans behind us as we emptied them. We gunners carried a 12-inch screwdriver to rotate red-hot barrels as we primed the gun after loading. As we fired the last of the ammo, we collapsed in a sweat-sodden mass wherever we could find floor space." Often, Shadow crews saw enemy responses to their lethal rain of fire—gray smoke trails from rockets, or red, green, or yellow tracers probing for their fat target, which, in daytime, would have been difficult to miss. Yet, enemy rounds often found their mark.

Like their Spooky brethren, Shadow crews got their greatest satisfaction from preventing outposts and hamlets from being overrun. The enemy, who relied on the cover of darkness, was caught unprepared by Shadow's ability to rain fire without first dropping flares. The enemy now had to reconsider the danger of every approaching aircraft, learning the hard way that the AC-119Gs of the 71st SOS lived up to their motto, "Deny Him the Dark." That motto took on other meanings. On occasions when there was no target to be engaged, Shadow came to the rescue providing light from its flares and powerful searchlight. There were obvious advantages to continuous light over the flickering and relatively brief light from flares, especially when flares could endanger people on the ground. Shadow illuminated emergency landing sights for aircraft in trouble and provided light so that the urgent repair of equipment could be made. Noteworthy is a mission during which Lt. Col. Burl Campbell and his crew held a circular pattern while lighting a compound that lost electrical power during heavy ground attack. Ignoring ground fire, for more than 30 minutes, the shadow's light allowed doctors in the camp to operate on a wounded soldier; the soldier survived.

Shadow crews flew their first TIC mission on 15 February. AC-119G pilot William Hamilton of the 71st SOS continues:

"The next one occurred the night and morning of February 22 and 23 in support of Fire Support Base Thunder II on Highway 13 north of Saigon. We flew two sorties totaling 9.8 hours and fired 150,000 rounds. It was during these two missions that ground forces found out that, with our equipment, we could fire right up to their perimeter wire without exposing their posi-

tions. We stopped the base from being overrun that night and for our efforts were awarded the Distinguished Flying Cross. But more importantly to us, we were made honorary members of the 1st Infantry "Big Red One," and we became the most requested air asset in-country at night. Our success was underlined by a GI, who during a later encounter with the Viet Cong, and about to be overrun, said, 'Screw the F-4s. Get me a Shadow!'"

In March, Shadows began working with FACs directing air strikes. Besides providing suppressive fire and lighting positions, Shadow crews marked targets with Mk 6 "log flares." As the summer of 1969 wore on and Shadow's reputation spread, AC-119G missions not only increased but became more varied. Navy patrol boats, which were often attacked by large enemy forces hidden along shorelines, knew they had only to fire tracers at enemy positions to mark targets for Shadow crews. Missions supporting Australian troops and Navy SEALs in the IV Corps delta region were on the rise. When AC-119Ks began appearing in September, Shadow operations shifted west in support of units in the U Minh Forest region. Shadows also became regular participants in SAR operations, not only keeping the enemy away from downed aircrew, but keeping track of everyone on the ground with the night observation sight. Shadows also saw an increase in sorties supporting Special Forces teams, often flying as diversion for team insertions and extractions, and providing fire support when teams found trouble.

The nose art of this AC-119G included the Roman numeral III, taken from the original project name for the Shadow, Gunship III. (David E. O'Mara)

Although night missions were the norm for Shadows, some day missions were flown. For example, in early June 1969, a Flight B crew led by Lt. Col. Rostkowski had completed its night mission, but was roused from sleep to help Vietnamese Marines pinned down attempting a beach landing. After Phan Rang-based F-100s attacked the enemy, Shadow went to work firing 21,000 rounds under the direction of an FAC. The crew was certain they had set a new record when gunner Sgt. Wade Dunn kept the guns hot, firing 18,000 rounds in six minutes. During another 1969 mission, a Shadow piloted by Lt. Col. William Long was called to help a unit under intense automatic weapons fire. In a daring move, the crew turned on its powerful light, hoping the enemy would fire and reveal its position. Long stated, "It worked. Charlie opened up on us with .50-cal. machine guns. We shot back, destroying three of the six positions and causing four secondary explosions."

During May 1969, replacements for the Reserve 71st SOS began arriving, and on 1 June the unit was re-designated the 17th SOS.

Before the Reservists of the 71st SOS departed Nha Trang on 5 June, 7th Air Force commander Maj. Gen. Royal N. Baker stated, "They've come from civilian life, worked with a new weapon system, brought it into the country, and have done a tremendous job." After arriving at Bakalar AFB, the 71st was deactivated on 18 June. As the only Air Force Reserve unit deployed to the war zone, and equipped with a vintage airplane that had endured a troubled rebirth, the 71st SOS had been met with skepticism upon its arrival in Vietnam. Shadow crews quickly proved their skills and the ability of their AC-119Gs. Besides having successfully defended every outpost it supported, Shadows suffered no fatalities, nor lost an aircraft during their combat tour. Despite ground attacks that damaged two Shadows and ground fire that hit six aircraft during missions, none of the AC-119Gs were damaged to the extent they were taken out of action for long periods of time. Shadow aircrews of the 71st flew more than 6,000 combat hours during 1,209 missions, expending 10,281 flares and more than 14 million

Nose art worn by number 52-5905 of the 17th SOS. (David E. O'Mara)

rounds of ammunition. Nearly 700 enemy troops were confirmed killed, along with 43 vehicles.

Besides the 18 AC-119Gs, the 17th SOS absorbed approximately 65 percent of the 71st SOS personnel. By the end of June 1969, the unit began dispersion as follows: Flight A to Tuy Hoa AB with four aircraft, Flight B to Phan Rang AB with seven aircraft, and Flight C to Tan Son Nhut AB with five aircraft. The two spares were left at Nha Trang. The 17th continued to boast not having lost an outpost while Shadows were overhead. Unfortunately, it could not say the same about its aircraft.

The first AC-119G loss occurred on 11 October 1969 when *Shadow 76* (S/N 52-5907), crashed on takeoff from Tan Son Nhut. The AC-119G's poor single-engine performance proved painfully evident when one of the heavy gunship's engines failed and caught fire. Five crewmen and an Air Force photographer were killed. In mid April, Flight A relocated to Phu Cat AB. Two weeks later, on the 28th, the second AC-119G loss occurred, again due to engine failure. Headed for a mission over the Trail, *Shadow 78* (S/N 53-8155), lost an engine during takeoff from Tan Son Nhut and crashed, killing six crewmen. Air Force leaders were forced to make a decision, which was to reduce the AC-119G's maximum takeoff weight by reducing fuel and ammunition loads. Shadow crews weren't any more reassured than they had been initially about a 150-foot-per-minute single-engine rate-of-climb.

Throughout 1969, 17th SOS Shadows teamed with AC-47D Spookies to defend outposts, claiming attacks repelled at 1,296 positions. However, Shadow's more sophisticated systems enabled it to be more offensive, and by December it had completely replaced Spookies. Shadows excelled at defending Special Forces camps, often working with AC-119Ks that had begun arriving in October. Testifying to these skills, both AC-119G and AC-119K gunships flew nightly sorties from 1 April to 22 May in defense of besieged Special Forces camps Dak Seang and Dak Pek in the Central Highlands. When an estimated 3,600 enemy troops staged a massive attack against these sites, the survival of the camps depended upon supplies air-dropped from C-7 Caribous. In the first five days, three C-7s were shot down over Dak Seang. Caribou pilot Col. Roger Larivee decided to try single-ship air-drops at night, using the Shadow's illuminator capability. When Shadow's light turned the drop zone into daylight, the Caribou's precious target was rolled down its tracks. At the Caribou crew's signal, the light was turned off, allowing the Caribou to escape into the darkness. Using this innovative tactic, 68 drops were made without a Caribou being hit, and the camp was saved.

Shadow pilot David O' Mara, who arrived in Vietnam in 1969, remembers:

"I was assigned to Phan Rang Air Base. Each of the 17th SOS's three flights generated up to nine sorties a night. Every squadron-level pilot started his first five flights in-country in the copilot's seat, with an Instructor Pilot as AC. The first takeoff was amusing because the pilot probably hadn't flown in well over a month. Each AC-119G, because it had been heavily modified,

required different and usually large trim corrections in all three axes to fly straight. It would be his first maximum-gross-weight takeoff in a C-119, keeping in mind that if you lost an engine before the landing gear was in the wheel well, you were guaranteed to crash. Adding to the excitement, minimum control speed, at 113 knots, was around 18 knots above takeoff speed. Every takeoff a pilot made was an instantaneous unusual attitude with rapid trim changes. After the first few, it became a routine flailing of controls and trimming. After losing the second aircraft to engine failure on takeoff, some pilots accelerated to 113 knots before raising the gear. I disagreed with this procedure as an IP for I felt I should follow standard procedure. Like all large reciprocating engine aircraft I have flown, the R-3350 was limited to only five minutes at takeoff power. I believed the longer the engine was at maximum power, the more likely it would fail. I reasoned that since the aircraft started her career at the end of World War II, every possible emergency had already been encountered. Pilots with far more years of C-119 experience than us had written the manual.

"On missions, if we found any suspicious activity such as a campfire, or some fool actually firing at us, we would make all the calls necessary for approval to fire. A prudent crew would either mark the target with a ground flare that was out of sight of anyone in the target area, or identify a prominent nearby terrain feature. The AC, copilot, nav, or NOS would memorize or write down the distance and bearing from the flare to the target. Hoping not to alarm the suspected enemy, the aircraft would then be flown away from the target area, while keeping in contact with the ground flare. If and when approved to fire, I liked to fly directly back to the target and on the tangent of the firing circle and commence fire as soon as I rolled in. I started with two guns

Unofficial patch worn by AC-119G Shadow crew members. (Author's Collection)

at low rate of 3,000 rounds per minute, or one gun at high rate of 6,000 rounds per minute. This would do a good amount of damage while keeping a huge amount of firepower in reserve."

During May 1970, Shadows were included in the evaluation of ground sensors. Equipped with portable UHF receivers, Shadows of Flight C could intercept signals that indicated movement in a sensor field. After firing into the area, scores of enemy were found dead, prompting the permanent placement of receivers aboard AC-119s.

When U.S. and South Vietnamese forces crossed the border into Cambodia on 1 May 1970, AC-119s were key participants in the incursion. As always, *Troops in Contact* was the priority mission, followed by armed reconnaissance missions during which trucks and vessels were targeted. Shadows regularly flew river patrol boat and convoy escort, often accompanied by an FAC. Throughout the month of May, Shadows of the Tan Son Nhut flight participated in the evaluation of a portable UHF receiver that monitored signals from ground sensors; the program was code-named Duffel Bag. On the nights of 18 and 19 April, a Shadow crew fired more than 34,000 rounds after detecting movement signals in a sensor field. Afterward, ground troops found 150 enemy dead and captured 17 enemy soldiers, along with nine heavy weapons. As a result, it was recommended that all AC-119s carry the new equipment. Although the invasion was short-lived, ending on 30 June 1970, AC-119s contin-

ued supporting Cambodian and South Vietnamese units. Since enemy anti-aircraft fire in Cambodia was found to be less severe than anticipated, some daytime missions were flown by AC-119s beginning 1 August. As AC-119Ks became more involved with the worsening situation in Laos, Shadows continued flying over Cambodia. Robert Atkinson, who flew AC-119Gs from March through September 1971, comments:

"I had two missions in Vietnam and 101 'across the fence' in Cambodia. I speak French, so I served as an aerial interpreter. I would talk to the Cambodian ground commanders and then tell the rest of our crew what to do, where to shoot, etc. About 70 of my missions were 0100 takeoff, so I have a memory or two of how things were in the dark. Toward the end, I also had several missions with VNAF crews. After we Vietnamized our airplanes, I spent the rest of my tour in and out of Cambodia on the ground in civilian clothes as a 7th AF liaison officer to the Khmer Air Force."

During nine months in Cambodia, until March 1971, AC-119Gs and Ks claimed 609 vehicles, 237 sampans with 494 damaged, and 3,151 of the enemy killed. After the 17th SOS with its AC-119G Shadows was deactivated at the end of September 1971, the AC-119K took center stage.

U.S. Air Force AC-119Gs

52-5892   *Buzzard Eyes, Charlie Chasers*; later to VNAF
52-5898   4413th CCTS; later to VNAF
52-5905   *Charlie Chasers*: later to VNAF
52-5907   4413th CCTS; *Hoosier Hunter*, first AC-119G to fly combat, detached to Det. 1 at Tan Son Nhut AB, crashed following engine failure on takeoff on 11 October 1969. *Shadow 76* became the first AC-119G combat loss.
52-5908
52-5925   4413th CCTS; later to VNAF
52-5927   *Devil's Advocate*, first AC-119G combat damage 7 March 1969; later to VNAF
52-5938   4413th CCTS
52-5942   4413th CCTS; later to VNAF
53-3136   4413th CCTS; *Burk's Law*; later to VNAF
53-3145   later to VNAF
53-3170   later to VNAF
53-3178   later to VNAF
53-3189   first AC-119G to arrive Southeast Asia with 53-8069 on 27 December 1968; later to VNAF
53-3192   *Ghost Rider*; later to VNAF

53-3205   4413th CCTS; later to VNAF
53-7833   4413th CCTS; later to VNAF
53-7848   *The Charlotte Representative*; lost engine during night combat mission 31 May 1970 and made emergency landing at Bien Hoa AB; later to VNAF.
53-7851   later to VNAF
53-7852   4413th CCTS; *Midnight Special*; later to VNAF
53-8069   4413th CCTS; first AC-119G delivered to USAF, accepted at Robins AFB on 19 May 1968; first to arrive Southeast Asia with 53-3189 on 27 December 1968; *City of Columbus*; later to VNAF.
53-8114   4413th CCTS; later to VNAF
53-8115   later to VNAF
53-8123   later to VNAF
53-8131   later to VNAF
53-8155   4413th CCTS; detached to Det. 1 at Tan Son Nhut AB; on 28 April 1970 *Shadow 78* experienced engine failure during takeoff and crashed two miles from base, killing its six crewmen.

Other aircraft names were *Oklahoma Representative* and *Egg Sucking Dog*.

*Named the Oklahoma Representative, **this Shadow flies near Tan Son Nhut Air Base in 1969.** (Larry Davis)

CHAPTER FIVE

THE AC-119K: SMARTER AND STRONGER

From below, the Stinger appeared as an all-black aircraft. (U.S. Air Force)

Although the designation AC-119K identifies the addition of jet engines in the second phase of the *Gunship III* program, this model introduced a number of additional improvements over the AC-119G. Both were structurally the same aircraft, however, their weapons and avionics systems differed significantly. In addition to the K model's two Wright R-3350 radial engines, two under-wing General Electric J85-GE-17 engines rated at 2,850 pounds of thrust each allowed a takeoff weight of 80,400 pounds, more than 15,000 pounds greater than the AC-119G. With added jet power, the AC-119K had a greatly increased rate-of-climb and even with one radial engine out the aircraft could climb at 500 feet-per-minute. Its speed was increased to 180 knots and it had greater endurance, being able to stay aloft for 5 hours with a 30-minute fuel reserve. Gunship navigator Bill Bryden noted: "There were several challenges to this conversion. The recips on the C-119G used aviation fuel, not jet fuel, so the jets would have to be configured to run on aviation gas. This in turn required that their turbine blades be cleaned frequently. We never had a serious problem with these engines and they got me and my crew home safely more than once when a recip failed."

Unofficially named Stingers, the 26 AC-119Ks retained the Shadow's four podded or module miniguns which were given more punch with the addition of two linkless-feed M61A1 20mm Vulcan cannons. The M61A1 was a six-barrel, hydraulically operated, electrically-driven rotary cannon with a rate-of-fire of 2,500 rounds per minute, and a muzzle velocity of 3,450 feet per second. GE developed this weapon during the late 1940s, with the M61A1 first being used operationally in 1959 on the Lockheed F-104D Starfighter.

The AC-119K's night observation sight, semi-automatic flare launcher, illuminator, and fire control system were carryovers from the AC-119G, but that's where the similarities ended. The Stinger's significantly upgraded avionics capability included FLIR, terrain avoidance radar, and an advanced communications package. The Motorola AN/APQ-133 Beacon Tracking Radar (BTR), also called Side-Looking Radar, was included initially, but beginning in 1970, it did not remain in constant use. Since the weight of these systems reduced the AC-119K's time over the target, and since the aircraft was designed for close support of ground troops, its installation depended on where the aircraft would be based. The BTR was an X-band system that worked in conjunction with a transponder for offset firing when the target could not be visually identified. To provide an effective target designation system that could penetrate dense jungle or marginal weather, a ground beacon marked a fixed reference point for the guns. Distance and bearing to the target could then be sent to the fire-control computer which determined an offset aiming point for the pilot.

The BTR's angular tracking function was critical since the aircraft flew in a 30-degree left bank for firing. The initial test phase of the BTR was called *Combat Rendezvous.* The Texas Instruments AN/AAD-4 FLIR was a passive system that could view images in total darkness by detecting infrared radiation, which was instantly displayed on a viewer. That data could then be fed to the fire control computer, which had automatic, semi-automatic, manual, and offset firing capability. The FLIR unit was mounted in the aircraft's lower nose section, offset from and immediately forward of the nose landing gear. Housed in the aircraft's nose section was a Texas Instruments AN/APQ-136 search radar with moving target indicator. Doppler AN/APN-147 terrain following radar and APQ-25/26 electronic countermeasure units were also installed. Additionally, 2,000 pounds of armor was used to protect crew stations and ammunition containers.

The C-119G, S/N 53-3142, was the first to be outfitted with J85 jet engines, becoming the YC-119K prototype. The jets were added to broaden the C-119's safety margin, in addition to improving its performance. Number 142 is seen here in August 1968 wearing an abundance of patriotic markings. (Frank MacSorley via David Menard)

Despite this array of equipment, the aircraft had ample room for the large crew of ten necessary to perform the mission. Besides two pilots, three navigators were aboard—a table nav, night observation sight operator, and radar/infrared operator. The remaining crew comprised an illuminator operator, flight engineer, and three gunners.

Due to the complex nature of their sophisticated systems, AC-119Ks were slow in becoming fully converted to gunships. Much of the delay centered on the FLIR system, the first of which did not reach Fairchild Hiller's conversion facility until 3 May 1969. Testing began by the end of the month and the last FLIR would not arrive until April 1970. Since 7th Air Force was intent on expanding its gunship force, three Stingers were deployed to Southeast Asia, with the first aircraft arriving at Phan Rang AB on 3 November 1969. Their

The AC-119K's gunsight, built by Chicago Aerial Industries, was an improvement over sights used on the AC-47D and AC-119G. Mounted to the left of the pilot's seat, the sight was linked directly to the fire control computer. (via Larry Davis)

combat evaluation began immediately, however, without FLIRs, they flew the Shadow's mission profile until FLIR units arrived.

The Stingers were to form the 18th SOS, which had been established on 25 January 1969. The 4413th CCTS at Lockbourne AFB, which had trained Shadow crews, was tasked with training AC-119K crews. Edward Pinkham recalls:

"When I received my assignment to the 18th Special Operations Squadron at Lockbourne AFB, little did I know that the squadron didn't even have aircraft yet. I had no idea what kind of aircraft I was going to be flying. Although the Air Force just spent a ton of money training me as a Flight Engineer on EC-121 aircraft, everybody knew that Lockbourne AFB did not have them. The EC-121 was an early warning aircraft that was usually based near the coasts where they watched our skies over the oceans. Then I heard that Texas Instruments was at Lockbourne teaching ground support personnel how to maintain some new high tech infrared equipment. I just assumed they were modifying some 'Connies,' and wanted to keep them secret and we would be flying over Southeast Asia from some other location. When I was informed that we were getting C-119 aircraft, I couldn't believe it. I thought they were all in the boneyard. I really had no desire to fly an aircraft with a nickname like Widow Maker. It got worse. These aircraft were to have guns sticking out the sides. Sure, I heard of Puff, the Magic Dragon, but a C-119 gunship?

"As the newly refurbished K models started their first test flights, I was sent to St. Augustine, Florida, as part of an acceptance team. We eventually formed crews and began practicing on the Atterbury firing range in Indiana. Since we had terrain avoidance radar coupled to the autopilot, we also flew low-level flights over the Hocking Hills in southeastern Ohio and Kentucky. On one trip, as we were hunting for targets in the hills of Kentucky, the NOS or FLIR picked up a police car. We circled him for a while, and the officer got out of the squad and started looking for us. When he shined his spotlight at us, we decided to have some fun. The illuminator operator had the light working in the infrared mode, so someone decided we should show the officer our light. It was switched to clear, and when this poor officer's whole world lit up, he jumped in his car and took off like he just saw a Martian. He was not the only one who saw strange objects in the sky. We had many reports of UFO sightings while we were searching for targets. We also got some very interesting views of night activities on the beaches and in backyard swimming pools of unsuspecting participants. This job could have actually been fun if we didn't have to go to Vietnam."

The 18th SOS received its first AC-119K on 8 November 1968. The first K model assigned to the 18th arrived at Lockbourne on 5 March 1969. The squadron's advance element arrived at Phan Rang AB on 11 October, and on 21 October, the first six AC-119Ks left Lockbourne for the many-legged trip to Vietnam. Although three

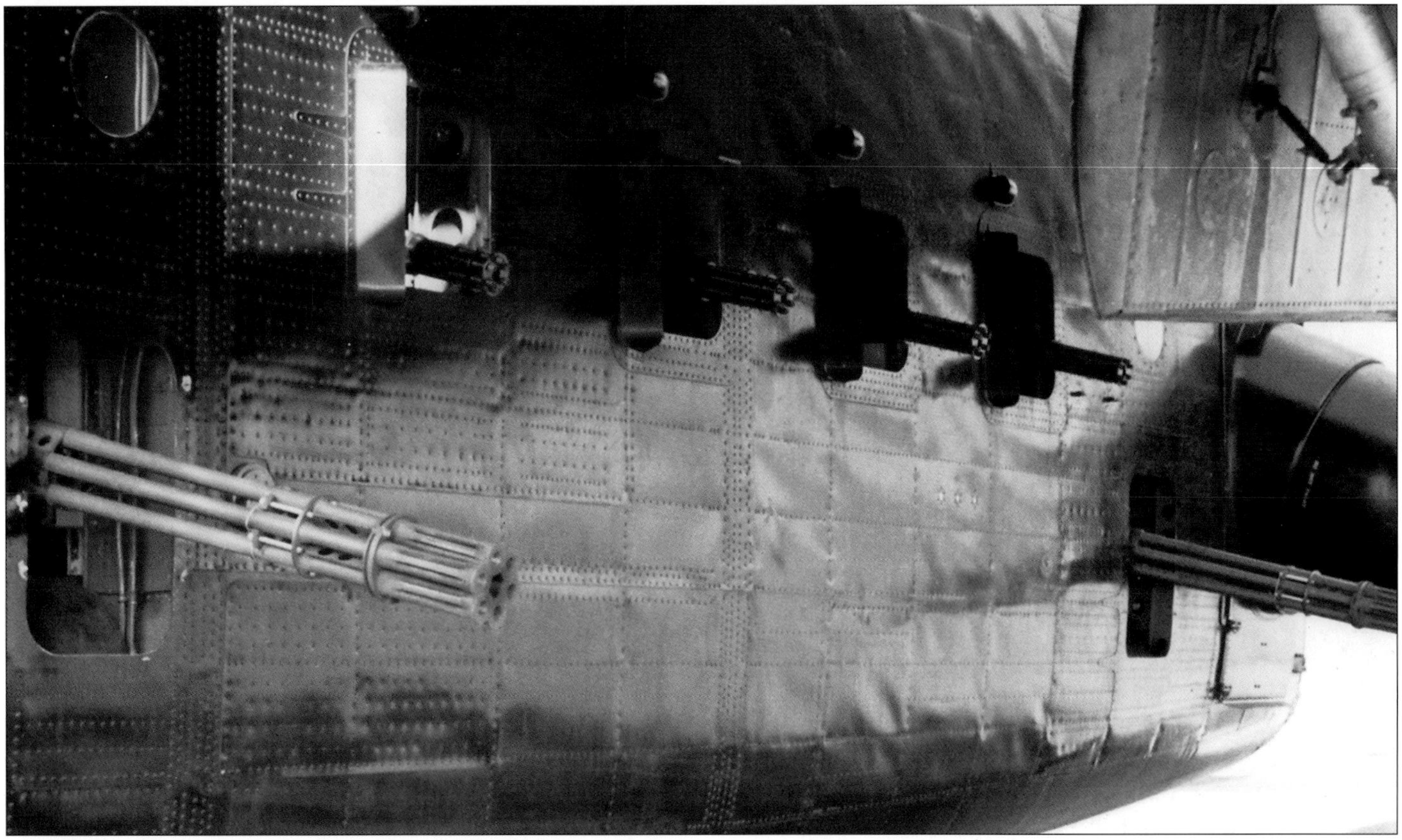

The M61A1 20mm cannons were positioned forward and behind the rear miniguns, which were podded SUU-11/A units or MXU-470/A modules, depending on availability. (Author's Collection)

The addition of jet engines to the AC-119G resulted in the designation AC-119K. The J85's air intake doors were closed when the engine was not in use. The J85 of AC-119K, S/N 53-7831, seen here has multiple punctures from a rocket attack at Da Nang Air Base. (Tom Novak)

Although use of the AN/APQ-133 side-looking radar was discontinued in December 1970, its bulbous housing was retained. Stinger's AVQ-8 20kw Xenon light was variable beam, producing 1.5-million candle-power to turn night into day. (Stephen Miller)

The AN/AAD-4 FLIR allowed Stinger crews to see in total darkness. The unit's housing and sensor were mounted considerably offset of the aircraft's centerline. The last three numbers of the aircraft's serial number were usually worn on the nose landing gear doors. A tow bar is attached to the landing gear. (Larry Mersek)

Rare view of the AC-119K's cargo area clam shell doors pen, showing the number two 20mm cannon's vertical ammunition drum and stand. The drum was positioned directly behind the weapon, while gun number one's drum was located forward of the weapon. The illuminator is in the opposite doorway. (Tom Novak)

Mounted vertically, the MXU-470/A minigun modules allowed more room in the cargo area than SUU-11/A gun pods. Weapons placards appear on the control boxes of these later style modules, along with safety devices attached to familiar "Remove Before Flight" streamers. Work lamps, although used sparingly, were attached above the gun systems. (Larry Mersek)

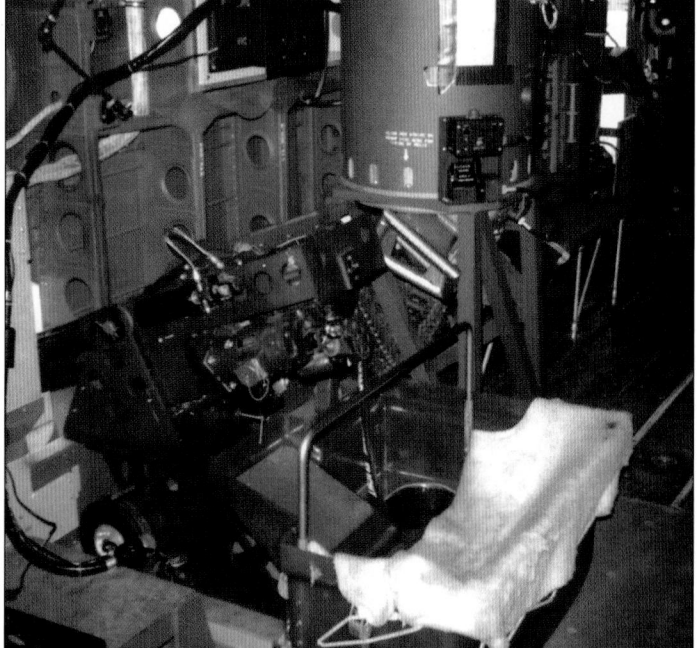

View looking forward of the AC-119K's number one 20mm M61A1 cannon. A container for catching spent cartridges has been added below the gun. The cannon's 200-round capacity vertical ammunition drum is mounted on a stand to the right of the weapon. In keeping with Air Force regulations for labeling ordnance, it wears a red and white ammunition placard. Visible in the upper right corner in the doorway is the armor plate for the night observation sight operator. (Larry Mersek)

The aircraft commander occupied the left seat of the Stinger's cockpit. The flight engineer was positioned centered and behind the pilots, from where he could monitor instruments and work controls. Sun visors covered upper cockpit windows. (Tony Bautz)

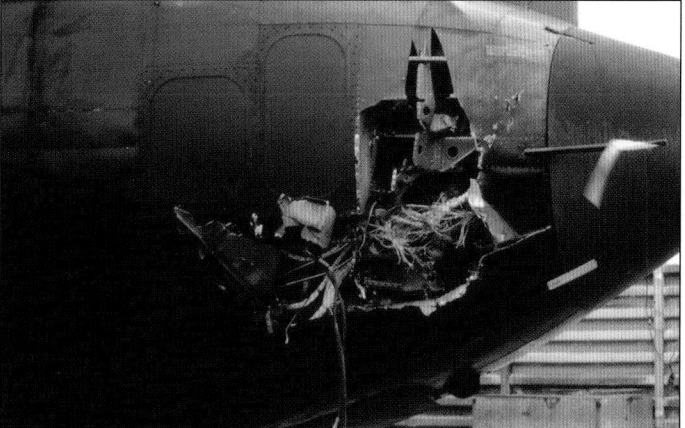

Doppler terrain following radar was housed in the AC-119K's nose. The lower cockpit windows of this Stinger were painted over with black, and its rear cockpit windows are covered. Lights inside the aircraft were kept to a minimum since the Stinger relied on total darkness to avoid detection by enemy gunners. (Tony Bautz)

On the night of 4 February 1970, this Stinger (S/N 53-7826) was over Laos lining up for an attack on a truck when it was bracketed by heavy anti-aircraft guns. A 37mm shell struck the Stinger, injuring the copilot and knocking out the radios, instruments, and some hydraulics. The AC-119K was able to land safely at Da Nang Air Base. (Larry Mersek)

500-gallon Benson fuel tanks were installed in the aircraft's cargo bay, the AC-119 did not have the fuel reserves to fly directly across the Pacific. Robert Leach, who was among the crewmen of that first group, describes the troubled beginnings:

"I was a former KC-135 driver who was selected for Aircraft Commander duty in the first group of AC-119Ks. We reported for duty in Ohio only to find that the planes were not ready. We established the squadron and made several trips to Fort Lauderdale, Florida, to accept planes from Fairchild Hiller, and we trained extensively in southern Ohio. In 1969 I started the first trip to Vietnam. After aborting back into Ohio twice with maintenance problems, I finally made it to Malstrom AFB, Montana. On touchdown, I broke a scissors link in the right main gear. After we stopped on the runway, no two gear were pointing in the same direction. The only thing that saved my butt was that I touched down in front of the supervisor of flying and he witnessed the whole thing.

"After another aircraft was ferried out to us two days later, we left for Anchorage, Alaska. In the meantime, another crew had the same thing happen to them in Anchorage, except that the landing gear strut came up through the wing. We then proceeded to Adak, Alaska, where we spent a week waiting on winds and weather to launch for Hawaii. Since we were running so far behind the pack, we were chosen to be the first guinea pigs for jungle survival school at Clark AB. After that we were scheduled for another aircraft delivery in-country. We took off from Clark, reached cruising altitude, and when the flight engineer switched from the external tanks we used for takeoff and landing to internal tanks, all four engines and the auxiliary power unit quit. Boy, did it get quiet up there. I put the plane in a glide back to Clark and we got two recips back on line. Two days later we made it to Phan Rang."

Stinger gunships often fell victim to anti-aircraft guns, one of which scored hits on this AC-119K's jet engine and wing. The doorway with a boarding ladder was a crew entrance added as part of the AC-119K modification. (Author's Collection)

Although the jet engines alone were not designed to sustain flight of the AC-119, Bill Wait recounts a fuel system test flight at Lockbourne AFB during which the radial engines were intentionally shut down to prove the aircraft could fly on jets only:

"The pilot calmly reached over to the throttles for the piston engines and pulled off the power, shut down the engines, and feathered the propellers. Did it ever get quiet. We were still in a shallow dive and were flying just on the little J85 jet engines. Slowly descending is probably a better way to describe our flight path, as there is no way we could maintain level flight just on the jets. As we made our pass over the field with both props standing still, we could see people pointing and staring at the crazy AC-119, which everyone knew was about to crash. As we crossed the base boundary, still slowly descending, our pilot restarted the piston engines. After hearing the growl of the big R-3350s, we all began to breathe a bit easier. The next day, our squadron commander had a few choice words that he shared with the pilot. That was our last 'pure jet' AC-119 flight."

As a Captain, Wait was the aircraft maintenance officer assigned to an Enroute Support Team (EST), which flew the route of the AC-119Ks being ferried to Vietnam. Flying faster than the AC-119Ks, the EST's C-130 aircraft usually arrived ahead of the gunships. According to Wait:

"Onboard the C-130 was the EST and a spare parts kit. The EST consisted of 12 aircraft maintenance technicians from the various maintenance disciplines, a supply technician, and an aircraft maintenance officer. We had an electrician, a hydraulics repairman, a jet mechanic, a piston mechanic, a fuel systems technician, an instrument repairman, and several avionics types. The spares kit, referred to as a 'War Readiness Spares Kit,' contained the components that past experience had shown would be most likely to fail. The kit was quite complete, but in accordance with Murphy's Law, we knew that we would need something that wasn't in the kit."

Bill Bryden, who was an instructor navigator flying T-29s, describes the beginning of what he calls his "gunship adventures:"

"In the fall of 1968, while stationed at Los Angeles Air Force Station, I received orders to report to 119 upgrade training in early December, with a follow-on assignment to gunship training, and then on to Vietnam. This did make for a rather down weekend. I did a little research into the Fairchild C-119 and found the results rather discouraging. Here was a two-engine aircraft that had trouble staying airborne on a single engine, and it had the unfortunate nickname of 'The Flying Coffin.'

"I went to Clinton County AFB, Ohio, for 119 ground school. The pilots were learning how to handle the two big reciprocating engines and the long landing gear, while we navigators were trying to make sense out of the rather sparse instrumentation in the

aircraft. My first flight in a C-119G was on 31 December 1968, and we flew for 2.3 hours on a low-level navigation mission over the Ohio countryside. We would see much more of this over the next ten months. After a few more flights and an over-water check flight, we graduated and were reassigned to Lockbourne AFB, Ohio. We now got into training for the AC-119K mission in earnest, and after 15 missions, I received my tactical evaluation on a night live-fire mission on the 3rd of March, 1969. Normally I would have been on my way to Vietnam; however, we were missing some equipment. The FLIR had not yet been delivered for all of our aircraft and it had not received its tactical acceptance. Because most of the navigators in this first group were from Air Force Systems Command and had extensive testing backgrounds, the Tactical Air Command had us form a test group and we became the primary testers for the FLIR system. Many of us were sent to school at the contractor's facility in up-state New York to learn about infrared surveillance systems and the FLIR in particular. The FLIRs were slow in coming so the Air Force decided to make our assignments permanent.

"I flew 61 missions over the next seven months, flying more than 210 hours of test and training time. We finally had all the systems checked out and began sending the aircraft and our crews over in November 1969."

The AC-119K got its first taste of combat on 13 November when a Stinger supported *Troops in Contact* at a fire base near Da Nang. The second group of AC-119Ks deployed to Vietnam on 27 December, and by year's end, the dozen were dispersed among three bases; six aircraft formed A Flight at Da Nang AB, three formed B Flight at Phu Cat AB, and C Flight at Phan Rang, the main support base for both AC-119Gs and AC-119Ks, had three aircraft. With both squadrons in-country, the 17th SOS with 16 AC-119Gs, and the 18th with 12 AC-119Ks, USAF

Stinger gunner Ronald Julian loads 7.62 ammunition in preparation for a mission. (Larry Mersek)

AC-47 operations in Vietnam came to a close. Eight K models were retained in the states for training by 4 February 1970. Eighteen Stinger gunships were in Vietnam and combat ready, with each detachment assigned six aircraft. Since the Stinger was configured specifically for attacks against vehicles and vessels, Da Nang and Phu Cat-based AC-119Ks were quickly scheduled for missions over the Ho Chi Minh Trail in Laos. Confirming their success was the establishment at Udorn RTAFB of D Flight, with three aircraft and four crews drawn from Phu Cat AB. Their primary mission was armed reconnaissance in the Barrel Roll region, with the secondary mission of Lima Site support. Two aircraft were sent aloft, while the third stood alert. On all missions, three F-4Ds from either Korat or Udorn RTAFB provided escort, along with F-4Ds of the Da Nang-based 366th TFW. Seventeen F-4s of the 13th Tactical Fighter Squadron were committed to the gunships. Edward Pinkham shares this view of the Stinger escorts:

"After MiG threats and missile launches, the Air Force decided to send fighter escorts with us. In the early days, we had two A-1 Skyraiders as escorts. These aircraft carried a huge load of armament, could stay with us while circling the target, and could nail a Triple-A sight without our giving directions. In fact, they worked with us so well the Air Force decided to take them away, and gave us three F-4s, not that the Phantoms were a bad aircraft, but the AC-119 was a slow, low-flying aircraft, and the F-4 was just the opposite. I don't believe the F-4 could even fly at our airspeed. It was a poor match. It took three very expensive aircraft to replace two old surplus birds, and the three could not get the job done. In addition to flying much faster and higher than us, and not seeing half the action from the AAA sites, we were lucky to have one long enough to get established on target. The F-4 needed so much fuel at low altitudes that one would have to be with Yellow Bird, the KC-135 tanker, and another enroute. By the time we started taking AAA again, it was time for our escort to get a drink."

The first mission was flown from Udorn on the 17th, and two days later, the 18th SOS lost its first Stinger. *Stinger 61* crashed short of Da Nang when both left engines lost power due to fuel starvation. The crew of ten survived; however, the aircraft, S/N 53-3156, was destroyed. By the end of February 1970, Stinger crews had flown 410 missions beyond Vietnam's border and 228 in South Vietnam. Flying more than 2,000 combat hours, the Stingers had fired nearly 1,400,000 rounds of minigun ammunition and nearly 600,000 rounds of 20mm cannon ammunition, claiming 302 trucks destroyed, along with 26 sampans.

Over Laos, Stinger crews, mindful of their slow speed and predictable attack pattern, were careful to avoid known anti-aircraft gun sites. The normal working altitude on truck-killing missions was 5,500 feet, while 7,000 feet was the norm in heavily defended areas. Ammunition loads also varied according to missions. Those flown over Laos had crews loading 8,000 minigun rounds and 3,000 cannon rounds, plus 12 flares, while loads for missions in South Vietnam comprised up to 20,000 minigun rounds, up to 3,000 cannon rounds, plus

Not until the Stinger was at very low altitude were its upper camouflage surfaces visible. This view illustrates the long, sturdy main landing gear necessary to clear the aircraft's boxy fuselage. (U.S. Air Force)

AC-119K S/N 52-5910 of the 415th Special Operations Training Squadron, 1st Special Operations Wing in September 1972. After replacing the 4413th CCTS, the 415th used tail code AH when it came under the 1st SOW. Number 910 wears a TAC emblem on its tail fins, and the 1st SOW emblem below the cockpit. (Stephen Miller)

Number 910 in the markings of the 415th SOTS in September 1972. Unusual is the area separating upper and lower camouflage painted dark gray. Its four-blade props have been replaced by three-blade Hamilton Standards. Following its service as a trainer, number 910 was transferred to the Vietnamese Air Force. (Stephen Miller)

When assigned to the 4413th CCTS, 4410th CCTW, 1st SOW at Lockbourne AFB, Ohio, during early 1969, number 52-5910 wore the 4413th's IH tail code. (Clyde Gerdes)

24 flares. Both loads also included red marking flares, called Lulus, which burned on the ground for 90 minutes. As 18th SOS crews quickly gained combat experience, they discovered that the FLIR, the sensor upon which they relied most, was kept operational only with constant attention from Texas Instruments technicians. And the 20mm cannon, although highly effective, frequently failed due to problems with its feed system. Bill Bryden explains concerns about noise:

"When the hydraulic steering mechanism for the illuminator was running, the gas turbine at full power, all four engines running, and all six guns firing, the noise level in the cargo compartment was measured at 156 decibels, well above the level of pain and beyond the point where instant hearing damage would occur. All AC-119K crew members were fitted with specially designed helmets which had heavy noise-blocking padding. On top of this, all were required to wear earplugs in addition to the helmets. Even with all this protection, our hearing would lack all but the lowest frequencies after a mission. We all respected the need to protect our hearing."

Bryden takes us through a typical Stinger mission:

"Following successful check-out, our crew was sent to Phu Cat Air Base. We began flying combat missions along the Trail at night, looking for truck. Missions started with our crew being scheduled for either the early mission, arriving on target just after dark, or the late mission, covering the day's target through the late hours of the night. On alert, we pre-flighted the aircraft for any need to support Troops in Contact, or to attack a high-value target found by another gunship or a FAC. The pre-mission intelligence briefing attempted to define the anti-aircraft artillery locations, the last known activity in our patrol region, and the location of planned B-52 Arc Light missions. This was followed by our crew briefing where we reviewed our assigned target area, types of targets expected, intended flight route, frequencies for our cover F-4s and later A-1s, frequency for the Airborne Command Post, and the altitude reporting factor. This was a number we added or subtracted from our actual altitude so we could talk in the clear on the radio without giving away our working altitude. We always believed that it took the bad guys about ten minutes to figure out the night's factor.

"After the briefings we rode to our aircraft and went through our preflight checks. The pilots and flight engineer checked the engines, radios, instruments, and flight control systems. Our navigator checked his equipment, and the gunners tested each gun and made sure we had the proper ammunition for the mission. The illuminator operator checked out the searchlight, its infrared lens, and the gas turbine generator that provided power for onboard equipment. The NOS operator checked his equipment and sighted it on something to verify that the pilot's sight was centered on the same point. The FLIR operator started the cool-down process for his infrared sensor, which took over ten minutes. When these checks

were completed, we started engines, taxied to the active runway, and with our two jets at full power, advanced the recips to takeoff power. Following a rather long and rumbling ground roll, we stumbled into the air and started our climb to 8,000 feet, the average enroute altitude. With all the openings in the aircraft, we stayed below 10,000 feet to avoid the need for oxygen.

"Once in the working area, we began our patrol, first descending to our working altitude, from 3,500 to 6,500 feet, looking for targets. Our briefings helped define available targets, but they were routinely given as anything moving along a line of communication (LOC), usually defined as a road, trail, or waterway. We were allowed to engage any target within three miles of an LOC. In the process, we were allowed to do our own target acquisition and identification as we had the necessary sensors to accomplish the task.

"Along the Ho Chi Minh Trail, the NOS located a distant set of lights, usually belonging to a truck carrying goods from the north to troops in the south. We had meters that allowed one sensor to home in on any other sensor's target so the FLIR could locate and track the same target. Once the trucks heard our aircraft approach, they would turn out the lights. That worked against earlier patrol aircraft, but not against the AC-119K. With the FLIR on the truck, we could follow its hot engine. Turning off the lights did nothing to help him hide. We approached the target off-set to the right and as it came abeam, we initiated a firing circle. Keeping the FLIR on the target and depressing the consent switch would tell the pilot that we were ready to fire. He directed the gunners to put one or more guns on line, and when all was ready, he depressed his trigger, putting several hundred 20mm rounds on the target. Together, the 20mms would fire up to 4,800 rounds per minute. With a ten-second burst from both cannons, we fired 1,600 rounds. Every fifth round was a tracer so we could see where the rounds were hitting and correct. When hunting trucks, we carried armor-piercing rounds and high explosive incendiary (HEI). The side-firing concept could be extremely accurate, concentrating a high rate of firepower within an area of les than 50 yards square from more than 3,500 feet. At full rate of fire, with all six guns on line, the AC-119K was capable of firing more than 33,000 rounds per minute. The Air Force had transformed the old 'flying coffin' into a devastating war machine.

"We were the first AC-119K to take a hit, which occurred on the night of 4/5 February. With our F-4s flying cover, and the night cloudy with a thin overcast at 7,000 feet, we had formation lights atop the aircraft on. These shined directly upward to help cover aircraft keep us in sight, while preventing the enemy from seeing us. We also ran our recips slightly out of synch to make us less visible in the night sky. We located a truck and headed in for a firing pass. Our illuminator operator, who was watching for anti-aircraft fire, yelled, 'Break right—break right—triple A!' Almost at the same time our copilot yelled, 'Break left—break left!' We were bracketed by two AAA sites. One missed but the other hit somewhere on the nose of our aircraft. The next 30 sec-

onds were pandemonium. The copilot had been hit in his foot or lower leg. The cockpit was filled with smoke and dust, and the smell of gunpowder. The flight engineer had debris in his eyes but noticed that the engine gauges for number-two engine had gone to zero, telling him the engine had quit. He reached out and pushed the throttle for number-two, but nothing happened on the gauges. He said that both engines had quit! The navigator gave the pilot a heading toward an area that was recommended for bailout because it was dense jungle and offered a good chance of evasion until rescue.

"Our pilot looked out of his window and could see that the left engine was still running; the copilot did the same. We had two engines, just no engine instruments. In fact, as we took a deep breath and began checking, we found that we had lost everything but one airspeed indicator and one compass system. We could not receive radio transmissions from the outside. We learned a good lesson. We assumed that since we could not receive radio transmissions that no one could hear us broadcasting. That was not the case and we should have been communicating our intentions. We later learned that our formation lights had reflected off of the cloud cover and made our position easily seen from the ground. Add a new procedure to the gunship handbook.

"After realizing that we could stay airborne, we got a heading from our navigator directly to the nearest U.S. base, Da Nang. An hour later, with our F-4 escorts staying with us all the way, we flew directly over the airfield. We went out over the ocean a short distance to unload all of our ammunition and excess fuel prior to making an emergency landing. Hydraulics were out; however, the main gear fell into place and the nose gear had to be cranked down by hand. The nose wheel was flat so we landed holding the nose wheel off as long as possible. Once off the main runway and stopped, we were most happy to leave the aircraft. We saw a three-foot hole in the right side of the nose, where the large wire bundle to the cockpit instruments had been completely severed. We had been in-country about two months and thought that our mission was a relatively safe one. The fact that we could be hit by anti-aircraft fire made us think more about the safety of our tactics and our missions."

Larry Mersek, a Stinger gunner, provides insight to enemy anti-aircraft artillery, which crews commonly called AAA or Triple A:

"The AAA was very real, with airbursts below, beside, and above us on missions we flew 'across the fence' into Laos. Some nights we encountered very heavy AAA and others none at all. We encountered some type of ground fire on 35 percent of our missions. Depending on who you talk to, that percentage could change dramatically. We normally encountered small-arms fire up to .51-cal. ZPU in-country. Over the fence typically it was 23mm, 37mm, and 57mm AAA with and without tracers. The latter were set for airbursts, exploding at various preset altitudes, or on impact. Some were radar-guided. A gunner on the left and

the illuminator operator on the right stood in open doors reaching as far out of the airplane as they could to scan for either ground bursts or tracers being fired at the gunship. It was their job to call for a break right, break left, or dive to avoid the AAA. The pilot immediately complied with their commands. Flying in a 30-degree left-hand orbit, if there was a break right called, the pilot would go to 100 percent on the jets and bank hard, sometimes to 70 to 90 percent bank angle, pulling about 3 gs in the turn. The IO on the right sometimes would see the horizon come into view. The scanners did not wear parachutes but they were strapped in to avoid falling out. Oh how exciting. Oh how scared. It was just another night at the office. The aircrews were all very professional and worked very well together as a team."

Due to the worsening situation in the Barrel Roll region of Laos, 7th Air Force requested that the trial period for the detachment of Stingers at Udorn be indefinitely extended. After the Thai government granted a four-month extension ending 20 July, a fourth AC-119K was added. During March, 16 Stingers were divided between Da Nang AB and Korat RTAFB. The Da Nang element flew

This is what a 20mm cannon barrel looks like after exploding while the gun is firing; a rare occurrence. It was believed that a round traveling too slow through the barrel was detonated by the next round. (Larry Mersek)

The Stinger presented a menacing image, a far cry from its previous role as an airlift platform. (U.S. Air Force)

The added FLIR and 20mm cannons gave the Stinger a capability far superior to that of the Shadow in the search and destroy role. An armor panel covered the lower half of the forward doorway to protect the night observation sight operator. Two smoke-clearing air scoops immediately rearward of the doorway are closed. On the forward fuselage of S/N 52-5910 is the emblem of the 1st SOW. On some AC-119s, the two lower cockpit windows on both sides of the fuselage were painted over with black. (Stephen Miller)

This impressive view of a Stinger firing one of its four miniguns illustrates the importance of wind spoilers used to direct gun smoke and gasses into the slipstream. (U.S. Air Force)

Serial number 53-7854 at Phan Rang AB in 1969. The upper air scoop of the smoke-clearing system is open. Montezuma's Revenge was lost in Thailand in 1972. (via Jeff Kolln)

The crew of 53-3154 prepares for a mission from Nakhon Phanom RTAFB in 1971. Stingers were regular residents of NKP, flying interdiction missions in Laos. Heavy exhaust from the gas turbine stains the aircraft's mid-fuselage. (Tony Bautz)

the Steel Tiger region of Laos, and the NKP flight flew mainly in support of *Troops in Contact* in the Barrel Roll region. To capitalize on the Stinger's capabilities, the Air Force teamed with the Army, using the Grumman OV-1 Mohawk to seek targets. Beginning in late April, Udorn-based Mohawks, equipped with infrared sensors (OV-1C) and Side Looking Airborne Radar (OV-1B) found targets for the Stingers to attack. The tactic was simple and successful if all systems functioned properly, up until the rules of engagement came into play. The Mohawk pilots had to report targets to the C-130 command aircraft, which then relayed the information to the U.S. embassy in Laos. If validated, target information was sent back to the airborne command post, which then gave the gunship the go-ahead. In the meantime, if the target had moved, the validation process had to be repeated.

A second test in the fall of 1970 produced even less favorable results, and the concept was dropped, since AC-130 gunships had already proven their success with finding and destroying their own targets. Robert Leach recalls working with AC-130s on missions: "Missions were interesting when we all flew at about the same altitude. This improved significantly when the high/low techniques were implemented. We would come in low at about 5,000 feet to fly our mission. We were followed by an AC-130 that came in high at about 10,000 feet. Then we would come back in low again. It screwed up the bad guys' aiming techniques and improved our outlook tremendously."

On 21 April 1970, the Da Nang Stinger detachment, the largest, with nine AC-119Ks, claimed the squadron's 1,000th truck. The landmark kill was among 13 trucks claimed, with many more unconfirmed, given the number of secondary explosions. The AC-119K aircraft commander, Capt. Ronald J. Dean, commented, "The trucks we got won't be carrying any more rockets and mortars to hit our

On the night of 8 May 1970, Capt. Alan Milacek and his crew landed their Stinger at Udorn RTAFB successfully after having a large portion of its right wing shot away during a truck-killing mission. The hard luck AC-119K (S/N 53-7826) would become the only Stinger shot down. (Larry Mersek)

bases." When the Cambodian incursion began on 1 May, the Stingers provided support of U.S. and South Vietnamese ground forces. Thankfully, the skies over Cambodia were not a high-threat AAA environment. As lessons were learned, changes were made in equipment and tactics to keep pace with the changing tactical environment, and to broaden the safety margin. The AC-119K's beacon-tracking radar, which lagged in development and had seen only intermittent use in combat, was again brought into focus. Although ground commando teams equipped with transponders relied upon Stingers for all-weather close support on high-risk cross-border forays, the system was used sparingly. The demand for and subsequent success of gunships inevitably took their toll on aircraft and crews. An example of such heightened activity occurred on the night of 8 May 1970.

Stinger pilot Capt. Alan D. Milacek and his crew were having success hunting trucks near Ban Ban, Laos. After destroying two, Milacek began his firing circle to attack three more when six anti-aircraft batteries opened up. The F-4 escort went to work on the gun sites, and the Stinger bored back in for another truck kill. Surviving AAA batteries kept up their relentless attack, this time finding their mark on the Stinger's right wing, jarring the aircraft. Milacek remembers, "We had been flying in a 30-degree left bank, but we swung violently into a 60-degree right bank and began diving." Milacek called "Mayday, Mayday, we're goin' in," and told the crew to get ready to bail out. The aircraft plummeted more than 1,000 feet; however, both pilots were able to regain control and headed for friendly territory. The navigator warned that they were too low to clear mountain ranges. Milacek said, "We had to gain altitude if we were going to safely clear the mountainous terrain. I told the crew in the cargo compartment to dump ammo and anything else to lighten the aircraft. As soon as this was done, I started to climb rapidly to a fairly safe altitude." Meanwhile, the F-4 escorts had climbed well above the crippled Stinger to provide navigational assistance. The crew's problems were not over. The flight engineer discovered that they would run out of fuel about 30 minutes short of the base. Milacek continues, "In order to conserve fuel, once we cleared very high terrain, I pulled off power which put the aircraft in a slow descent." Improved fuel consumption rates prompted Milacek to decide to make a dash for base.

By this time, additional escort aircraft had arrived and Jolly Green rescue helicopters were inbound. After a one-hour-and-twenty-minute flight, using full left rudder and aileron for a straight-in approach to Udorn, the pilots brought it down without flaps at 140 to 150 knots. Milacek said, "Looking over the right wing after parking we discovered 14 feet of its leading edge and 17 feet of the trailing edge shot away. We also had lost one aileron, and had a hole in a hatch and one in the right vent." Bill Bryden remembers the crew saying that if it had been daylight and they could have seen the damage to the right wing, they probably would have left the aircraft. For their superior airmanship and teamwork, the crew was presented the Mackay Trophy for the "Most Meritorious Flight of the Year."

Having long been plagued by runaway props, the AC-119Ks underwent a program to have their four-blade Aeroproducts propellers replaced by Hamilton Standard three-blade props. The change increased the safety factor of emergency prop oil replenishment. Although both types used oil reservoirs, the Hamilton could replace its oil with engine oil if its supply was depleted, whereas the Aeroproducts could not. From a performance standpoint, the three-blade prop increased the aircraft's takeoff roll. The prop switch was accomplished at Phan Rang by a team from the Warner Robins Air Material Area. Bob Leach recalls, "After I had been in-country for a while, I was transferred back to Phan Rang to run the flight test section of the squadron. We had many incidents of props not feathering in Vietnam during test hops. In one incident, I refused to release an aircraft about a half dozen times because the prop would not go to full feather. Maintenance personnel even flew with me and confirmed that something was wrong. Finally, the wing maintenance officer released the aircraft over my objections. I never heard anything more about that aircraft."

The prop change would not come soon enough for one hapless crew and aircraft. On the night of 6 June 1970, shortly after departing Da Nang Air Base, S/N 52-5935 and crew had the prop of their number-one engine go into overspeed. As the pilot tried to return to Da Nang, the Stinger became uncontrollable and he ordered bailout over the South China Sea, just off the air base. All survived with the exception of one crew member. The AC-119K continued on its course unmanned, causing concern as it headed for the Chinese airspace of Hainan Island. Thankfully, it crashed into the sea well short of Hainan.

Other changes made in-country to enhance the Stinger's effectiveness involved the 20mm cannon. The AC-119Ks first used 20mm high-explosive incendiary (HEI) loads, but found these ineffective against armored sampans and vehicles. During November 1970, a mix of HEI and armor-piercing incendiary (API) was tried to see if the AC-119K's sting could be made even more lethal. Findings were inconclusive until a Stinger engaged tanks in early 1971, erasing all doubt as to the effectiveness of mixed ammunition.

During the second half of 1970, AC-119G and K gunships remained not only the primary interdiction force in Cambodia, their operations were expanded. They were considered the main reason why towns and the provincial capital of Kompong Thom remained in friendly hands. During the last three months of 1970, Stingers had destroyed 312 vehicles and damaged 196, along with 279 sampans. Among those tolls was a record 29 trucks destroyed in one night, on 16 December, by a Stinger crew over Laos. The Stingers were good at their business, and business was good. Statistics jumped dramatically during the first quarter of 1971, with AC-119K crews credited with 1,845 trucks destroyed or damaged.

The 18th SOS became heavily committed to the 1971 South Vietnamese offensive into Laos, called *Lam Son 719*. The operation marked the AC-119K's first encounter with tanks. On the night of 28 February, Stinger 04, with Maj. Earl R. Glass and 1st Lt. Charles T. Robertson, Jr., at the controls, detected hot spots on their sensors moving toward the convoy they were protecting. The crew was certain that they were tanks, which was confirmed by ground elements. When the crew of a nearby AC-130 heard this, they begged the Alleycat airborne controller for the target. But Stinger had found

them and the request was denied. Soon eight tanks came into view, which the FAC confirmed were Soviet PT-76s. *Stinger 04* was cleared onto the target, and with a mix of HEI/API 20mm ammunition, and dodging intense anti-aircraft fire, made short work of all eight tanks. During *Lam Son 719*, AC-119Ks would claim 10 tanks, sharing the total with AC-130s, which had claimed 14.

During a period of four months, the Stingers had shifted operating bases to meet tactical requirements. Both AC-119Gs and Ks were divided among only four bases; Tan Son Nhut, Da Nang, Phan Rang, and NKP. Scoreboard tallies mounted, with one Stinger crew, nicknamed the "Polish Bandits," destroying a record 40 trucks on the nights of 10 and 11 May. Despite such successes, plans were made to turn over the AC-119G program to the Vietnamese Air Force in September, in keeping with the goal of Vietnamization. Realizing that the VNAF alone could not shoulder the interdiction campaign with large, sophisticated gunships, the concept of min-gunships was brought to the fore.

Meanwhile, back in the States, the AC-119 training unit, the 4413th CCTS, had been transferred in June from Lockbourne AFB to Hurlburt Field and re-designated the 415th Special Operations Training Squadron (SOTS). Eight AC-119Ks and six AC-119Gs were assigned to the squadron. The 4410th CCTW, which had switched locations and components with the 1st SOW at England AFB in July 1969, was re-designated the 4410th Special Operations Training

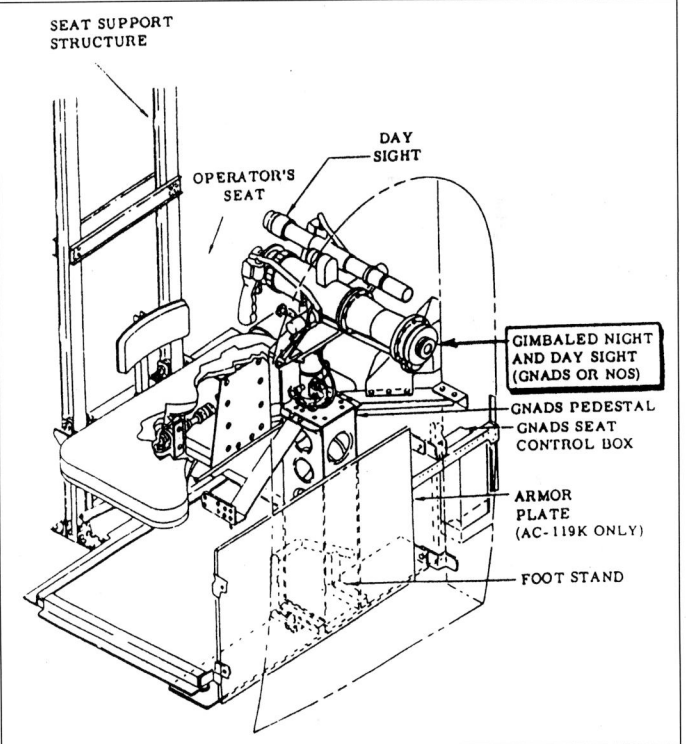

The NOS/NOD Operator's Station; the seat shown was seldom used.

After numerous problems with the Stinger's massive four-blade Aeroproducts propellers, a program was begun to replace them with more reliable three-blade Hamilton Standards. The conversion was done at Phan Rang Air Base, South Vietnam, with most Stingers eventually undergoing the change. (Larry Mersek)

AC-119K S/N 53-3187 was one of eight Stinger gunships assigned to the 4413th CCTS at Hurlburt Field in 1971. Unusual is 187's fuselage cheat line that separates its black and green camouflage colors. (David W. Menard)

This imposing view shows to good effect the AC-119K's massive, boxy fuselage that enabled it to carry the equipment and weapons loads that made it an effective gunship. Lurking behind the Stinger is an AC-130 Spectre gunship. (U.S. Air Force)

This AC-119K, S/N 52-5926, was assigned to the 4413th CCTS at Lockbourne AFB, Ohio, for crew training. It is seen here in early 1969 wearing fresh paint. The door for the NOS operator's station in the forward fuselage usually was removed. (Kenneth Buchanan)

Group. Base realignments in Southeast Asia during early 1972 simplified AC-119K operations, using only Da Nang and NKP in Thailand. With the drawdown of U.S. forces, the North Vietnamese launched major offensives, increasing the Stingers' workload in South Vietnam, Laos, and Cambodia. When the provincial capital of An Loc, 60 miles north of Saigon, came under siege, six AC-119Ks were staged at Bien Hoa AB during mid April to counter the offensive. Impressive kill totals were tempered with the 18th SOS's third Stinger loss, which was the only AC-119 lost to antiaircraft fire.

During a daylight mission on 2 May near An Loc, *Stinger 41* was to take its turn destroying a C-130 ammunition drop that landed in enemy territory. Although daylight missions were rare, it was vital that the ammunition not fall into enemy hands. A 37mm gun scored hits on the Stinger's right wing, which caught fire. The right jet engine had been blown off and the radial engine failed. The right main landing gear carriage swung downward, causing extra drag. The aircraft was uncontrollable and seven of the crew bailed out. Capt. Terrance Francis Courtney fought with the controls, but he and two others were killed when the Stinger crashed. The FAC that had been working with the AC-119K contacted the airborne command post, which summoned two HH-3E Jolly Green helicopters of the 3rd Aerospace Rescue and Recovery Squadron. The pair rescued six crewmen, while an Army UH-1 Huey helicopter snatched the remaining survivor. Just three days later, the enemy introduced the dreaded infrared-seeking SA-7 Strela surface-to-air missile. The grind of battle took its toll not only on the aged aircraft, but on crew-

men, who often suffered ailments from exhaustion and spending hours in the cold slipstream watching for ground fire. Amid growing concerns about the worsening situation, two AC-119Ks of the 415th SOTS were ferried to Vietnam.

Despite the grim tactical situation, which included a rise in tank sightings, and the accidental bombing of Da Nang Air Base by five fighter-bombers, which damaged six AC-119Ks, Air Force leaders moved ahead with plans to turn over the AC-119K program to the Vietnamese. Under *Project Enhance*, 16 in-country AC-119Ks were transferred to the VNAF on 1 October 1972. Another six were sent from the 415th SOTS at Hurlburt, thereby eliminating the USAF Stinger force. The 18th SOS became a training squadron, with the first Vietnamese training flight taking place in S/N 53-7831 on 18 December. Although the 18th SOS was officially deactivated at the end of December 1972, a number of its personnel remained at Da Nang AB for training VNAF Stinger crews. Two final missions with U.S. Air Force Stinger crewmen aboard were flown on 1 March 1973. One of those, flown in AC-119K S/N 52-5911, would end successfully. The other, flown in number 53-7839, would not. In what he calls the "Bailout of Stinger Number 839," pilot Lt. Col. Roy "Tony" Simon provides insight not found in official aircraft loss reports:

"It was just a routine night training mission when we departed Da Nang Air Base with a crew of 13. Our pre-mission weather briefing contained no information regarding adverse weather conditions for our arrival time at the base following the training

Stingers of the 415th SOTS in their element at Hurlburt Field in early 1972. (Dwayne Meyer)

Daytime photos of AC-119s in flight were often taken during flights to and from Phan Rang AB, where major maintenance was performed. AC-119s often were flown at unauthorized low levels down the coast. (David E. O'Mara)

Stinger S/N 52-5910 with the new three-blade props in September 1972. (Stephen Miller)

mission. Normal duration of these training flights was approximately three hours, therefore our aircraft had been fueled to allow for a maximum flight time, including fuel reserve, or approximately 3.75 hours. We flew a dry fire mission south and southwest of Da Nang for two-and-a-half hours. My VNAF student pilot was having difficulty with landings on previous missions, so I decided to return to Da Nang a little early to give him some landing practice. When we called for weather information 30 minutes before returning to base, I remember being able to see the lights of Da Nang in the distance. I called the tower for landing instructions for a visual approach and landing, then to remain in the traffic pattern for a couple more practice landings. We were instructed to enter downwind for a visual approach and landing to the south.

"The weather appeared good with the base and runway lights clearly in sight. As we approached, I could see scattered-to-broken clouds beginning to move over the base. Just as I reported on downwind, the VNAF tower controller advised me that the weather on the field was now below visual approach minimums and asked for my intentions. He said weather conditions were above TACAN non-precision approach minimums, so I requested we be cleared as soon as possible for TACAN approach to the south. The controller cleared us to the TACAN initial approach

fix [IAF] ten miles north of the base, and told us to expect immediate clearance for the approach. We switched to an approach control radio frequency and were advised that the field was now below minimums for all approaches, including precision approaches. Again, he asked for our intentions.

"The next few minutes were a blur. I was vaguely aware of our fuel situation, but not overly concerned. The next few minutes would quickly bring me to the stark realization that the 'pucker factor' was about to go through the roof. We were told the whole coastline was socked in with fog, with no alternate airports available within our range. I declared an emergency and requested an immediate Ground Controlled Approach [GCA] to the south, even though I knew the weather was reported below GCA minimums and the runway was closed. We entered the holding pattern at the TACAN IAF. The controller reported that GCA was shut down. I very adamantly requested that a U.S. controller be brought on board and fire up their precision radar with all due haste.

"I advised control I was about to begin a TACAN approach to the south, hoping precision radar would be available on final. I had no choice but to try an approach before the weather got worse, if that was possible. Maybe we would get lucky and catch a break in the fog long enough to get the bird on the ground. I

This 18th SOS AC-119K (S/N 53-3156) was returning from a night mission over the Trail, when, about two miles from Da Nang AB, both left engines lost power due to fuel starvation. Unable to maintain control, the pilot crash-landed in a small lake. (Larry Mersek)

Business card used by AC-119K air crews of the 18th SOS.

requested control to have the U.S. controller contact me as soon as he arrived, announced that I was departing the final approach fix inbound, and started a descent to the runway.

"Fuel was now a major concern. I figured we had enough for the TACAN approach, plus a missed approach, followed by a precision approach if necessary, and without a bailout procedure. I didn't have a good feel for how much time it might take to position the aircraft at a bailout point and get 13 people out safely.

"The TACAN approach went well. I tried desperately to remain calm. Never before had I started down a non-precision approach, without clearance, with the intention of busting minimums severely. Somewhere down final, the unmistakable voice of a G.I. broke the silence and my hopes soared. He said he'd stay with us, but he didn't yet have his precision radar operational. I

Amazingly, number 156's crew of ten escaped with minor injuries when their Stinger crash-landed, destroying the aircraft. Engine problems accounted for the majority of AC-119 losses. (Larry Mersek)

settled 839 down to 300, leveled off and stingily eased the throttles forward to maintain altitude and airspeed. I told the copilot to keep his eyes peeled outside and let me know when he saw runway light. As we approached the runway on short final, we were still in a wall of fog. When I determined we were about a half mile out, I started a descent to 150 feet and leveled off. The copilot reported what looked like strobe lights starting to pass under the aircraft. I looked up briefly to see the strobes barely pulsing up into the fog as we passed, and then they were gone. Once again, all was black. I flew level a few more seconds, hoping for a glimpse of a runway light or two, but to no avail. We applied power and executed our missed approach."

The approach controller told Simon he was still trying to bring up the precision radar, and suggested he try a northern approach in case the visibility was better at the opposite end of the runway. Simon knew they would have only enough fuel for another missed approach and would then have to fly to a bailout point. As the gear was lowered, flaps set, airspeed pegged, and checklists completed, 839 was on course. Simon continues:

"There was a tenseness in the air as I had never felt before as I called on my 10,000 hours and 18 years flying experience to make

this approach the finest of my career, for I felt it might be my last. The growing possibility of a bailout kept flashing through my mind. All was quiet except for the droning of those beautiful 3350s. All we had to do was keep everything centered, nail the airspeed, ease old 839 down to 200 feet, find the runway, and not run out of fuel."

Simon repeated the southern approach and suddenly the strobes disappeared as quickly as they came into view. Simon said:

"I allowed 839 to settle through 100 feet and decided to land in the blind, lights or no lights. But, no runway lights. I had a split-second image of the aircraft in a not-so-controlled crash, scattering crew and aircraft all over the field. I screamed to myself, 'This is no way to go,' and rammed the throttles to the stops. I yelled, 'Go around,' and the copilot responded immediately by toggling the jets to max power. Thank God the recips didn't cough."

Ground personnel later told Simon that they were about 50 feet above the runway when he applied power, and some said they could see the underside of the aircraft. "We sucked up the gear and prayed her into a climb," said Simon. The controller

Douglas A-1 Skyraiders initially escorted AC-119Ks on missions over the heavily defended Ho Chi Minh trail, until they were replaced by F-4D Phantoms. Stinger crews preferred the A-1s since they could loiter longer and were more accurate in ordnance placement. This AC-119K, S/N 53-8121, had the round fairing of its beacon tracking radar replaced by a blunt cover. (U.S. Air Force)

almost begged him to try again, but Simon knew he had only enough fuel to make it to a bailout point. More bad news from the controller advised that the base rescue unit had been transferred. The Stinger orbited at 3,500 feet with the jet engines shut down as the crew prepared for bailout.

A crewmember told Simon he couldn't get any of the five VNAF crewmen to jump. Simon commented:

"Some of the VNAF had to be literally dragged to the exit and forced out."

Both engines started losing power and fuel gauges read empty. Simon pointed 839 toward the sea.

"With [the] aircraft on autopilot and steady on course, I set up a 200 to 300 foot-per-minute rate of descent, advised the controller I was bailing out and got out of the seat. I took one last look at the fuel gauges, all of which read zero or less. I was amazed the engines were still running. I couldn't find my life raft. Time was running out. If I didn't get out of the aircraft soon, I'd be much farther out to sea than the other crewmembers. I vaguely remember ripping off my helmet and giving it a sling. I hate hats. When I reached the right side door, I quickly checked my 'chute and other equipment, stepped to the threshold and looked outside. It was pitch black. For an instant I thought,

'What the hell am I doing here?' I grabbed hold of the sides of the door to shove myself out. I hesitated. Then I walked to the other side of the cabin, turned around and headed for the opening in a dead run. No turning back now. I dived out head first and it seemed like I did a lot of tumbling as I was trying to count to ten. I felt like I was falling way to fast, so at the count of 'one thousand four' I figured, 'To hell with ten' and jerked the D-ring as hard as I could.

"After the chute had deployed, during an emotional moment, I looked up in an attempt to get one final glance at Stinger 839. There she was, lights flashing and engines humming faintly—a perfectly good airplane descending gently to her watery doom. I felt I had let her down. If ever there was an aircraft to which I experienced a special attachment, this was the one. Tonight she had done all that could possibly be expected of her. Silently, I thanked her for hanging on just long enough."

After four hours in the water, Simon and 11 other crewmen were rescued. A VNAF navigator drowned when his parachute, which he did not release, got caught in the propeller of his rescue boat. During the investigation that followed, Simon was told that the VNAF would not release the control tower tape recordings to the investigators. The tapes would have told much of the story. Simon summarizes, "It was never revealed to me why we were not advised of impending weather conditions. I thank God that twelve survived,

The AC-119K, S/N 52-9982, was named **The Super Sow.** (Author's Collection)

Crewmen prepare to board their Stinger aircraft at sunset, a scene replayed countless times in Southeast Asia. The AC-119K was named City of Columbus, Indiana. (U.S. Air Force)

A Stinger crew of D Flight, 18th SOS prepares for a mission at NKP in 1972. Parked beyond the trio of AC-119Ks are HH-53 rescue helicopters. (Larry Mersek)

The removed flap showing the devastating effect of 37mm fire. (Larry Mersek)

The 18th SOS advertised not only its prowess, but its VNAF training role with this holiday sign at Da Nang AB in December 1972. (Author's Collection)

Besides damage to its flap, which had been removed, this Stinger had 122 holes following an encounter with a 37mm anti-aircraft gun in 1970. All 122 holes, some of which are visible on the tail boom, were patched and the Stinger resumed flying combat missions. (Larry Mersek)

but the fate of the thirteenth will forever haunt me." The incident not only ended AC-119K training for the VNAF, it brought *Project Enhance Plus* to a close.

The AC-119K, along with the AC-119G gunship, like its descendant, the Dollar Nineteen, endured such dubious endearments as Widow Maker, Flying Coffin, and Fairchild's Pregnant P-38, but in the end, they proved themselves premier weapons platforms for defending forts, *Troops in Contact,* and as a truck killer, surpassing the F-4 Phantom in truck kills. Although the AC-119K eventually shared the gunship role in Southeast Asia with the larger, newer, and more sophisticated AC-130, the latter owed much of its success to the lessons learned during Stinger operations.

The few AC-119K crews that remained during 1972 and 1973 to train VNAF gunship crews came under the Base Defense Division at Da Nang AB. The VNAF transition program was termed Project Enhance Plus, during which instructors conducted a 45-day Stinger training course. Here, Flight Engineer Instructor MSgt. Lee Keyser works with his VNAF counterpart checking the AC-119K's main landing gear. (Lee Keyser Collection)

In January 1973, Da Nang AB was attacked with a barrage of Soviet 122mm rockets, one of which damaged this high revetment. AC-119K S/N 53-7831 in the background was so extensively damaged by the attack that it was reportedly written off. (U.S. Air Force)

Freshly painted AC-119Ks prior to arrival in Southeast Asia. In the foreground is serial number 53-8121. (Author's Collection)

Các bạn cán binh trong hàng ngũ Cộng Sản,

Các bạn vừa bị phóng pháo cơ AC–119 tấn công như vũ bão. Loại phóng pháo cơ cận chiến này được trang bị 2 đại bác cỡ 20 ly và 4 tiểu liên cỡ 7.62 ly xạ tốc của mỗi khẩu là 6.000 viên mỗi phút, đủ để bắn 6 viên đạn vào mỗi thước vuông nơi vị trí trú đóng của các bạn, trong giây phút. Phi cơ có thể mang một số lớn đạn dược đủ để bắn phá quét sạch mục tiêu. Ngoài ra, phi cơ AC–119 còn được trang bị những dụng cụ điện tử tối tân để khám phá, xác định vị trí nơi các bạn ẩn núp, ngay cả vào ban đêm.

Chúng tôi còn tiếp tục tấn công các bạn. Liệu lượt sau các bạn có thoát khỏi tử thần được không? Mong các bạn nên sáng suốt quyết định ra hồi chánh với chính nghĩa Quốc Gia để sớm đem lại cảnh thanh bình cho đất nước và tránh được cái chết khủng khiếp.

4 – 47 – 70

MƯA ĐẠN GIEO CHẾT CHÓC

ĐÂY LÃ PHÓNG PHÁO CƠ AC–119 VỪA TẤN CÔNG CÁC BAN

The psychological effect of the AC-119K Singer's firepower was exploited by dropping this propaganda leaflet following an attack by the 18th SOS. One side of the leaflet had a photograph with the heading caption, "Rain of Death." Below the photo read, "Here is the AC-119 Gunship which just attacked you." On the reverse side of the leaflet was the clear warning, "Men in the communist ranks, you were just attacked by the AC-119 Gunship. This gunship is equipped with two 20mm cannons and four 7.62mm miniguns. Each has a rate of 6,000 rounds per minute, meaning that it can fire six rounds into each square meter of your area in a few seconds. The aircraft can carry great quantities of ammunition, enough to saturate its target. Moreover, the AC-119 is equipped with modern electronic devices to determine your positions, your hideouts even at night. We will continue to attack you. Next time, will you escape death? We hope you will make the clearsighted decision to rally to the national just cause to bring peace soon to the nation and allow you to escape a dreadful death."

Most Stinger nose art was applied at Midway, one of many stops for aircraft being ferried to Vietnam. After serial number 53-7864 of the third group of six AC-119Ks was painted, crewmen found a Navy Chief to paint nose art on serial numbers 52-9982, 53-3154 and 53-7830. The nose art was short-lived since it was felt that large graphics on the Stingers' slab sides could be used by gunners as aiming points. (Larry Mersek)

The AC-119K S/N 53-3154 in 1970. Three mission markings appear below the cockpit. Already 17 years old when this photo was taken, the C-119 was proving to be the optimum aircraft for the upgraded gunship mission of the time. (Larry Mersek)

Another example of Stinger nose art, with the name Fly United and winged graphic having been worn by number 53-7830. The aircraft commander and flight engineer's names were painted below the cockpit, while the illuminator operator and crew chief's names appear below the nose art. (Larry Mersek)

The AC-119K S/N 52-9982 was named The Super Sow. Since the Stinger's camouflage was a heat magnet in Southeast Asia's tropical climate, the astrodome over the flight deck was kept open to help dissipate heat. The door of the night observation sight opening was removed for combat missions. (via Larry Davis)

During the short time that Stinger nose art was worn, few limits were placed on its often unsavory nature. This is in stark contrast to the politically correct Air Force nose art regulations of today. (Larry Mersek)

Nearly every major component of 831 was badly damaged from the rocket attack. (Tom Novak)

Emblem of the 18th Special Operations Squadron.

Extensive damage to number 831's left rear fuselage from the attack at Da Nang. (Tom Novak)

Emblem of the 18th SOS in Southeast Asia.

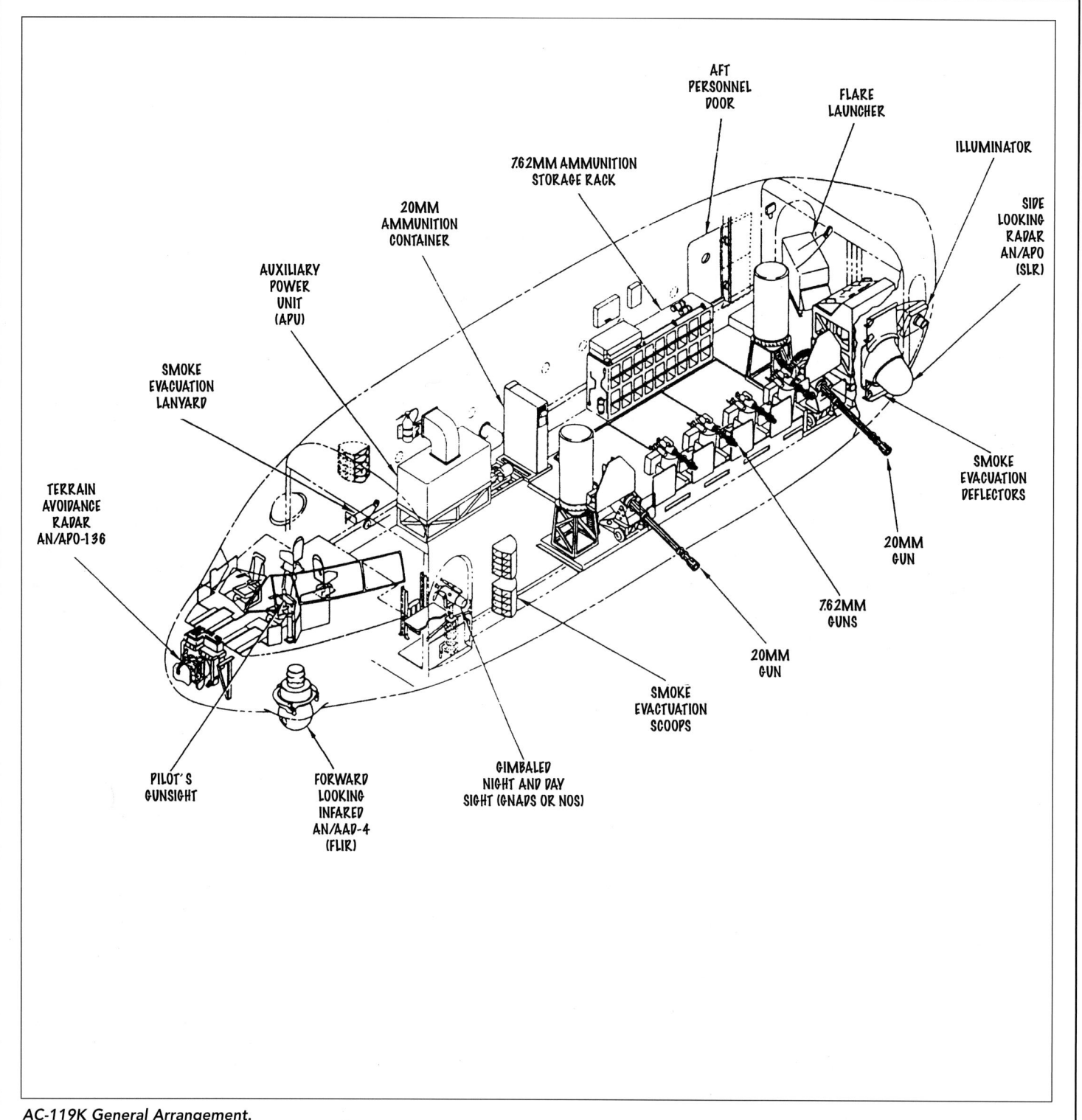

AFT
PERSONNEL
DOOR

FLARE
LAUNCHER

ILLUMINATOR

7.62MM AMMUNITION
STORAGE RACK

SIDE
LOOKING
RADAR
AN/APO
(SLR)

20MM
AMMUNITION
CONTAINER

AUXILIARY
POWER
UNIT
(APU)

SMOKE
EVACUATION
LANYARD

SMOKE
EVACUATION
DEFLECTORS

TERRAIN
AVOIDANCE
RADAR
AN/APO-136

20MM
GUN

7.62MM
GUNS

20MM
GUN

PILOT'S
GUNSIGHT

FORWARD
LOOKING
INFARED
AN/AAD-4
(FLIR)

GIMBALED
NIGHT AND DAY
SIGHT (GNADS OR NOS)

SMOKE
EVACTUATION
SCOOPS

AC-119K General Arrangement.

The *AC-119K, S/N 53-7830,* named Black Killer Duck, *prepares to depart on the last Stinger mission over Laos on 4 November 1972.* (Steve MacIsaac)

U.S. Air Force AC-119Ks

52-5864	later to VNAF
52-5889	later to VNAF
52-5910	4413th CCTS; later to VNAF
52-5911	4413th CCTS; flew last AC-119K mission 1 March 1973; later to VNAF
52-5926	4413th CCTS; later to VNAF
52-5935	detached to Da Nang, on 6 June 1970 had runaway prop during takeoff, crew bailed out over sea, one crewmen lost
52-5940	4413th CCTS; later to VNAF
52-5945	later to VNAF
52-9982	*The Super Sow*; later to VNAF
53-3154	*The Pea-nut Special*; later to VNAF
53-3156	flew first AC-119K combat mission, 15 November 1969, *Stinger 61*; detached to Da Nang, on 19 February 1970 crashed short of Da Nang when both left engines lost power, crew of ten survived, aircraft written off
53-3187	prototype AC-119K; 4413th CCTS; later to VNAF
53-3197	4413th CCTS; later to VNAF
53-3211	later to VNAF
53-7826	on 8 May 1970 had large portion of right wing shot off, crew received Mackay Trophy; detached to NKP, *Stinger 41*, on 2 May 1972 shot down during daylight mission at An Loc, three crewmen KIA, Courtney (AC) Air Force Cross
53-7830	*Fly United, Black Killer Duck,* flew last Stinger mission over Laos on 4 November 1972; later to VNAF
53-7831	4413th CCTS; later to VNAF, flew first VNAF training flight, extensively damaged in rocket attack at Da Nang in January 1973, reported in some records as written off
53-7839	4413th CCTS; in VNAF possession on 1 March aircraft was ditched over South China Sea due to fuel starvation, radar problems, and weather; one VNAF crewman killed, among a crew of eight VNAF and five U.S. instructors
53-7850	later to VNAF
53-7854	*Montezuma's Revenge* lost in Thailand on 2 August 1972
53-7877	first AC-119K delivered to USAF; later to VNAF
53-7879	
53-7883	
53-8121	later to VNAF
53-8145	4413th CCTS; later to VNAF
53-8148	later to VNAF

CHAPTER SIX

THE BIRTH OF SUPER SPOOKY

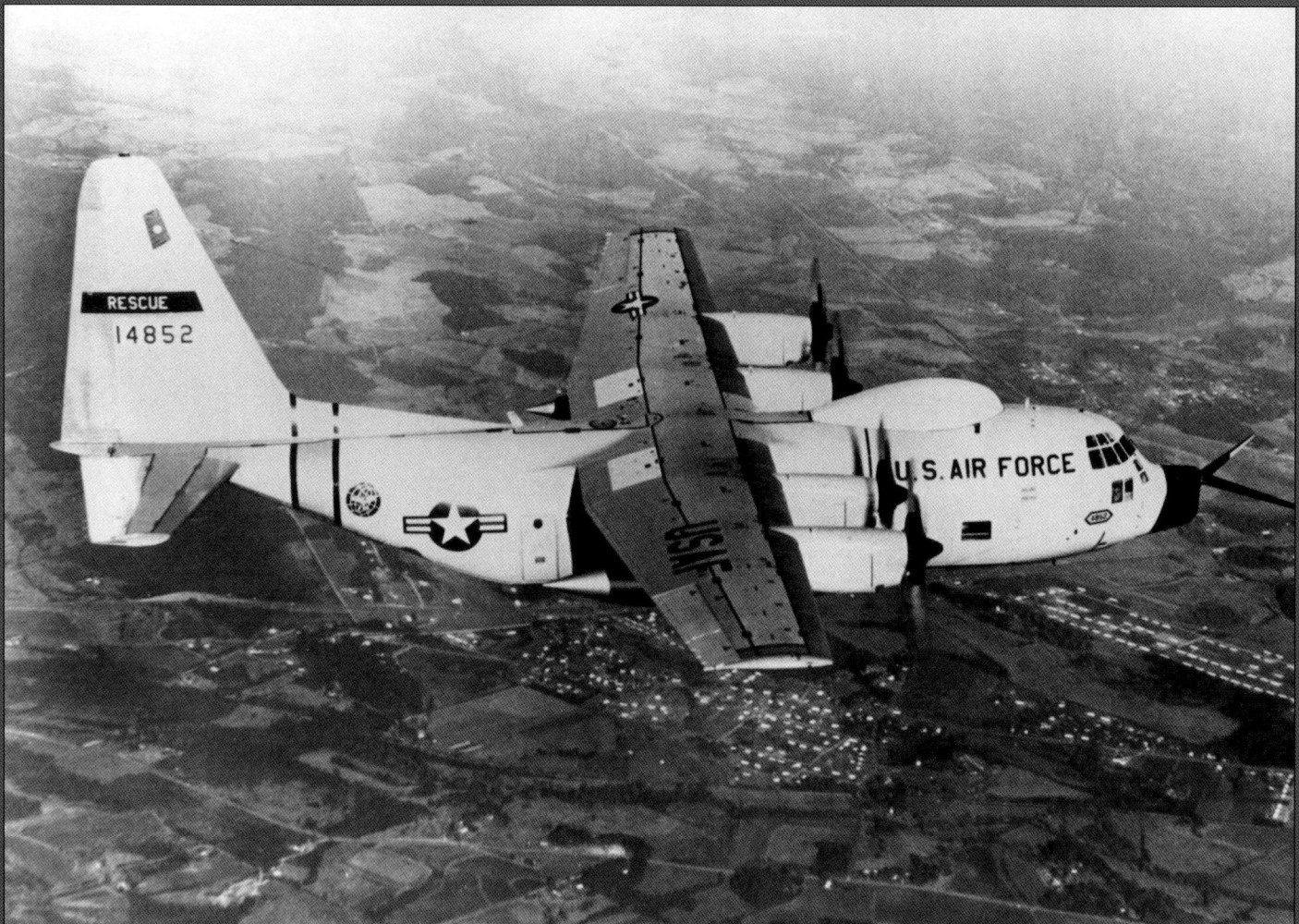

Among the C-130's wide variety of special applications was its role with the Aerospace Rescue and Recovery Service. Proving its multi-mission capabilities, in the rescue role alone there were at least seven variants. This HC-130H of the 305th Aerospace Rescue and Recovery Squadron featured the Fulton Recovery System, the nose-mounted arms of which could be extended to snag the tether of a balloon connected to a harness worn by personnel on the ground. The unique system saw use in special operations, rescue, and space capsule recovery operations. (U.S. Air Force)

It seemed that the Air Force was saving the best for last. Although in the overall gunship plan, *Gunship II*, the AC-130, preceded the development of *Gunship III*, the AC-119, the AC-130 would actually take center stage after its brother gunships had been fully committed to combat. After all, transforming the C-130 into the ultimate war machine would take considerable time and engineering effort. Meanwhile, Spooky, Shadow, and Stinger went to war, writing the book on gunship operations, not only proving the concept of transport aircraft modified with sensors and side-firing weapons, but providing valuable research data that benefited the development of their big brother—Spectre.

When work first began on the C-130 Program back in the early 1950s, Lockheed officials expressed that they would be content with producing 300 airplanes. The absurdity of that conservative view would become evident when the C-130 became king of the Air Force's multi-engine turboprop heavyweights, and is today the longest continually produced airplane in military history.

Having realized during the Korean War the need to improve tactical airlift capabilities, Air Force planners in 1951 and 1952 sent Requests for Proposals to aircraft manufacturers for a heavy airlifter. Rigid specifications called for a long-range aircraft capable of carrying a 37,800-pound payload 950 nautical miles and back without refueling. Designs, predictably, were submitted by leaders in the industry; Boeing, Douglas, Fairchild, and Lockheed. Although lacking in tactical airlift design experience, Lockheed was ahead of the game in an innovative design sense, submitting its proposal for the C-130. Its name, Hercules, would prove to be an understatement. The prototype first flew on 23 August 1954, farther back in time than most people realize. While not the sleek design expected from the company responsible for the classic C-121, the fat, round fuselage Herc was every inch a powerful, brutish workhorse. Its cranked fuselage with upswept tail allowed rear ramp loading into its flat-floored interior. The four-wheel main landing gear was housed in external sponsons, allowing maximum use of the cargo area.

While the Herc's little brother, the C-119, was called the Flying Boxcar, the C-130's cargo area was the actual dimensions of a railroad boxcar. Its cavernous fuselage, power, and high-wing design would easily draw the attention of gunship planners. The C-130's four Allison T-56A turboprop engines gave the big transport a speed of 360 mph. The first production C-130A made its first flight on 7 April 1955, with the type becoming operational with the 463rd Troop Carrier Wing at Ardmore AFB, Tennessee in December 1956. The first of countless changes made to the airplane was the change from three-bladed Curtiss Electric propellers to the more manageable four-bladed Hamilton Standard hydraulic props which became standard.

In 1958, the B model introduced more powerful 4,050 shaft horsepower (shp) T-56-A-7 engines, although the payload was unchanged. The landing gear and horizontal stabilizers were strengthened, and fuel capacity was increased to extend range. Early in the Herc's life, the U.S. Marine Corps showed a keen interest in the C-130 as an assault transport and aerial tanker, and soon placed orders. Next came the C-130E which was strengthened overall to support a maxi-

mum takeoff weight of 175,000 pounds, an increase of 40,000 pounds over the B model. Fuel capacity was increased also allowing flights to Europe with a 35,000-pound payload. External 1,360-gallon fuel tanks were relocated from outboard stations to a position between the two engines. The Air Force took delivery of the first E model on 1 June 1961 with production of 488 E models more than doubling the combined total of A and B models built. However, production records would not end there.

Topping production figures was the C-130H model, with 565 built. Introduced in 1964, the C-130's wing structure was again beefed up and the engines upgraded to 4,591 shp. The Hercules was now faster and able to fly twice the distance of the A model. Structural improvements were again made in 1969 and 1972. With advances in technology came an encyclopedic array of electronic systems. Additional electrical power was derived from an auxiliary power unit, and hydraulics were improved as well.

The latest version of the Hercules is the C-130J, the fuselage of which has been stretched 15 feet. Its maximum takeoff weight of 164,000 pounds is possible with Rolls Royce AE 2100D3 turboprops rated at 4,700 shp each, driving Dowty six-blade, composite, scimitar propellers. The J model flies at a maximum speed of 417 mph and has a range of 3,700 nautical miles with a service ceiling of 28,000 feet.

More than 2,000 C-130s have been built in more than 40 models, and through innovative engineering over the years, Lockheed has steadily improved the C-130's basic design enabling the stalwart aircraft to perform a seemingly endless variety of tasks. Besides transport and re-supply, the Herc has proven its versatility by serving as a drone platform, hurricane hunter, and fire fighter. The amount of specialized equipment it could carry in the Electronic Warfare role was unlimited while the U.S. Marines found it useful for transport and aerial refueling. In the hands of U.S. Navy and Air National Guard pilots, ski-equipped versions supported scientific exploration of the Arctic and Antarctic. The U.S. Coast Guard was quick to pick up on the airplane's attributes, and a C-130 was even flown off an aircraft carrier. During the war in Southeast Asia, the Herc saw duty as a tactical transport, bomber, flareship, and Airborne Battlefield Command and Control Center (ABCCC), while "MC" variants found a home in special operations. It premiered in the Air Force Aerospace Rescue and Recovery Service. More than 500 are currently in service with the active U.S. Air Force, Reserves, and Air National Guard. Worldwide, it continues to fly under the flags of more than 60 nations, and has even become popular with commercial cargo carriers. But its most awesome application, exclusive to the U.S. Air Force, has been, and remains—gunship.

Bigger and Better

Ron Terry didn't stop with the AC-47D. He knew the advantages of applying the side-firing concept to larger and faster aircraft that could carry more sensor systems and guns, selling the idea to Air Force officials at every opportunity. Air Force Systems Command officials shared Terry's foresight, urging during evaluation of the

The C-130A, serial number 54-1626, shortly after gunship modifications were completed in 1967. Pairs of 20mm cannons can be seen forward and rearward of the landing gear sponson, while two pairs of miniguns are located above the sponson. The bulbous radome of beacon tracking radar is immediately aft of the rear cannons. Early C-130 models featured a Roman nose, which followed the slant of the cockpit section. This was soon replaced by a protruding nose section, which housed, among a variety of electronic equipment, AN/APN-59 radar. (U.S. Air Force)

A freshly camouflaged C-130E at Da Nang AB in 1966. Although it was the largest tactical airlifter during the war, the C-130 had a short field capability that enabled it to operate from most airstrips. (Tom Hansen)

Wearing the black and green camouflage familiar to Air Force special operations heavy lift aircraft, this Hercules is believed to be one of the few MC-130E aircraft used in Southeast Asia for Operation Combat Spear. The specially equipped C-130s not only dropped Vietnamese agents into North Vietnam, crewmen reported that a number of them were extracted with the Fulton gear. The Fulton system was used for training in Southeast Asia and remained on special operations C-130s long after the war. (Tom Hansen)

The FLIR operator's position in the AC-130A. Unlike the rest of the crew, systems operators saw little of a firing mission beyond their scopes. (via Larry Davis)

An early gunship's fire control console, which incorporated flight instruments, radio equipment, a sensor angle display, and an oxygen panel. (via Larry Davis)

This sensor cluster, termed the AN/AJQ-24 Stabilized Tracking Set, was located in the AC-130's forward left fuselage. At center is the AN/ASQ-145 LLLTV narrow lens, while the lens at upper left was for wide TV. The lens at upper right served the AN/AVQ-19 laser target designator, and the smallest lens was the range finder. (via Larry Davis)

AC-47D that a better transport be considered. The North Vietnamese, unknowingly, helped push the plan along. As American gunships hammered the extensive and complex Ho Chi Minh Trail, the enemy countered by increasing the number and size of its anti-aircraft guns. Most of the enemy's supply route weaved through more than 1,500 square miles of jungle, which challenged reconnaissance efforts. It was painfully obvious that vastly improved gunships were needed to meet the challenge and Terry made it obvious that he had a solution. His involvement with the AC-119 invariably led to his work with the AC-130 program.

In January 1967, Terry was given the go-ahead to modify a C-130 (S/N 54-1626) in the shops of the Aeronautical Systems Division at Wright-Patterson AFB. The aircraft and personnel were assigned to the ASD's 4950th Test Wing. Teamed with James Wolverton, Terry was put in charge of the gunship System Program Office. Air Force officials apparently had accepted Terry's unique management style, which produced results despite established rules and regulations. The C-130 program, which initially was dubbed *Project Gunboat*, and later, *Prototype Gunship II*, became a scrounging operation, which was familiar territory for Terry and his tight-knit group. Equipment included excess or discarded military hardware, commercial and hand-made items, rudimentary engineering model design packages (termed Breadboard), all of which combined into something loosely referred to as a system.

The AC-130 was based on the AC-119, with the addition of two M61A1 20mm cannons. The proven FLIR and night observation system, side-looking radar, and guns were linked to an analog computer that gathered sensor inputs to correct the pilot's side-looking sight for wind, airspeed, and attitude. Also included were a Bell optical sight, an illuminator with two 20kw Xenon arc lamps capable of visible, infrared, or ultraviolet light, a semi-automatic flare launcher, Doppler navigation radar, armor, and inert fuel tanks. Beginning in June 1967, a C-130A named *Vulcan Special* was tested at Eglin's ground and water ranges. After much trial and error, various ad hoc components were shaped into a single system while two crews became intimately familiar with its operation. It was decided that a crew of 11 was required to maximize the gunship's potential. These positions were: aircraft commander, pilot, fire direction officer, navigator, navigator/sensor (night observation system) operator, navigator/sensor (infrared and radar) operator, flight engineer, loadmaster, master armorer/scanner, minigun armorer, and cannon armorer. The time had come to put the Gunship Prototype II to the test.

Majors Terry and Wolverton, along with MSgt. Bunch from the original Pirates, plus crews and support personnel, left Eglin for Southeast Asia, arriving at Nha Trang on 20 September 1967. There, the aircraft and crew were assigned to the 14th Air Commando Wing. The *Gunship II* Task Force flew their first mission one week later, defending *Troops in Contact.* Anxious to be released from the TIC mission, the Super Spooky finally was given the opportunity to show what it did best—kill trucks. On the night of 9 November, the C-130A's FLIR operator detected six trucks moving on the Ho Chi Minh Trail in Laos. Within 15 minutes, all six were reduced to burning hulks. Super Spooky, now named Spectre, made an impression initially defending ground forces, an impression made indelible as a truck killer.

Air Force officials were sold on the C-130 gunship, and quickly ordered seven more. Their enthusiasm, however, would be dimmed when Secretary Brown questioned not only the ability of the sensors to do their job, but the need to replace the AC-47 and the AC-119 gunships. A few months earlier, the Air Staff had emphasized the importance of C-130s remaining dedicated to airlift, having studied other cargo aircraft as follow-on gunships, specifically the Douglas

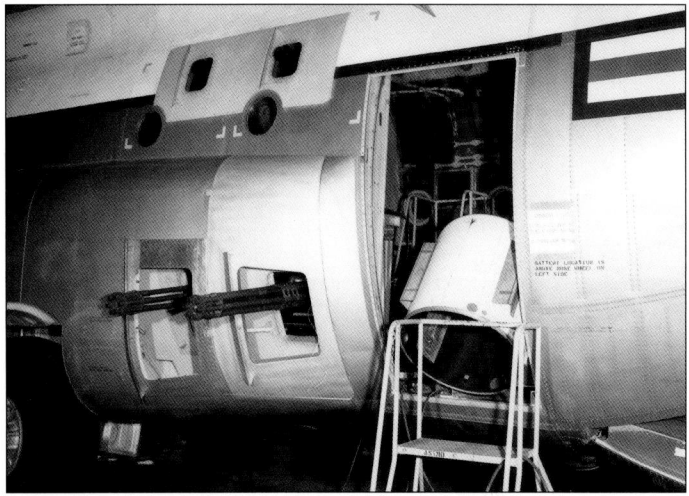

The prototype Gunship II during modification showing the rear 20mm cannons, rear miniguns above the sponson, and the housing for beacon tracking radar. (U.S. Air Force)

C-54 and C-118, the Boeing C-97, and even the Navy's Lockheed P-2 Neptune patrol bomber. General Momyer, 7th Air Force commander, pushed for the C-130, citing its four-engine survivability, greater speed, loiter time, and growth potential. Secretary Brown relented, calling the C-130 gunship, "The most effective breakthrough we have experienced in tactical aviation." The controversy seemed to dwindle, and the C-130 was again back in the limelight. The follow-on gunships would be designated AC-130As, and they would be culled from a small fleet of JC-130As, which served as test and research platforms. The Air Force couldn't spare C-130s from front-line units since they were heavily committed to tactical airlift in Southeast Asia. Meanwhile, by the end of 1967, the Vulcan Special and her crews had detected 94 trucks, 38 of which they destroyed.

This airplane was also experiencing problems commonly associated with new systems, so it was returned to the U.S., refurbished, and then arrived back in Southeast Asia on 12 February 1968. It was assigned to Ubon RTAFB and on 27 February began flying combat missions. Soon, the prototype proved to be the most effective means of destroying enemy traffic at night along enemy supply routes. The combination of monsoons over Laos, a decline in truck traffic, and a more threatening anti-aircraft environment prompted officials to transfer the Vulcan Express to Tan Son Nhut AB, South Vietnam. From June to November, the gunship flew throughout most of South Vietnam defending *Troops in Contact,* attacking trucks and sampans, and even hunting for enemy helicopters reported in the Demilitarized Zone. Weary from strenuous testing and combat, and plagued with equipment problems, number 1626 flew its last mission on 18 November 1968. Its crew had detected 1,000 trucks, destroying 228 and damaging 133. Another 481 trucks were attacked. Of 32 vessels the crew had detected, it destroyed nine and damaged eight. Leaders of the 7th Air Force and the 14th ACW were hopeful that the aircraft could be used in the enemy's forthcoming offensive. When they discovered that it suffered extensive equipment failures, they recommended that it be replaced by another AC-130A as soon as possible. On 26 November, the Vulcan Special arrived back at Wright-Patterson, where it served as a test bed for new systems earmarked for the gunship program.

In early 1968, the Air Staff had recommended that a mix of AC-47s, AC-119s, and AC-130s be used throughout the combat theatre. As expected, this stirred new controversy and deliberations continued throughout the year. This brought consideration of a Boeing AC-97 back into the picture. During preliminary evaluation of the C-97, which served mainly as a cargo hauler and aerial tanker, officials of the Air Force Logistics Command noted that the C-97 was large enough for the gunship package, and that it was available. On the downside, not only did it require more maintenance, it required a longer runway for takeoff, even with turboprop engines or auxiliary GE J47 jet pods. Secretary Brown limited the total number of gunships to 110 aircraft, 40 of which could be AC-97s. The Air Staff was able to convince Brown that J47 jets would add 10,000 pounds to the C-97, thereby reducing its performance at altitudes normally flown by gunships. So popular had the AC-47 become that what began as a search for its replacement culminated with a mix of gunship types. The decision to retain the AC-47 was based on the fact that it was being transferred to Allied air arms. The C-130, however, would come out on top in view of its ultimate growth potential.

The conversion of follow-on gunships converted from JC-130As was given high priority. LTV Electrosystems (later E-Systems) was awarded a contract with delivery of the first AC-130A scheduled for June 1968. Key modifications included the addition of Texas Instruments AN/AAD-4 FLIR, a Singer-General precision fire con-

As sensor systems and their related antennas were added to AC-130As, the Roman nose seen here on the prototype gave way to an enlarged nose section, which became the standard. Foremost among the gunship sensor systems installed in the prototype were the fire control radar and moving target indicator. (U.S. Air Force)

trol computer, and Texas Instruments moving target indicator (MTI) radar. Mounted to the rear ramp was an LAV-74 flare launcher. Later additions included AN/ALE-20 flare launchers in the rear section of both landing gear sponsons. Eventually mounted under both wings on pylons was a pair of AN/ALQ-87 electronic countermeasure units, used mainly for anti-radar. Outboard of those were SUU-42A/A rearward-firing, eight-tube ejector pods. The right pod launched flares, while the left pod ejected chaff cartridges. Four of the aircraft were to be sent to Southeast Asia, while the remaining three would stay behind for crew training. The directive calling for a force of eight AC-130As included the prototype after it was refurbished and updated, but when Ron Terry decided that work on the prototype would be too costly and time consuming, a standard C-130 was selected to undergo conversion.

Although E-Systems was slated to modify the eight aircraft, the innovative Terry had another idea. He decided to take on the job of converting the eighth AC-130A at ASD's shops at Wright-Patterson, managing all of the engineering, procurement, and ground and flight testing. Since Terry had proven his abilities and there was no point in stopping him now, he received uncontested approval. Terry's new endeavor, called *Project Surprise Package*, would be one of many steps taken to exploit the AC-130. The project introduced ten new subsystems, the most notable of which was the addition of twin M2A1 40mm cannons, which were labeled Bofors L60s after modification. The L60's rate of fire was 100 rounds per minute, usually fired in rapid three-to-five round bursts. These guns replaced the rear 20mm cannons, along with the two rear miniguns. The AC-130A S/N 55-0011 was the first gunship to have the guns installed. A digital computer fire control system was added, along with GE-ASQ-145 Low Light Level Television (LLLTV), Motorola APQ-133 beacon-tracking side-looking radar, a video bomb damage assessment (BDA) recorder linked to the LLLTV, and a Korad AVQ-19 laser designator/range finder. So vital was the fire control system's reliability to ensure that friendly forces were not hit while providing close support, that it embodied nine cross-check subsystems, which gave detailed readouts and displays.

Training for AC-130 crews initially was done at Lockbourne AFB, where flight training sorties were often flown to free other AC-130s for combat. Training was later moved to Hurlburt Field, where the 415th Special Operations Training Squadron put the new guys through their paces. Gunship crews learned the array of systems and flew 11 sorties each over Eglin's vast ranges.

Terry's in-house modification management program was labeled *Pave Pronto*. As the go-between for the acquisition of government furnished equipment and contractor systems, Terry's office foresaw better management of the conversion process, with shortened delivery schedules and the ever-important overall cost savings. When deployed to Southeast Asia, the enemy would indeed find the improved gunship a lethal surprise package. He could not hide on the darkest of nights, given the FLIR operator's ability to detect the heat emitted by truck engines and exhaust, not to mention body heat. The AC-130 was a resounding success, and there was even more to come.

The AN/ASD-5 Black Crow direction finding radar on AC-130A, S/N 54-1626. On the AC-130A, the dome incorporated a hinged baffle, which smoothed airflow and kept debris from sensors in the open forward doorway. Behind the perforated baffle was the battery compartment access and external power plug access. (Stephen Miller)

When the prototype modification was complete, the aircraft was camouflaged and tested over the water ranges at Eglin AFB, Florida in summer 1967. Unusual is the aircraft's level flight attitude while firing its side-firing weapons. (U.S. Air Force)

This AC-130A, S/N 55-0011, still wears the tail code of the 40th Tactical Airlift Squadron at Lockbourne AFB, to which it was assigned prior to gunship conversion in 1968. The gunship was named Surprise Package after the project name for the twin 40mm cannon installation. (Larry Davis Collection)

Wearing the emblem of the 4950th Test Wing near its cockpit, the pro-totype AC-130A is seen here at Wright-Patterson AFB in late May 1971. Number 54-1626 also wears the red fin flash worn by aircraft assigned to the 1st Special Operations Wing. With a small amount of black paint applied to the aircraft's tail fin, someone added a bit of character to the gunship. After two evaluation periods in the combat theatre, number 626 would return to combat in 1972. (Jack Morris via Stephen Miller)

During its evaluation deployment to the combat theatre, the proto-type was further darkened with camouflage paint, in addition to being named the Vulcan Special. It is seen here at Eglin AFB in mid-February 1968 prior to returning to Southeast Asia. The tail ramp of early AC-130s was kept open, even during firing missions, to allow crewmen to watch for ground fire. (U.S. Air Force)

The working side of AC-130A, S/N 55-0011 after it was modified with the Surprise Package twin 40mm cannons. Forward of the sponson are two 20mm cannons, and above the sponson are two miniguns. The twin 40mm L60 Bofors cannons project at the rear. The black ball unit was the AN/AAD-7 infrared detection unit, behind which was located the gas turbine compressor. This was a battery-started unit which ran an air turbine motor powering a generator. The compressor supplied high pressure air for engine starting and ground air conditioning on the flight deck, as well as hydraulic assist. Air deflectors were added forward of all openings in the aircraft's fuselage. (U.S. Air Force)

While in Southeast Asia, number 626 wore the name Vulcan Special in addition to zaps, which included the original Spooky ghost emblem. (Larry Davis Collection)

The business end of the AC-130 Pave Pronto's twin 40mm Bofors cannons had flash suppressors. It is ironic that the 40mm cannon was originally designed as an anti-aircraft gun, having been used extensively as such during World War II. (Larry Davis Collection)

Flying at dusk over an Eglin range, an all-black Spectre of the 919th Special Operations Group fires its 40mm cannons. (U.S. Air Force)

Interior view of the 40mm cannons showing their breech assemblies. The hinged curved pieces on the ends of the breech housings directed spent shell casings into large barrels. (U.S. Air Force)

CHAPTER SEVEN

BEHOLD, SPECTRE

One of the first AC-130As at Can Ranh Bay AB, South Vietnam, in March 1969. Spectres drew a great deal of attention when they made stops at air bases. In keeping with the fictional cosmic nature of its name, Spectre, AC-130s usually wore a large rendition of the hooded, skeleton-like character as nose art. Nurtured through comics since the 1940s, Spectre was depicted as a dark, destructive avenging entity, aptly characterizing the AC-130 gunship. (Ed Holcomb via David Hansen)

Under *Project Pave Spectre I*, E-Systems initially was contracted to convert nine C-130Es to gunships. The new gun platform combined the E model's capabilities with the Surprise Package gunship arrangement with one major change: the addition of a sensor called Black Crow (BC). This sensitive system was able to detect radiation signals emitted by automotive ignition systems. The ignition systems of Soviet and Chinese-built trucks that plied the Trail nightly were unshielded, proving that the enemy had underestimated the technology being brought to bear against its movement of troops and supplies. Blind Bat C-130 flareships had been operating in Southeast Asia serving as test beds not only for the Black Crow system, but other night sensors, including the LLLTV, night observation device (NOD), and laser target designator. The Black Crow's laser illuminator could also be used to mark targets for smart bombs delivered by F-4 Phantoms. Systems configurations varied from aircraft to aircraft, often creating a complex maintenance nightmare.

The AC-130E also introduced a change that greatly increased crew safety and comfort. During missions with the AC-130A, the illuminator operator, whose parachute harness was attached to a cable, laid in the open cargo doorway, watching for anti-aircraft fire. In the AC-130E, the door was kept closed, with the IO watching through an observation blister built into the lower section of the cargo door. The increase in weapons and sensors required a corresponding increase in crewmembers to 13, comprising seven officers: AC, copilot, naviga-

tor, IR operator, TV/NOD operator, Black Crow operator, and fire control officer (FCO), along with six enlisted men: flight engineer, three weapons mechanics/gunners, and two scanners.

In keeping with the theory of *Pave Pronto,* Terry gave the job of creating two prototype AC-130Es to the Warner Robins Air Material Area. After comparing the cost savings of WRAMA and industry, Terry gave the WRAMA the additional task of completing six additional AC-130Es. The AC-130E, having the E model's increased fuel capacity and payload capability, meaning more ammunition and armor than earlier AC-130s (now dubbed Plain Janes), was viewed as the model for future gunships. Three more AC-130Es would be built, bringing the total to 11. All were low-time airframes, having 1969-dated serial numbers. Despite Terry's innovative genius and flexible thinking, he was resolute in claiming that there was no better airframe for the gunship job than the C-130. He added, "It has proven to be a very good airplane and very survivable, and we have done much to improve on that. We've taken a beating over there, with many, many hits from 37mm and 57mm, and the aircraft came home with the crews uninjured for the most part."

Terry believed that the AC-130's success in combat was derived from keeping new equipment and tactics a surprise, and soliciting ideas from and communicating with the many agencies and laboratories involved in the gunship's ongoing development. True to his reputation for sidestepping bureaucracy, Terry said, "We normally have stuff out, bought, tested and over in combat before you could even

The AC-130A number 56-0469 of the 16th SOS at Ubon RTAFB in 1970. Some gunships wore the squadron's tail code FT in red on the tail fin. The Spectre is armed with 40mm cannons in addition to miniguns and 20mm cannons. Electronic countermeasure pods are mounted under its wings. (Don Jay)

finish the first step of the source selection process." Terry was adamant about improving systems, versus seeking revolutionary breakthroughs, and he made it his business to find out what had been successful. The AYK-9 digital computer fire control system used in the AC-130, for example, was a slight modification of that in the Navy's A-7E attack aircraft. Terry also considered it important to learn from gunship air and ground crews, and that he and his staff fly actual combat missions to evaluate systems first-hand. Between February 1968 and January 1970, Terry had flown 56 AC-47D and 140 AC-130 combat missions.

In December 1968, four AC-130As arrived at Ubon RTAFB, where they formed the 16th Special Operations Squadron, formerly Detachment 2 of the 14th Air Commando Wing, which had been attached to the 8th Tactical Fighter Wing. Of a total of 19 AC-130As built, 12 were normally flown from Ubon, sharing truck kills with AC-119Ks. Although frequently diverted to other missions, truck interdiction was the AC-130A's main mission. Within three months, the four Spectres claimed 607 trucks destroyed, more than one-fourth the theatre total. As AC-130A crews gained experience, they added new chapters to the gunship manual by devising new tactics when the North Vietnamese brought in more guns to defend the Trail. Spectres teamed with F-4 Phantoms, whose pilots called the gunships "Fabulous Four-Engine Fighters," a name not taken lightly by Spectre crews, or, for that matter, by anyone else. The F-4s were unlikely wing men, given the dissimilar speed of both aircraft types. Yet, when enemy guns opened up on the gunship, the F-4s flew through the Spectre's orbit to eliminate the threat, usually with cluster bomb ordnance.

On 8 May 1969, a Spectre achieved an unusual first when the crew of number 54-1629 detected and shot down an enemy helicopter, much to the chagrin of the fighter community. Underscoring the hazards of the Trail's high threat environment was the first loss of an AC-130, which occurred on 24 May 1969. While entering the firing circle to attack trucks in southern Laos, AC-130A (S/N 54-1629) was hit by two 37mm rounds. The aircraft became uncontrollable and most of the crew bailed out over Thailand, and were rescued. The illuminator operator died instantly but not before he was able to warn the crew of the incoming fire. The pilots nursed the crippled Spectre back to Ubon, where it crash landed and caught fire, killing the flight engineer.

A Spectre crewman reflects:

"We fired 40mm rounds that left the barrel at 2,930 feet per second. About six seconds later the round would slow to Mach 1 just as it hit the target. So the ground folks seldom heard the whistle of an approaching round. I don't know what the muzzle velocity of the 37mm rounds was that were fired at us, but they always used tracer rounds that looked like roman candles that would curl off to the side if not coming close, so we felt that their rounds took about the same time to get to our altitude. The IO would lay out in the breeze behind the aft ramp with heavy clothing (it was cold), a clear face mask, and a mike stuck between his teeth to minimize wind noise. He could see everything below the gunship, including under and well in front of the plane. The enemy usually fired four to five rounds at a time—one in the chamber and a clip of four ready to drop in place. The IO would call out rounds that were fired at us. If the rounds looked like they might come close, he would scream for right or left break. When the AC heard that, he would pull a hard right or left to evade the upcoming rounds. I have been in planes that went from a firing position of a 30-degree left bank to a 120-degree right

The aircraft commander, copilot, and flight engineer on the busy flight deck of an AC-130A prior to taking off on a night mission from Udorn RTAFB in 1972. (U.S. Air Force)

bank in four seconds, without breaking the redline g loads.

"Sometimes the enemy would set up a flak trap. They would bait a truck out in the open with its motor running to attract attention from the Black Crow ignition sensor and the IR sensors on our bird. They would set up 30mm AAA guns on hills surrounding the truck. When a crew saw a single tracer round going straight up, they knew they were in a flak trap and immediately broke hard to get out of there because that was the signal to the surrounding guns to all fire at once, bracketing the gunship."

Built into the AC-130's center right fuselage was the "booth," in which three crewmen operated the night eyes of Spectre's sensors, and where the fire control officer oversaw the mission. Since the navigator needed light, he worked over his table behind a curtain on the flight deck. The rest of the crew was in the dark; the cold and noise seemed to make conditions even worse. Beginning in May 1970, five AC-130As were rotated back to the U.S. for installation of bomb damage assessment equipment, 40mm cannons, moving target indicator, and 2-kw illuminator. Hayes International was contracted to do the work, and Lockheed Air Service of Ontario, California, installed the Black Crow, which was tested on C-130A S/N 56-0471. Later that year, more effective high density 20mm rounds were approved, along with 40mm Misch ammunition, whose more intense incendiary characteristics set trucks afire, even with near misses.

Henry Zeybel, who served in Southeast Asia as a C-130 navigator and logged 135 Specter missions as a television/night observation device operator, vividly recalls:

"During the dry season, AC-130s were fragged for armed reconnaissance of the Trail from the end of evening twilight until the first light of dawn. Unless battle damaged, every airplane flew every night. 'On target' time over an assigned sector of Steel Tiger was three to four hours. Although the NVA [North Vietnamese Army] had deployed AAA there, its primary defense was darkness. Few trucks moved during daylight. In the booth, while the navigator directed the gunship through systematic sweeps of a target sector, the sensors randomly searched for trucks. Usually the Black Crow made initial contact. On its oscilloscope, a target appeared as a green blip. Using computer direction, the pilot homed on the target. Closer in, the IR or TV/NOD located it. Pilots preferred TV for firing guidance because it was more stable. From an operating altitude, the pilot orbited the target in a bank at a constant airspeed and aimed the guns by aligning electronic symbols on a computer display. He had the option of firing manually or automatically when the symbols were near or in coincidence. Unless a target burned or exploded, the pilot never saw it.

"The boys in the booth ran the ball game and, by consensus, decided what was destroyed or damaged. Action that appeared on the IR and TV sensor screens was videotaped. With a photo interpreter, damage assessment was reviewed and, if necessary, reevaluated during post-flight debriefing. No special skill was needed to interpret what took place. Watching the sensor screens and the videotapes was like watching ordinary black-and-white television. The NOD-equipped gunships had no video recorders and operated on an honor system.

"Because of the volume of videotape, only footage of the most interesting or unusual events was saved by converting it to 16mm film and calling it 'AC-130 SEA Gunship Activity—Best of the Week.' Distributed Air Force-wide, the motion picture showed the destruction wrought by the gunship and also much of the anti-aircraft fire directed at the plane. A soundtrack of interphone conversations provided a vivid and often X-rated background. The Best of the Week was a novelty that grew into a form

A portion of the "booth" of an AC-130A in 1971. The booth, later called the Battle Management Center, was an enclosure in the center of the aircraft, where operators monitored sensor inputs and controlled Spectre's mission. (U.S. Air Force)

of entertainment rather than a battle report. At times it resembled a Keystone comedy. It showed NVA drivers who were frightened by near misses swerve their trucks off roads and crash into trees, tumble down ravines, or drive up steep hillsides before turning over. In one sequence, a driver abandoned his truck without setting the brake; the truck rolled backward down a steep grade while others swerved wildly to avoid it. On another occasion, a heavy tank reacted like a plastic bear in an electric-eye shooting gallery. Each time a 40mm round bounced harmlessly

off the tank's thick armor, the tank driver reversed course. The only thing needed to complete the farce was the 'Anvil Chorus' on soundtrack.

"Despite the pictures, the truck count was periodically questioned. For example; one night a crew found a truck park with 65 vehicles. The crew hit each one with a 40mm shell, and none of the trucks burned. In accordance with the damage assessment criteria, the crew claimed 65 destroyed, the largest single mission total of the season. In the morning, on orders from 7th Air Force,

The AC-130E, S/N 69-6567, of the 415th Special Operations Training Squadron, 1st Special Operations Wing at Eglin AFB in June 1973. Number 567 wears a TAC emblem on its tail fin and the 1st SOW emblem on its nose. The long probe attached to the nose was an Angle-of-Attack antenna for the groundspeed system, which was carried over to the AC-130H. (Jack Morris via Stephen Miller)

After flying two combat evaluations in Southeast Asia, the prototype Spectre, often referred to by its earlier JC-130A designation, served as gunship component test bed at Wright-Patterson AFB. Number 54-1626 is seen here while assigned to the 4950th Test Wing in July 1972. (Jack Morris via Stephen Miller)

When this photo of AC-130A, S/N 56-0509, was taken at Ubon in 1970, its Spectre nose art had been removed, possibly because it could be seen by enemy gunners. To further reduce the aircraft's visibility, propeller blade tips were painted red, versus the standard yellow. Spectre gunships wore a bare minimum of standard camouflage on their upper surfaces, with the majority of the aircraft, including its massive tail, painted black. (Don Jay)

an OV-10 Bronco pilot visually checked the area but found no signs of trucks. As a result, the 7th Air Force staff asked questions that were accusations: Did the crew actually hit that many targets? Were the targets trucks or things that looked like trucks? If the former, where did they go? If the latter, what were they? In reply, the crew asked some questions of its own: Did the recce bird overfly the correct coordinates? Did enough time elapse for the NVA to sweep up? What about the pictures?

This AC-130A, S/N 55-0029, at Ubon RTAFB shows the effects of combat missions in Southeast Asia. (Don Jay)

"For the crews, every night was a new battle and the dry season provided little time to reflect. From experience, sensor operators knew the speed with which maintenance teams cleared the Ho Chi Minh Trail. Sometimes when we had damaged a single vehicle, we would then fly elsewhere, hoping to find a convoy. If we found nothing, we would circle back to the lone vehicle ten minutes later and frequently find a repair crew there with a second truck. According to intelligence, the population of the Trail provinces was a quarter of a million Laotians, with an additional 75,000 NVA troops supervising work. It was our impression that everybody in the Trail provinces worked on trucks.

"For every mission that was questionable, there were dozens that were absolutely convincing of Spectre's truck-killing ability. Many convoys died spectacularly. Trucks traveled either singly, in small convoys of about five, or in large convoys of about 15. Often, by the time a gunship finished with a large convoy, the road was ablaze with flaming vehicles. Burning fuel from 8,100-gallon tanker trucks ran down the roadside ditches. Tankers erupted anew, and fires gained in size and intensity as flames spread from one fuel cell to another. Ammunition trucks exploded when intense heat cooked off their cargo; exploding tracer rounds pin-wheeled into the sky before falling back into the holocaust. Nothing escaped the flames. The destruction was breathtaking, and much of it was recorded on videotape.

A Pave Pronto AC-130A Gray Ghost in 1974 painted in overall Gunship Gray. The change from Southeast Asia camouflage to this scheme was introduced in 1973. (Kenneth W. Buchanan via David Menard)

"Seventh Air Force Awards and Decorations helped create the controversy that surrounded the truck kill figures. Using data from 1969 to 1970, Awards and Decorations decided that a gunship crew would be given the Distinguished Flying Cross if it stopped 25 trucks (total of destroyed and damaged) on one mission, and encountered ground fire (say, 200 rounds of AAA). Since the previous season, however, not only were more 37mm guns deployed along the Trail, but 57mm was added at key locations. The salvation for Spectre was that none of the guns were radar controlled. During two months, our crew averaged more than 300 rounds of AAA per mission. Therefore, half the criteria for a DFC were automatically fulfilled. It was axiomatic that trucks and AAA went together. As our navigator explained to new guys, 'You're going to get shot at if you do your job properly. The NVA doesn't position guns to protect trees or karst. Find guns, you find trucks.'

"Twenty-five trucks was a good night's work during the first half of the 1970-71 season, but few crews attained that figure. However, when American and South Vietnamese soldiers drove into Laos during Lam Son 719 in February and March, a total of 25 became a joke. Each night at least one gunship destroyed that many or more. The incursion into Laos interdicted the Trail's eastern roadways and forced traffic to the fewer roads along the less complex western part of the Trail. Because the NVA did not reduce its volume of traffic, jams resulted, and convoys backed up into each other. From Spectre's viewpoint, the same number of targets had been compressed into an area half as great. Searching was eliminated. The Trail was a shooting gallery. This was the only time that NVA maintenance teams could not keep the roads cleared. Hulks sat untouched for days, and bottlenecks developed where convoys piled up in ruin. Moving vehicles were forced to

In December 1971, AC-130A, S/N55-0044, was hit by a large caliber weapon, shearing off number four engine's gearbox and propeller. Its prop then struck the number three engine. After the crew lightened the aircraft, its pilot was able to stabilize the aircraft at 4,000 feet for the 45-minute flight back to Ubon. Spectre and crew, with only two left engines, landed safely, attesting to the pilot's skill and the C-130's durability. (U.S. Air Force)

One of the first AC-130A gunships built, S/N 55-0011 was the first to have 40mm cannons installed. Number 011 is seen here in 1972 equipped with pairs of under-wing ALQ-87 ECM pods, and wearing the FT tail code of the 16th SOS. Besides upper wing surfaces, only a small portion of the AC-130's upper fuselage wore tri-tone camouflage. (U.S. Air Force)

In Pave Pronto configuration, AC-130A, S/N 56-0469, stands alert at Ubon RTAFB in May 1972. (U.S. Air Force)

Serial number 69-6573 was one of 11 AC-130E Pave Spectre Is. The E model introduced the Black Crow sensor, which was identified by the radome seen above the nose landing gear. Number 573 was upgraded to AC-130H standards, becoming a training gunship during the late 1970s. The change from Curtis Electric three-blade props to Hamilton Standard four-blade props was introduced in the C-130B model. The four-blade unit created less vibration and noise. (U.S. Air Force)

weave around scattered wreckage. In the eyes of the Spectre sensor operators, it was lovely chaos.

"The wealth of vehicles influenced the sensor operators' attitude regarding damage assessment. When targets were scarcer, they hit a vehicle with several 40mm rounds in hopes of making it burn. They succeeded about half the time. Nearly as decisively, those trucks that did not burn, nevertheless, did sustain multiple hits. The large number of truck sightings during Lam Son caused a shift in tactics. Crews spent less time on each truck in order to strike more trucks. The single-hit criterion was liberally applied. As a result, crews burned or blew only about one out of four targets. Spectre's March 1971 figures were 3,361 trucks destroyed and 819 damaged, a third of the season's total.

"After the rains came, Lt. Col. Ken Harris, 16th SOS Commander, met with our pilot and the navigators from our crew. Harris read a message from 7th Air Force that talked about re-struck and twice-counted vehicles, decoys, and armored trucks. Instinctively playing cover-your-ass, one of our crew said, 'Nothing in there we didn't already think about.' We knew the NVA drivers had tricks, probably more than we recognized. Like most crews, we had learned by trial and error. When we first started, we would find a convoy and blast away at the leader who took off like a scared rabbit. By the time we stopped him and then punished his truck, the others in the convoy were nowhere to be found. We fell for that three or four times before we decided to ignore the escaping leader who probably had an armored cab and, instead, plowed into the others before they had time to vanish.

"While trucks and their cargo traveled the overall length of the Trail, drivers worked only short segments that they knew perfectly. They could nestle vehicles into side roads or beneath overhanging branches so that IR signatures disappeared. We once watched four trucks fade from sight right before our eyes, just slip off the road and be gone. We hammered through the foliage at where we thought they had hidden and, before we departed, had a pair of fires raging. We also watched drivers pull up near a burning vehicle in order to mask their IR signature in the glow of the blaze. We often wondered just how much the drivers knew about our capabilities."

According to Air Force intelligence, during the 1969–1970 dry season (October to April), when truck traffic peaked, the North Vietnamese moved 68,000 tons of material down the Trail to maintain offensives in the south; 21,000 tons reached its destination. During the 1970-71 dry season, the same tonnage went down the trail by truck, but only 9,500 tons got through. During that season, the Spectre fleet was increased from 12 to 18 gunships. And the arrival in the theatre of the first AC-130E on 25 October 1971 couldn't have been better timed.

As the North Vietnamese increased the number and size of guns along the Trail, and more armored vehicles appeared, 7th Air Force officials sought a weapon that increased Spectre's stand-off distance, yet allowed crews to still kill trucks. Ron Terry's team at Wright-Patterson went to work researching various weapons, including the 57mm anti-tank gun and the 106mm recoilless rifle. They finally settled on another time-honored stalwart, the M102 105mm Howitzer artillery piece. The Howitzer could fire a 42-pound shell with a 33-pound warhead, 6.5 pounds of which was high explosive, a distance of 12,000 meters. The new gun package was named *Pave Aegis* and on 17 February 1972, a modified version of the 105 was installed in AC-130E number 69-6570 at Ubon RTAFB. The gun was fix-mounted in the left rear door, replacing one of the 40mm cannons and relocating the side-looking radar. The gun was hand-loaded and it recoiled 3-1/2 feet into the fuselage when fired. Henry Zebel commented:

"After this AC-130 sustained battle damage to its right wing, the howitzer was installed in gunship number 69-6571. The 105 came close to what designers at the ASD laboratory had anticipated when they modified the 40mm for use on the AC-130; a single hit inflicting major damage on a vehicle. In the fall of 1971, I participated in live fire missions out of Hurlburt Field. From what I saw, I conservatively estimated that there was no more than a ten-percent chance that a truck would be operable after being hit with a 105 round. Seventh Air Force retained the criteria ruling that vehicles had to burn or blow up to be counted as destroyed. Despite that, during 32 missions, the howitzer-equipped AC-130 received credit for destroying 75 trucks and damaging 92 with the 105, while destroying 27 and damaging 24 with 40mm fire."

Eventually, all Pave Spectre AC-130Es had the 105 installed, although on trainable mounts that were linked to the computer sighting system. Although a 105mm high-explosive shell is considered lethal within a 35-foot radius, Spectre crews were able to deliver accurate fire to defend troops, and soon, ground commanders were requesting "The big gun."

On 11 January 1972, Air Force intelligence confirmed the enemy's deployment of the SA-2 Guideline missile. Although Spectres were not intended to fly in surface-to-air-missile (SAM) environments, they continued to fly missions in Steel Tiger, although at higher altitudes, up to 9,000 feet. Spectre continued to amass truck kills, but would soon feel the sting of SAMs. On the night of 28 March, AC-130A (S/N 55-0044) departed Ubon in search of trucks over the Trail in southern Laos. An SA-2 from a newly built SAM site found the Spectre, which burst into flames, crashed, and exploded. All 14 crewmen aboard were killed. Just two days later, *Spectre 22* was entering its second firing orbit to attack trucks when 57mm rounds hit its right wing and fuselage. The AC-130E caught fire and Capt. Waylon Fulk turned toward Thailand, hoping to reach Ubon. Conditions worsened, forcing the crew to bail out, which set in motion one of the largest and most complex SAR effort of the war. All 15 crewmen were rescued. A few days later, on 2 April, rescue forces would again be put to the test during the equally massive rescue effort for *Bat 21*.

In the AC-130's cramped quarters, gunners continually scooped so many minigun links and spent cartridges that they devised a patch with the wording, "Shovel Qualified." Despite containers kept nearby for the refuse, long missions and the guns' high rate of fire accounted for tens of thousands of rounds. (U.S. Air Force)

The 105mm Howitzer installation added to the crowded interior of the AC-130E. Since the gun recoiled 3.5 feet when fired, a safety frame was added to the back of the weapon. At right is the storage rack for 40mm and 105mm ammunition. (Author's Collection)

On some AC-130Es, an AN/APQ-150 beacon-tracking radar was re-installed between the 40mm and 105mm guns. Visible under the forward section of the sponson is the AN/AAD-7 infrared detecting unit. (Author's Collection)

The 105mm Howitzer installation was code named Pave Aegis. The Howitzer replaced a 40mm cannon and beacon-tracking radar, which previously had occupied the space between the two guns. After initial use of the Howitzer, it was discovered that the gun's large opening caused stress cracks in the fuselage skin. The solution was a rigid ribbed panel above the mount to absorb the gun's recoil forces. At upper right is the 20kw illuminator. An air deflector was installed immediately forward of the illuminator opening. Mounted on each side of the lower cargo door ramps were air deflectors, which also served as armor. (U.S. Air Force)

The round object to the right of the illuminator is a Trim-7A antenna. The rectangle immediately to the right of the illuminator port is a portion of the national insignia that had been removed. In the shadowy world of special operations, gunships periodically were flown without such insignia. (Author's Collection)

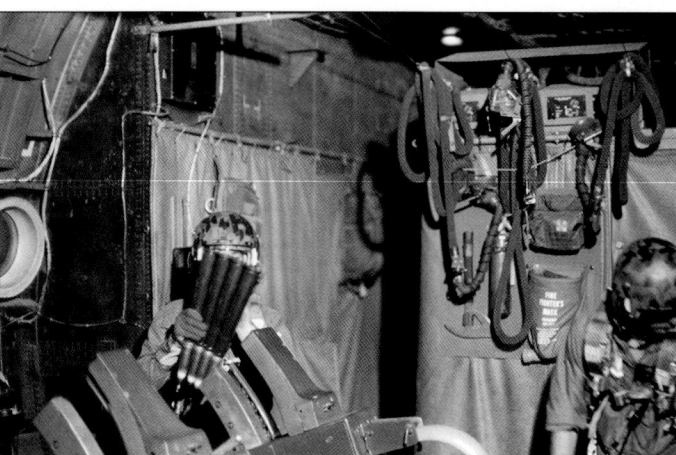

A Spectre gunner loads a four-round clip into the 20mm Bofors cannon. At right is an enclosure for systems operators. Crewmen in the aircraft interior endured a cold, dark and noisy environment. (Larry Davis Collection)

Stenciled on the top ammunition feed chute of this 20mm cannon are the words "TIC LICKER." TIC was the abbreviation for Troops in Contact, a mission commonly flown to support ground forces engaged in combat with the enemy. (Frank Murray via Larry Davis)

Personnel of the 16th SOS advertised their presence after the unit was transferred from Ubon to Korat RTAFB in mid-1974, embellishing their reputation as "Fabulous Four-Engine Fighters." As expected, the fighter community didn't concur. (U.S. Air Force)

Serial number 69-6567 was upgraded from an AC-130E to an H model in 1973. Like all AC-130Hs, it was painted overall Gunship Gray. Number 567 is seen here in 1974 after returning from Southeast Asia, when it was assigned to the 415th SOTS. (Kenneth W. Buchanan via David Menard)

After the war, AC-130As were assigned to the Air Force Reserve 711th SOS. Number 55-0046 is seen here at Dobbins AFB in July 1979. The gunship mission of this C-130 is not readily apparent from the right side. (R. Ray Leader via Stephen Miller)

While displayed during Armed Forces Week at Andrews AFB in 1977, AC-130H, S/N 69-6567, was equipped with its full complement of under-wing countermeasure devices. (Stephen Miller)

Painted overall flat black, AC-130H, S/N 69-6573, undergoes maintenance at Korat RTAFB in July 1975. This paint scheme might have applied to any number of C-130 missions. (Don Jay)

The AC-130A, S/N 55-0040, of the Reserve 711th SOS, 919th SOG at McChord AFB, Washington, in July 1975. Besides its white propeller tips, unusual is the absence of weapons, indicating that this Spectre may have been in a modification phase. The A model AC-130s are differentiated from other models in having their external fuel tanks mounted outboard of the engines, while on other models, they are mounted between the engines. A small white Spectre emblem appears on the plate where the Black Crow radome was installed. (Doug Remington via Stephen Miller)

After the war in Southeast Asia, the prototype AC-130A was returned to the 4950th Test Wing at Wright-Patterson AFB. Although stripped of its guns and once again called a JC-130A, number 1626 continued to serve as a gunship component test bed. It is seen here in May 1978 wearing an Air Force Systems Command emblem and a large marking, which served as a photographic reference point during test flights. If this cross was painted red, it would signify a medevac mission aircraft. (Author's Collection)

Shortly thereafter, the North Vietnamese introduced the infrared-seeking SA-7 Strela missile, with the first recorded firing at an AC-130 occurring on 5 May. Spectres were able to avoid more Strela firings until 18 June 1972 when an AC-130A (S/N 55-0043) was hit over South Vietnam 25 miles southwest of Hue. The missile hit the aircraft's number three engine and the wing blew off when the fuel tank exploded. Three of the 15-man crew were able to bail out and survived. A Spectre crewman later reported that one of the onboard sensors may have been responsible for the aircraft's demise. The Illuminator Operator saw the missile inbound, but made a "no sweat" call when it appeared to arc far behind the aircraft. The TV operator directed his sensor toward the missile to view it, overlooking the fact that his infrared sensor was activated and slaved to the TV. This appeared to have caught the missile's attention and it swerved toward the gunship and streaked into the rear ramp opening and exploded.

Anti-aircraft threats increased at enormous rates, forcing gunships to higher altitudes, from where their miniguns and 20mm cannons proved less effective. This threat, combined with mounting Spectre losses and the enemy's refinement of camouflage and convoy discipline, prompted 7th Air Force to drastically curtail gunship missions in the dangerous skies over Laos and Military Region I, south of the DMZ. Eventually such high-threat areas were left to "fast mover" jet aircraft.

At the end of March 1972, the North Vietnamese Army launched a major three-pronged offensive in South Vietnam. As troops, tanks, and artillery rolled across the DMZ, battalions of enemy troops attacked key provinces in the south. The widespread onslaught, intended to break the South Vietnamese Army, was called the *Easter Offensive*, and required an all-out effort from AC-119Ks and

AC-130s flying from bases in Thailand and South Vietnam. The enemy brought scores of Soviet T-54, T-55, and T-76 tanks into the battles. Again the combination of Specter and F-4 came into play, with the AC-130 holding tanks mercilessly with its laser marker as Phantoms rolled in to finish the job. The Pave Aegis proved especially successful, using the 105mm gun to kill tanks, along with trucks and artillery. In a remarkable display of skill, one Specter crew destroyed 12 trucks within 15 minutes. Spectres also provided support of South Vietnamese troops, and when its guns were silent, flew as FAC platforms for other aircraft. As Spectres supported U.S. and South Vietnamese troops in defense of Quang Tri and Hue in the

The emblem of the 415th Special Operations Training Squadron at Eglin AFB.
(Larry Davis)

After a distinguished career, the prototype AC-130A, S/N 54-1626, was put on display at the USAF Museum at Wright-Patterson AFB, Ohio.
(Stephen Miller)

north, they attacked enemy forces that had encircled the key city of An Loc to the south. Spectres flew around the clock, finally helping to break the siege in June. The NVA brought the SA-7 into the offensive, one of which scored a hit on a Spectre on 8 May. Luckily, the crew was able to fly it back to Tan Son Nhut Air Base.

Beginning in 1973, all but one of the AC-130Es was upgraded as part of a program aimed at improving the entire C-130 fleet. This massive undertaking focused on replacing the engines with more advanced T56-A-15 turboprops delivering 4,910 shp. This powerplant shortened the aircraft's takeoff roll, gave it a better rate-of-climb, and improved its overall performance, especially in hot climates. The improved gunship had a maximum speed of 328 mph, a service ceiling of 34,000 feet, and an unrefueled range of 4,848 miles, although with the addition of an air refueling package, range was unlimited. Pave Spectres included in the program were given updated radio and avionics equipment, while those not armed with the

AC-130As

53-3129/3001	First production C-130A; became JC-130A in September 1957; after a series of assignments, number 129 was assigned to the 6650th Strategic Wing when it was converted to AC-130A; ensuing assignments were the 4413th CCTS, 415th SOTS, and 16th SOS in Vietnam and Thailand from 1968 to 1970, wearing the names *The Arbitrator* and then *First Lady*; it served the 711th SOS beginning in 1976; then became a reserve gunship in 1995; it is displayed at Eglin AFB		1977; flew three missions in *Desert Storm*; displayed at the National Museum of the Air Force
		55-0011/3038	40th TAS; then AC-130A in 1968 *Surprise Package*; 4413th CCTS 1970; 415th SOTS, 1st SOW 1971; 16th SOS, 8th TFW at Ubon RTAFB 1972 *Night Stalker*; 711th SOS in 1976; *Desert Storm*; arrived AMARC November 1994
		55-0014/3041	40th TAS; converted to AC-130A in 1968; 16th SOS, 8th TFW at Ubon RTAFB 1973; 711th SOS in 1973 *Jaws of Death*; flew 20 missions in *Desert Storm*
54-1623/3010	16th SOS, 8th TFW at Ubon RTAFB 1971 to 1972 *Ghost Rider*; 711th SOS in 1978; *Desert Storm*; displayed at Warner Robins AFB	55-0029/3056	AC-130A in 1970; 16th SOS, 8th TFW at Ubon RTAFB 1972 to 1973 *Midnight Express*; 711th SOS in 1977; arrived at AMARC in November 1994
54-1625/3012	previously a JC-130A with AFSC; 4413th CCTS; 4410th CCTW 1968 to 1969; 16th SOS at Ubon RTAFB *War Lord*; shot down over Laos on 21 April 1970 *Adlib One* ten crewmen KIA	55-0040/3067	16th SOS, 8th TFW at Ubon RTAFB 1972 to 1973; 711th SOS 1975 to 1976; arrived at AMARC in June 1976
54-1626/3013	Prototype AC-130A; 4950th TW 1966 and 1967; 16th SOS, 14th SOW at Nha Trang *Vulcan Special, Super Spooky*; crashed in Vietnam in March 1972 but repaired; 711th SOS; 4950th TW; displayed at the National Museum of the Air Force	55-0043/3070	AC-130A in 1970; 16th SOS, shot down by SA-7 in South Vietnam on 18 June 1972, 12 crewmen KIA
		55-0044/3071	AC-130A in 1970; 16th SOS, 8th TFW at Ubon RTAFB *Prometheus*, damaged by ground fire December 1971 (both right engines lost); shot down by SA-2 over Laos on 28 March 1972, 14 crewmen KIA
54-1627/3014	converted from JC-130A; 16th SOS, 8th TFW at Ubon RTAFB 1969 to 1972 *Gomer Grinder*; 415th SOTS 1973 to 1974; 711th SOS in 1975; arrived at AMARC in June 1976	55-0046/3073	AC-130A in 1969; 21st TAS at Naha AB, Okinawa in 1970; 16th SOS, 8th TFW at Ubon RTAFB 1972 to 1974 *Proud Warrior*; 711th SOS in 1976; arrived at AMARC in November 1994
54-1628/3015	converted from JC-130A; 16th SOS, 8th TFW at Ubon RTAFB 1969 to 1973 *The Exterminator*; 711th SOS in 1977; arrived at AMARC September 1995	56-0469/3077	16th SOS, 8th TFW at Ubon RTAFB 1970 to 1973 *Grim Reaper*; 711th SOS in 1976; went into storage at AMARC but cockpit converted to AC-130U simulator at Sheppard AFB
54-1629/3016	converted from JC-130A; 16th SOS, 8th TFW; damaged from ground fire over Laos and written off after crashing landing at Ubon RTAFB on 24 May 1969, two crewmen killed	56-0490/3098	16th SOS, 8th TFW at Ubon RTAFB 1972 *Thor*; shot down over Laos on 21 December 1972, 14 crewmen KIA, two survived
54-1630/3017	converted from JC-130A; 16th SOS, 8th TFW 1979 to 1971 *Azreal-Angel of Death* (*Mores de Callis*); 415th SOTS 1971 to 1976; 711th SOS in	56-0509/3117	16th SOS, 8th TFW at Ubon RTAFB 1972 to 1974 *Raid Kills um Dead*, later *Ultimate End*, damaged at An Loc on 23 December 1972; 711th SOS in 1977; *Desert Storm*; displayed at Hurlburt Field

105mm gun, had it installed as well. An electronic warfare officer (EWO) was added to the "booth," which later was labeled the Battle Management Center. These changes resulted in the new designation AC-130H Pave Spectre II. Some aircraft arrived back at Ubon beginning in March 1973 in a new overall black color scheme, and all Spectres were eventually painted overall Gunship Gray, being commonly referred to as Gray Ghosts.

Spectres were not limited to warfare. In 1973, an AC-130H flew long duration orbits over the Florida Everglades, using its powerful light to help searchers locate the victims of a crashed airliner. The Vietnam peace accord took effect on 28 January 1973, and the last battle-weary Specter landed at Ubon RTAFB on 15 August, signaling the end of gunship operations in South Vietnam. But the Spectre-equipped 16th SOS would remain at Ubon until it was transferred to Korat RTAFB and attached to the 388th TFW on 19 July 1974. Having participated in every major campaign of the conflict, the Spectre covered the evacuations of Saigon and Phnom Penh in May 1975. When the U.S. merchant vessel *SS Mayaguez* was hijacked by the Cambodian Khmer Rouge the same month, Spectres flew in support of its disastrous rescue attempt on the island of Koh Tang.

Spectre and its valiant crews proved themselves to be the most lethal night-flying weapon system of the war. They were credited with destroying or damaging more than 10,000 trucks on the Ho Chi Minh Trail. Additionally, crews of the "Fabulous Four-Engine Fighters" of the 16th SOS flew an incredible record of 1,327 consecutive on-time combat mission launches. Such extraordinary performance in Vietnam, Laos, and Cambodia came at the very high cost, however, with a total of 52 crewmembers and 6 gunships lost in combat.

One method of countering the enemy's use of infrared and heat-seeking missiles was the installation of shields to mask engine exhaust. Since the shields increased fuel consumption, they were removed outside of the combat theatre. (via Larry Davis)

AC-130E/Hs

69-6567/4341	415th SOTS 1971 to 1972; converted to AC-130H in 1973; 16th SOS 1973. 415th SOTS 1974 to 1977; 16th SOS 1978 to 1981; *Ghostrider*; with call sign Spirit 03, lost to SAM near Khafji, Kuwait on 31 January 1991, 14 cewmen KIA
69-6568/4342	415th SOTS 1972; converted to AC-130H in 1973; 415th SOTS 1974 to 1977; 16th SOS 1978 to 1984 *Nightstalker, Bad Company*
69-6569/4343	16th SOS, 8th TFW at Ubon RTAFB 1972 to 1973; converted to AC-130H in 1973; 415th SOTS 1977; 16th SOS 1977 to 1984 *Excalibur, Fatal Attraction*
69-6570/4344	first Pave Aegis; 16th SOS, 8th TFW at Ubon RTAFB 1972; converted to AC-130H in 1973; 415th SOTS 1975 to 1977; 16th SOS 1978 to 1984 *The Hussy*
69-6571/4345	16th SOS. 8th TFW at Ubon RTAFB 1971 to 1972, shot down near An Loc, South Vietnam on 30 March 1972
69-6572/4346	16th SOS, 8th TFW at Ubon RTAFB 1972; converted to AC-130H in 1973; 415th SOTS 1976 to 1977; 16th SOS 1978 to 1984 *Grave Digger*
69-6573/4347	16th SOS, 8th TFW at Ubon RTAFB 1972; converted to AC-130H in 1973; 16th SOS 1975; 415th SOTS 1977; 16th SOS 1978 to 1984 *Heavy Metal*
69-6574/4348	16th SOS, 8th TFW at Ubon RTAFB 1972 to 1973; converted to AC-130H in 1973; 415th SOTS 1977; 16th SOS 1978 to 1984 *Iron Maiden*
69-6575/4349	16th SOS, 8th TFW at Ubon RTAFB 1973; converted to AC-130H in 1973; 415th SOTS 1975 to 1977; 16th SOS 1981 to 1984 *Wicked Wanda*
69-6576/4351	*Pave Spectre I* prototype; 16th SOS, 8th TFW at Ubon RTAFB 1973; converted to AC-130H in 1973; 415th SOTS 1975 to 1977; 16th SOS 1978 to 1984; with call sign Jockey 14, lost over Indian Ocean off coast of Kenya practice-firing 105mm, while supporting operations at Mogadishu, Somalia on 14 March 1994 *Bad Company, Widow Maker, Predator, Hell Raiser*
69-6577/4352	*Pave Spectre I* prototype; 16th SOS, 8th TFW at Ubon RTAFB 1973; converted to AC-130H 1973; AFSC 1974; 4950th TW 1975 to 1977; 16th SOS 1978 to 1984 *Death Angel*

CHAPTER EIGHT

NEW BATTLES,
NEW SPECTRES

Number 129 was among the first C-130s transformed into a gunship. While operating from Udorn RTAFB, 129's crew chief Randy Lawrence had named it The Arbitrator. When the 711th SOS relinquished its AC-130As during the early 1990s, The First Lady was retired, after having served more than 40 years and having flown 13,600 hours. The First Lady is seen here over Honduras in April 1987. (U.S. Air Force)

Late in 1975, the 16th Special Operations Squadron began relocating from Southeast Asia to Hurlburt Field, with the first gunship arriving on 12 December. The move was completed by the end of January 1976. The squadron's new parent command, the 1st Special Operations Wing, grew out of the 834th Tactical Composite Wing after Air Force officials waged a battle in the Pentagon against downsizing special operations aviation. Ten AC-130Hs comprised the 16th SOS, while the remaining mix of A and E models were assigned to the Air Force Reserve's 711th SOS, 919th Special Operations Group (SOG) at Hurlburt's remote Duke Field. "We're flying an antique," said the 919th's operations commander, Lt. Col. Norman Bowman.

The unit's maintenance officer, Lt. Col. Lawrence Wagner, added, "Our biggest problem is keeping the airplanes flying. Anyone can work on a new airplane and get good results. But, here it takes about 42 man-hours per flying hour; that's about double the time of regular A-model cargo types. Flights are aborted frequently because the old planes are falling apart. Years ago, the unique electronic stuff caused most of the problems, but today it's fluid leaks, corrosion and the availability of A model aircraft parts."

Demand for the gunships remained high and deployments created other problems since personnel at many bases on Spectre's flight plans were unprepared for handling their hazardous cargo, which included ammunition, flares, and nitrogen. Nevertheless, the Reservists, many of whom had years of experience, worked against all odds, flying the required 4,000 hours per year and maintaining the aircraft on overseas treks. Having been given in-flight fueling capability during upgrades, the much-improved AC-130H had unlimited range, enabling the Air Force to deploy the gunship across the globe.

Fully aware that simmering world trouble spots would soon become destinations on mission orders, the Air Staff kept Spectre modernization and crew training high on priority lists. Never losing their edge despite the military drawdowns following the war in Southeast Asia, Spectre crews participated in deployments across the U.S. and worldwide.

First on the "hot list," and proving Spectre's unlimited range, was the hostage situation in Iran. Spectres were flown from Hurlburt Field, Florida, to Andersen AFB, Guam, in November 1979, achieving a record distance flight that took 29.7 hours. The rescue attempt during which the Spectres were to provide cover would never take place, however, as complex bureaucracies involving the U.S. Government, the CIA, and the Air Force, Navy, and Marines coupled with service in-fighting spelled a recipe for disaster.

When rescue forces gathered at a rendezvous site in the Iranian desert known as *Desert One* on 24 April 1980, the mission was beset with both operational and meteorological problems, culminating with the collision of two aircraft, a parked Air Force MC-130E and a landing Navy RH-53D Sea Stallion helicopter, killing eight military personnel. The failed hostage rescue attempt made it painfully evident that the U.S. was unprepared for multi-service special sperations. From the ashes of *Desert One* rose a vow that the U.S. military would never again endure such an embarrassing military failure and special

The first production AC-130A and the oldest Spectre gunship, S/N 53-3129, was appropriately named The First Lady. *Following service in Southeast Asia, it was assigned to the Reserve 711th SOS, 919th SOW at Eglin AFB from 1976 to 1981. Number 129 is seen here armed with the Pave Pronto armament system. A subdued 919th SOW emblem appears above the forward 20mm cannon, while* The First Lady *is visible in stylish script above the stabilized tracking set doorway.* (Author's Collection)

operations suddenly became a high priority, leading to the formation of the Special Operations Command and the creation of specialized C-130s. The AC-130H spawned a variety of sub-variants for unconventional warfare, called Combat Shadow, Combat Talon, and Commando Solo. Surprisingly, the AC-130 gunship, which was thought to have seen its heyday over Southeast Asia, got a new lease on life.

In 1982, the responsibility for Air Force Special Operations was transferred from the Tactical Air Command to the Military Airlift Command, which led to the formation of the 23rd Air Force. In October 1983, the 23rd played a key role in *Operation Urgent Fury,* the neutralization of defenses on the Caribbean island of Grenada, and the support of local ground forces. When U.S. Army Rangers assaulted Point Salines Airfield on 25 October, they called on orbiting AC-130Hs to attack resistance fighters and 37mm anti-aircraft gun emplacements. In Central America during the 1980s, America waged undeclared war, pouring vast amounts of resources into training and equipping friendly nations that struggled with civil war and oppressive and brutal regimes.

The U.S. also sponsored the construction of huge air bases at Palmerola and La Ceiba, Honduras, along with four others whose locations were kept secret. Veteran air crews, who wore jungle fatigues and bush hats in the tropical heat, found the setting eerily familiar. In 1983, rebel forces in El Salvador had become such a formidable threat that the U.S. extended its training of Salvadorian troops in Honduras, and moved AC-130Hs of the 16th SOS to Howard AFB, Panama. The Spectres were void of markings and flown by crews with no military identification. Launching from Howard, the Spectres initially tracked guerilla activity at night, and later were given clearance to fire on targets they detected.

In Panama, when rule under Manuel Noriega became intolerable, *Operation Just Cause* took shape during late 1989 to end his regime. Spectres were heavily involved, with seven AC-130s—two from Howard AFB and five from Hurlburt—overhead during the 20 December invasion. The AC-130s conducted surveillance and provided intelligence to assault forces. Devastating fire from the Spectres against armor and artillery sites prior to the airborne assaults at Rio Hato and Torrijos Tocumen airfields allowed ground forces to achieve their objectives. Spectres also destroyed Panamanian Defense Headquarters and numerous command sites, using their sophisticated electronic systems for surgical placement of gunfire in urban areas. A secondary objective of *Just Cause,* named *Operation Acid Gambit,* was also under way—the rescue of American Kurt Muse from the Carcel Modelo Prison. As elite Delta commandos rescued Muse, two AC-130s along with two AH-6 attack helicopters, provided fire support in a superb display of coordination between completely dissimilar special operations aircraft. As the only heavy close air support platform in the operation, Spectres earned high praise for saving the lives of ground forces. By the end of December, AC-130s had flown 355 combat hours.

On 22 May 1990, Air Force Chief of Staff Gen. Lawrence Welch re-designated the 23rd Air Force as the Air Force Special Operations

Command (AFSOC). The creation of this specialized force proved timely, for on 2 August, when Iraq invaded Kuwait, the American military's response was swift and massive. On 6 September, five AC-130Hs and personnel of the 16th SOS deployed as part of *Operation Desert Shield,* arriving at alert bases in Saudi Arabia on the 12 September. When *Operation Desert Storm* kicked off on 16 January 1991, Spectres stood alert, and went into action in the Battle of Khafji, attacking an Iraqi armored column on 29 January. The next day, three Spectres provided covering fire for U.S. Marines, and began hitting Iraqi troops and vehicles that were moving south to reinforce positions north of the city.

On 31 January, the crew of AC-130H (S/N 69-6567), using call sign Spirit 03, decided to remain on station into the daylight hours to provide the Marines with continued support. Unfortunately, a surface-to-air missile found its mark on the Spectre and all 14 of its crew were killed. Spectres flew airborne alert throughout *Desert Storm,* racking up 50 missions before they returned to Hurlburt in late May 1991. The other four AC-130Hs of the 16th SOS that participated in *Desert Shield* and *Desert Storm* were serial numbers 69-6569, 69-6570, 69-6572, and 69-6576. Six AC-130As of the 711th SOS also served in *Desert Storm,* staging from Turkey. They were serial numbers 54-1623, 54-1630, 55-0011, 55-0014, 55-0029, and 56-0509. With the continual changes in AFSOC came the re-designation of the 1st SOW at Hurlburt to the 16th SOW on 1 October 1993.

During 1993 and 1994, the 16th SOS was sent to Africa in support of *Operation Continue Hope,* the United Nations relief effort in Somalia. Early in 1993, AC-130s that helped U.S. Marines quell civil war in the region had been withdrawn since the Clinton Administration considered them too war-like a component in its errant hope for a diplomatic solution. In late summer 1993, when U.S. Army commandos and Task Force 160 hunted for warlord Mohammed Aidid, the U.S. commander in the region requested heavy air and armor support, but was denied, and the world witnessed the debacle recognized in book and film as *Blackhawk Down.* In early 1994, Spectre crews were again deployed, flying from Djibouti to hit targets in Mogadishu, and were further deployed to Kenya to protect UN security forces as part of *Operation United Shield.* During this operation, AC-130H (S/N 69-6576) and eight of its 14-man crew were lost on a non-combat sortie. The tragedy occurred shortly after takeoff from Moi International Airport, Mombasa, Kenya, on 14 March 1994, when the crew of *Jockey 14* test fired its 105mm gun over the Indian Ocean and a round exploded in the gun's barrel.

In July 1993, in another part of the world, AC-130Hs deployed to Italy in the event that politicians decided to follow through on their threat to attack Bosnian Serb forces near Sarajevo. During the operation, dubbed *Deny Flight,* key targets in the Sarajevo region were targeted by AC-130Hs in support of NATO forces. In August 1995, *Deny Flight* was renamed *Operation Deliberate Force,* marking the largest NATO air operation in history. The gunships were part of a large search and rescue force, which rescued an F-117 stealth fighter pilot shot down over Yugoslavia. The Spectres operated only within specific safety margins, as Yugoslav forces did not challenge them with SAMs. On the first night of the operation, *Ghost 31,* AC-130H (S/N 69-6568) and crew attacked an artillery/mortar position near Sarajevo. During the first half of September 1995, 16th SOS Spectres flew combat search and rescue sorties, raining devastation upon radar and command sites in support of the rescue attempt of a French Mirage aircrew downed by a SAM. Throughout direct U.S. involvement in Bosnia-Herzogovina, which ended on 28 August 1995, a pair of Spectres stood ready at Brindisi, Italy.

Other hot spots around the globe demanded the attention of Spectres. For one month, beginning on 18 September 1994, the 16th SOS sent Spectres to Cuba to participate in *Operation Uphold Democracy,* the main purpose of which was the ouster of General Raoul Cedras and restoration of the democratic government of Jean-Bertrand Aristide in Haiti.

To best utilize its force of Special Operations C-130s, in late 1995 the Air Force changed the primary mission of the 711th SOS to that of long range clandestine infiltration and re-supply of special operations forces, replacing the aging AC-130As with MC-130E Combat Talon Is. The 919th SOG would eventually fly eight Talons and four HC-130 Combat Shadows; with the latter used to refuel special operations helicopters. Spectre gunships would now be flown by the 16th SOS and a newly formed squadron; the 4th SOS, which had been deactivated in 1969 after flying the original Spooky in Vietnam. The 4th was officially activated on 4 May 1995 at Hurlburt, with its Spectres and crews making their first deployment in October to Osan AB, South Korea as part of *Exercise Foal Eagle.* In September 1996,

the 4th SOS Ghostriders made its first deployment to Brindisi, Italy, to participate in the ongoing *Joint Endeavor* campaign in Bosnia-Herzegovina. That same year, the 19th SOS was established at Hurlburt for training crews in the AC-130 and MC-130.

Spectres of the 4th and 16th SOS maintained a strong presence in Italy, and in 1997, 16th SOS Spectres were called upon to provide support for U.S. and Allied ground forces during the evacuation of Americans in Albania and Liberia. Maintaining their dependability and popularity with U.S., Allied, and NATO commanders, Spectres were included in the show of force in 1998 to convince Iraq to comply with U.N. weapons inspections. During the 1999 Kosovo campaign, Spectres were credited with being largely responsible for ending hostilities. It became obvious, especially to opposing forces, that whenever U.S. and Allied troops went into action, Spectres were nearby. For all the missions that were given clever code names and covered by mainstream media, doubtless, there were as many worldwide operations in which Spectres participated that necessarily remain in the shadows.

Following the 11 September 2001 terrorist attacks in New York and Washington, D.C., in what is now known as 9-11, Spectres were staged at an undisclosed location near Afghanistan to support *Operation Enduring Freedom* in early November. The day after their arrival, they attacked Taliban and Al Qaeda terrorists near the city of Konduz to back Northern Alliance forces. Throughout the night of 26 November 2001, AC-130s turned the tide in the rebellion of terrorist prisoners at the prison fort of Qual a Jinga. Spectre crews also flew close

Changes to the AC-130H's armament saw the time-honored miniguns eliminated, along with one L60 40mm cannon. Taking their place were two 20mm Vulcan cannons on stationary mounts at the forward fuselage. The Vulcan fired 2,500 rounds per minute, with 3,000 rounds carried for each cannon. (U.S. Air Force)

Complementing the two 20mm cannons forward on the AC-130H was the 40mm Bofors cannon and the 105mm Howitzer in the rear fuselage. A total of 256 rounds were carried for the 40mm cannon, which fired at a rate of 100 rounds per minute. The Howitzer fired six to ten rounds per minute. Between the two guns is the radome, housing beacon tracking radar. Visible at upper left is the "Tub" installed around the engine exhaust to reduce the aircraft's infrared signature, to which infrared-seeking missiles are attracted. (U.S. Air Force)

air support and armed reconnaissance over Kandahar after an assassination attempt against Afghanistan's newly elected President Karzai.

During *Operation Anaconda* in Afghanistan in March 2002, three 16th SOS Spectres flew 39 combat missions, unleashing their firepower during a two-week period killing enemy troops and armor while supporting Allied troops who traded blows with enemy forces. Unsurprisingly, the 16th SOS had become the third most deployed unit in the U.S. Air Force. No longer taking a back seat to other programs and budget constraints as it had during the post-Vietnam era, the AC-130 gunship was deemed by military leaders as the aircraft most vital to keep in the inventory. On that premise, the go-ahead was given to make Spectre even better.

Gunboat: the AC-130U

When the gunship *The First Lady,* the first production C-130, was retired on 10 September 1995, along with four other AC-130As, its replacement had long been in the works. The acquisition program for the new gunship stemmed from a Congressional mandate during the mid 1980s to beef up special operations aviation capabilities. Since the active Air Force gunship force numbered less than 20 Spectres, it was decided to add 12 new models. A contract for the major rework was awarded to North American Rockwell's Aircraft Modification Division at Palmdale, California, in July 1987, with the end product becoming the most complex aircraft weapon system in the world. Officially designated the AC-130U, the new gunship was proudly called the Gunboat, or U-boat, by those who flew them. With more than 609,000 lines of software code in its mission computers and

The AC-130A, S/N 54-1630, at Warner Robins AFB in October 1979. The AN/ALQ-87 ECM pods, seen in white, were mounted in pairs on underwing mounts. (R. Ray Leader via Stephen Miller)

In the back of the AC-130U, three gunners operate the 105mm Howitzer, and one operates the 40mm Bofors cannon. The ammunition racks for both weapons are against the opposite side of the fuselage. (U.S. Air Force)

The AC-130H, S/N 87-0128, of the 6510th Test Wing at Edwards AFB, California, in October 1991. Near the nose landing gear is the infrared sensor. (via Larry Davis)

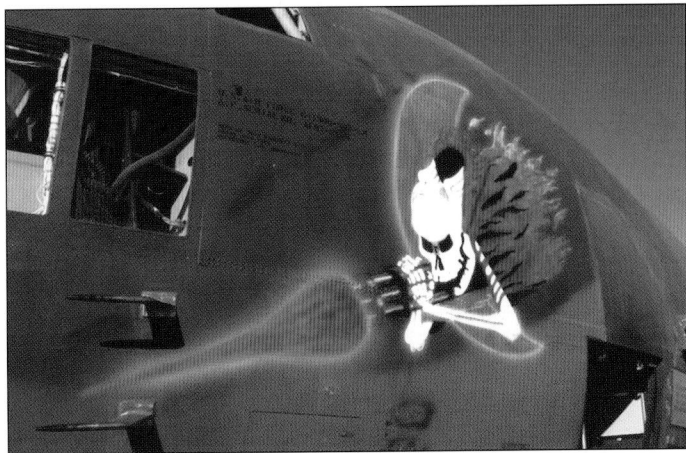

The Spectre's dramatic nose art seen on AC-130U, S/N 87-0128, Big Daddy at Nellis AFB, Nevada, in April 1997. (Sunil Gupta)

avionics systems, the AC-130U's guns were integrated with high-tech sensor, navigation, and fire control systems, enabling them to place their lethal ordnance on pinpoint locations, or as saturation fire, during longer on-station times, at night, and in bad weather. Sophisticated systems integration gave the crew the awesome ability to strike two targets one-half mile apart simultaneously using two different guns.

The first of these ultimate killing machines made its first flight on 20 December 1990, and after completing an intense three-year flight-test program at the Air Force Flight Test Center at Edwards AFB, the

When photographed in 2001, number 0513 showed extreme signs of weathering. Under-wing ECM gear matched the Gunboat's overall gray aircraft color. Immediately outboard of the ECM pylon is what appears to be an HF antenna resembling those found on the RC-135U. (Stephen Miller)

Air Force Special Operations Command took delivery of its first Gunboat on 1 July 1994. In 1992, a 13th AC-130U had been figured into procurement to replace the AC-130H lost during *Desert Storm*, but unlike their earlier modified brethren, these third-generation gunships were acquired from new Lockheed production. Although the U-boat retained the T56-A-15 engines and one 40mm cannon plus the howitzer, the two 20mm cannons were replaced by a single 25mm GAU-12 cannon on a trainable mount. A total of 3,000 rounds are carried for the new gun, which has a firing rate of 1,800 rounds per minute, and a standoff range of 12,000 feet. All three guns are computer-controlled, allowing them to be aimed at targets tracked by sensor operators.

Sensors aboard the AC-130U include Hughes AN/APG-180 main fire control radar, which was derived from the APG-70 system used in the F-15E. Gec-Marconi All-Light Level TV (ALLTV) is mounted in a turret under the fuselage with a 360-degree field of view. The Gunboat's survivability is enhanced with an ALR-69 radar warning receiver, AN/AAR-44 infrared warning receiver, AN/ALQ-196 jammer, AN/APR-46A RF panoramic receiver, and a Rockwell ALQ-172 countermeasures system that incorporates an AN/ALE-47 flare and chaff dispensing system. Synthetic aperture radar allows for long-range detection and identification of targets, giving operators the ability to track 40mm and 105mm projectiles to adjust fire. A Texas Instruments AN/AAQ-117 FLIR and GPS are also included, along with an inertial navigation system.

The AC-130U is pressurized, enabling it to fly at higher altitudes, thereby saving fuel and time and extending its range beyond that of the AC-130H. The AC-130U's crew of 13 (one fewer than the AC-130H, which carried an extra gunner for the 20mm cannon) comprises a pilot, copilot, flight engineer, loadmaster, and four gunners. Working in the booth in the center of the fuselage are the navigator, fire control officer, electronic warfare officer, and two sensor operators.

The AC-130A, S/N 55-0011, of the 919th SOG at Forbes Field in May 1988. (Jerry Geer)

In the AC-130H, the navigator and fire control officer positions are on the flight deck.

Following a study during the late 1990s that highlighted the gunship's role in Afghanistan and that recommended expanding the gunship fleet to more than 25 aircraft, the AFSOC in January 2003 awarded Boeing, which had absorbed Rockwell, a contract to modify four Air National Guard C-130Hs into AC-130Hs. Called the Plus Four, these aircraft had two Alliant Techsytems Bushmaster Mk 44 30mm cannons installed, which have greater range than the 20mm cannon, permitting higher altitudes in high threat environments. Since the AC-130H was unpressurized, better air conditioners and heating units were installed. The Plus Four entered service in 2007, the same year that the hard-hitting Mk 44s began replacing the AC-130U's 40mm and 25mm cannons. Besides requiring less maintenance, the Bushmaster is more accurate, weighs less, and has a firing rate of 200 rounds per minute.

Some Spectres of both H and U models have an observation dome in the aircraft's rear upper door. Besides the loadmaster, who uses this window, gunners also have the important duty of scanning for surface-to-air missiles. (Stephen Miller)

Built into the tail extension of the AC-130U is a cluster of Radar Warning Receiver antennas. The two curved antennas are part of the Large Aircraft Infrared Countermeasures (LAIRCM) system. (Stephen Miller)

The laser transmitter turret on the AC-130U's left rear fuselage is a component of the LAIRCM modification. This system automatically counters advanced IR missile systems by detecting an inbound missile and then using a laser beam to blind it and throw it off course. (Stephen Miller)

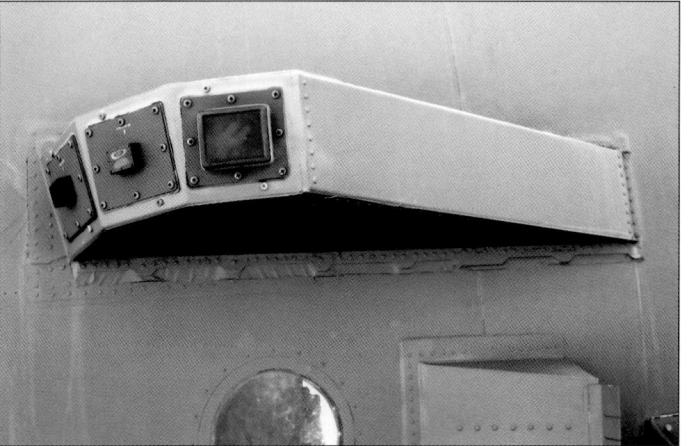

The Radar Warning Receiver (RWR) antenna grouping on the AC-130U's forward left fuselage is part of the ALR-69 system. It is interesting to note that none of this advanced technology existed when the C-130 first flew in 1954. (Stephen Miller)

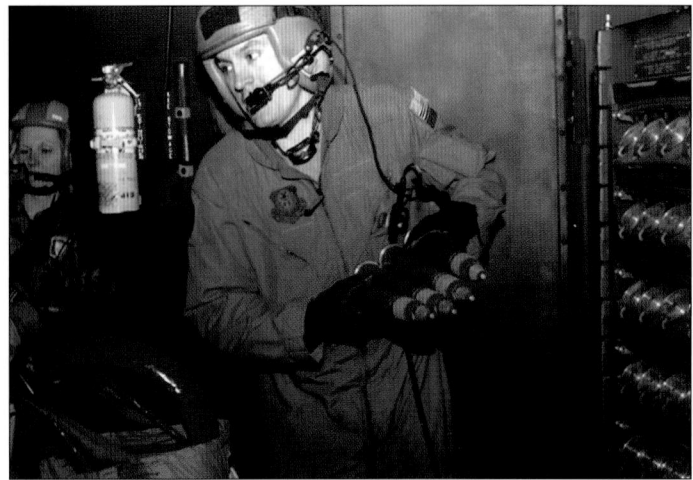

A gunner loads 40mm ammunition in the L60 Bofors cannon, whose curved shell ejection chute and container is seen at lower left. Note the relatively massive size of these projectiles. (U.S. Air Force)

Three gunners operate Spectre's 105mm Howitzer; one operates the breech mechanism, one loads the shell, and another handles ejected shell casings. (U.S. Air Force)

Gray Ghost AC-130U, S/N 89-0513, in April 2001. The infrared sensor is mounted next to the nose landing gear. A Radar Warning Receiver antenna atop the cockpit is part of the ALR-69 system. Faint nose art identifies the 4th SOS name Ghostriders. (Stephen Miller)

Since the Gunboat was pressurized, openings, including those surrounding the Bushmaster cannon, were sealed. At the forward end of the main landing gear sponson is the All-Light-Level TV. (Stephen Miller)

Concurrent with development of the AC-130U were major improvements done to AC-130Hs, termed the ALQ-172 ECM Upgrade. The ALQ-172 unit itself was modified with low-band jamming equipment and increased memory, the installation having been contracted to International Telephone & Telegraph. The H model's 40mm and 105mm ammunition racks, along with other components, were made lighter, and non-critical armor was removed. Such weight reduction measures improved fuel consumption, thereby increasing range and loiter time. In addition, firepower was sacrificed with removal of a 20mm cannon which was replaced by a scanner's dome, marking the first time that crew members could watch for ground fire from the aircraft's left side.

Like previous gunship models, the Gunboat underwent continuous upgrades. As the AFSOC took its gunships into the 21st Century, the decision was made to make the gunships more difficult to both see and shoot at. To accomplish this, a system called the AN/AAQ-24 Directional Infrared Countermeasures system, or DIRCM, was given the highest priority. The DIRCM maintains a focused beam of infrared energy on an inbound missile, sending the missile's flight data to a turret, which houses a target designator system that tracks the missile throughout its flight. The DIRCM was a joint American-British project, which proved successful on the MC-130H Combat Talon II. A more recent upgrade involves a system that allows crew members to receive live video feeds from unmanned reconnaissance aircraft.

When necessary, the AC-130U can be fitted with an Engine Infrared Suppression system (EIRS), making it more difficult for infrared-seeking SAMs to track the aircraft. The EIRS is used sparingly since it decreases the Gunboat's range and on-station time which is normally four-and-a-half hours. A dynamic equipment change, called a "fusion ball," combines the AC-130U's all-light level

Finished in overall Gunship Gray and showing wear, AC-130H, S/N 69-6569, Fatal Attraction in March 1988. Note how far the 105mm Howitzer barrel extends from the side of the fuselage. (U.S. Air Force)

CMSgt. Gerald Murray in the weapons control booth of a 4th SOS AC-130U in 2003 detects, identifies, and fires on targets with the 105mm Howitzer. (U.S. Air Force)

AC-130U, S/N 90-0165, in June 1998. The Gunboat carries a single ECM pod under-wing, and Spooky nose art is light gray. (Stephen Miller)

The AC-130U, S/N 89-0512, of the 4th SOS in April 1997. (Hans-Joachim Schroder)

television and infrared sensor, allowing the crew to better analyze the battleground scenario. Other improvements included software changes and updating the infrared detection set with an AAQ-26 to enhance target detection and recognition, thereby decreasing the gunship's vulnerability.

In the spring of 2003, the Gunboats and crews of the 4th SOS played a key role during *Operation Iraqi Freedom* by firing the first shots of the conflict. During the first two months of the campaign, the Ghostriders flew more than 1,000 combat hours from three forward operating locations. Gunships remained in high demand; in 2006, they deployed for 120 days, with the 16th SOS flying more than 1,300 combat sorties totaling more than 8,000 hours. The 21st Century gunship fleet peaked at 13 AC-130Us, flown by the 4th SOS, while eight AC-130Hs comprise the 16th SOS. Both squadrons are home-based at Hurlburt Field under the 16th SOW. Noteworthy is the fact that the name Spectre, so often associated with AC-130 gunships, has been replaced by Spooky, harking back more than four decades to a time when skilled and dedicated AC-47D gunship crews flew through night skies over troubled lands.

Indicative of the Air Force's intent to continually improve Spooky was the decision in 2006 to replace the 25mm and 40mm cannons with two 30mm Bushmaster II cannons. The 40mm weapon had become dated, while the 25mm cannon, although an excellent performer, requires excess maintenance of its loading system and lacks ammunition with airburst capability. The 30mm, on the other hand, offers greater ammunition commonality since it is in widespread use. The first Bushmaster II became operational in an AC-130U in January 2007, with plans to equip the entire gunship fleet by 2010. Plans were also laid to replace the howitzer with a breech-loading 120mm mortar, and to give Spooky a standoff capability using the AGM-114 Hellfire missile, the Advanced Precision Kill Weapon System (based on the Hydra 70 rocket), or the Viper Strike glide bomb.

How much more can be done to improve the AC-130 gunship in the future is questionable. Nevertheless, the intent is to take them to the year 2020, and possibly as distant a year as 2025. Talk of finding a replacement for the AC-130 was first heard in 2001, with a totally new design to be called the AC-X. Those in the special operations aviation community expressed a desire that a new gunship be smaller, have fewer crew members, possess stealth qualities, have the speed and maneuverability of a jet fighter, be armed with directed energy weapons, and be able to attack targets from any angle—a tall order for any manufacturer. Air Force Special Operations Command leaders agree that whatever replaces the AC-130 could be an unmanned vehicle, or even a space-based platform. They contend that it must be able to provide what the current AC-130 provides, something they call a Persistent Surface Attack System. As of this writing, little has come of a replacement. But as with other venerable aircraft throughout history that could never be replaced, the AC-130's replacement just may be another AC-130.

Logo used by Rockwell International in connection with its involvement of the AC-130U Gunship.

AC-130Us			
87-0128/5139	6510th TW; then 4th SOS, *Big Daddy*	90-0163/5256	*Bad Omen*
89-0509/5228	*Total Carnage*	90-0164/5257	*Bad Intentions*
89-0510/5229	*Gunslinger*	90-0165/5259	*Thumper, Medusa, Widow Maker, Death Before*
89-0511/5230	first production U model, delivered to the Air		*Dawn*
	Force in April 1992; *Predator, Lost Boys*	90-0166/5261	*Hell Raiser*
89-0512/5231	*Dead On*	90-0167/5262	*Azrael, Terminator II, Intimidator*
89-0513/5232	*Killer Instinct*	92-0253/5279	*Eight Ball*
89-0514/5233	*Maximum Carnage*		

Protruding from the side of this AC-130U are the long barrels of 30mm Bushmaster cannons, the newest addition to the gunship's arsenal. Having a firing rate of 1,800 rounds per minute, the cannon offers increased lethality, range, and accuracy than the 25mm cannon and 20mm cannons they replace. The Bushmaster is aimed and fired through computer links, and it is self-contained, requiring only that gunners throw switches and pull safety pins. The GAU-12's ammunition is beltless and spent cartridges are deposited into a container. The AFSOC expects to have its entire gunship fleet armed with Bushmasters by the year 2009. (U.S. Air Force)

The pilot's gun sight in the AC-130U shows its evolution from rudimentary sighting devices to a simplified head-up glass display. Crewmen of modern AC-130 variants wear earphones, which prove less cumbersome than the ballistic helmets required during earlier operations. (U.S. Air Force)

Sensors provide detailed images for video screens in the AC-130U's Battle Management Center, allowing operators to detect, identify, and fire on targets with pinpoint accuracy. (U.S. Air Force)

The copilot's position in the AC-130U. Gunboat cockpits are fully night vision compatible. (U.S. Air Force)

Painted in the "Shamu" two-tone scheme introduced in 2000, AC-130H, S/N 69-6572, is displayed at Andrews AFB in May 2006. (Stephen Miller)

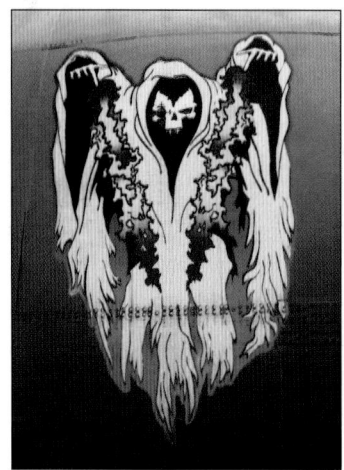

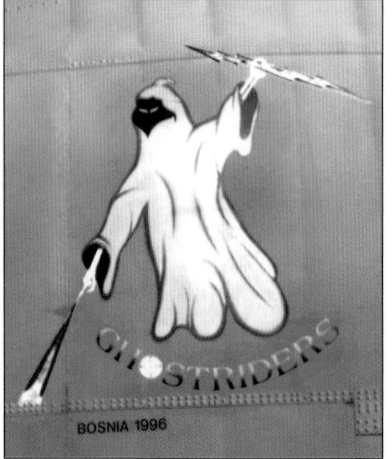

One of the variations of Spectre nose art seen on AC-130U, S/N 89-0513, in May 2005. Compared to most other nose art, which was applied with either flat color or very basic light and shadow, this image almost bears resemblance to the complex airbrushed "heavy metal" imagery of today. (Stephen Miller)

AC-130Us of the 4th SOS used this nose art, which is reminiscent of that worn by the original Spookies during the Vietnam war. In the 21st Century, AC-130U crews also resurrected the name Spooky. This AC-130U, S/N 89-0512, noted its service in Bosnia below the squadron name, Ghostriders. (Craig Kaston via Stephen Miller)

Following its combat duty during Desert Storm, AC-130A S/N 55-0014 of the 711th SOS wears nearly 20 mission marks on its forward fuselage in May 1991. (David Brown vie Stephen Miller)

In a dazzling display, an AC-130H launches its array of flares, creating what is often called an angel effect. The countermeasures system can dispense chaff cartridges, infrared flares, and active expendable decoys. Visible under the rear engine sections are IR shields, called tubs. (U.S. Air Force)

Similar to propaganda leaflets dropped in conjunction with gunship attacks during the war in Southeast Asia, this leaflet was used in Iraq by modern AC-130 gunships. It reads, "This is the AC-130H Spectre Gunship. This airplane is a heavily armed C-130 cargo aircraft and it has the 'green eyes.' This aircraft can find you, see what you are doing, and destroy you any time, anywhere, in any weather. This equipment has been brought to the people of Mosul by the provincial governor to provide security for the elections on January 30th, 2005." The "green eyes" mentioned in the leaflet refers to the green image of night vision equipment.

Painted in the Shamu scheme, this view of AC-130H, S/N 69-6570, shows the model's weapons arrangement and electronic systems external sensors. A FLIR is positioned beneath the nose, while long teardrop ALQ-137 V3 ECM antennas are mounted at center fuselage behind the cockpit. The Wasp Tail incorporates antennas for the ALQ-172, which also appear on MC-130E Talon Is. (U.S. Air Force)

The AC-130U, S/N 90-0164, in May 2000, freshly painted in the new Shamu two-tone camouflage scheme of Gunship Gray (36081) over Douglas Gray (3635). Although modern AC-130 variants differ greatly from their predecessors, their basic profile remains unchanged. (Lionel Paul via Stephen Miller)

CHAPTER NINE

BLACK SPOT

A small number of C-123s served in various special operations roles. They, along with specially configured C-130 variants, were called Blackbirds. One NC-123B, S/N 54-652, became the first modified with infrared equipment for detecting enemy traffic on the Ho Chi Minh trail. This Provider, in the special operations camouflage scheme applied to C-123s, has a nose-mounted sensor, probably infrared. It was void of markings when photographed in Vietnam in 1967. (Terry Love)

Following his success with initial gunship evaluations in 1964 using the Convair C-131B, Ron Terry returned to Wright-Patterson AFB to install the minigun package in a C-47 or a Fairchild C-123 Provider. Terry's team had initially set its sights on the C-123 since it was newer, larger, and more powerful, and most importantly, because it was a high-wing airplane. Having the wings mounted high on the fuselage, they reasoned, gave them more latitude in positioning the guns in the cabin area, and crewmen would have unobstructed visibility of the ground below. But since no C-123s were available when Terry and his pirates arrived at Wright-Pat, the proud distinction of becoming the first operational gunship went to the C-47.

Despite having missed its curtain call, the C-123 would come under the headings of both "Gunship" and "Special Operations," although on a very limited basis. The C-123 began life, oddly enough, as a transport glider for the U.S. Air Force. That failed plan led to powered versions, with Fairchild assuming production of C-123Bs from Chase Aircraft. The first production aircraft flew on 1 September 1954, and the Provider entered service in 1955.

Typical of cargo aircraft, the C-123 featured a high tail to facilitate rear loading. Giving it a maximum takeoff weight of 60,000 pounds were two Pratt & Whitney R-2800-99W Double Wasp, 18-cylinder engines, rated at 2,300 hp each. The Provider's maximum speed was 245 mph, with a range of 1,035 miles and a service ceiling of 29,000 feet. It carried 62 passengers and a crew of 3. Throughout its service life, a number of changes were made to the original design, ending with the C-123K model. Of 302 C-123Bs produced by Fairchild, 183 were brought up to C-123K standards with the addition of two under-wing podded General Electric J85-GE-17 turbojets developing 2,850 pounds of thrust each. The first C-123K flew on 27 May 1966.

The C-123 seemed destined for a short operational life cycle, having been overshadowed by the larger C-130 until the Vietnam War. The Provider had gone to the Reserves and only one USAF unit, the 464th Troop Carrier Wing at Pope AFB, North Carolina, flew them in front-line service. When the 1961 counterinsurgency panel cited the inadequate capability to airlift South Vietnamese troops, the C-123 got a new lease on life. Since the provider was able to operate from short, crude airstrips, the Air Force sent them to Vietnam to compete with the Army's CV-2 Caribou in the long-standing feud between the two services over tactical airlift responsibility. Soon, under *Operation Mule Train*, C-123s were not only airlifting South Vietnamese forces, they were supporting U.S. Army Special Forces. Providers in Southeast Asia also premiered as defoliant sprayers under *Operation Ranch Hand*, and were also pressed into service as special operations aircraft. Notable was their participation in *Project Duck Hook*, begun in 1964 as part of the highly classified Studies and Observation Group (SOG).

Modified with advanced navigation and radar equipment, six C-123Ks formed First Flight at Nha Trang, Vietnam. Trained, fittingly, at Hurlburt, Chinese and Vietnamese aircrew flew missions over North Vietnam, Laos, and Cambodia, first making leaflet drops and then inserting and re-supplying agents. First Flight C-123s introduced the distinctive black-and-green camouflage carried over to attack versions of the C-123. Under the code name Candlestick, C-123Ks of the 606th Air Commando Squadron at Nakhon Phanom RTAFB played an important part in night interdiction of the Ho Chi Minh Trail. Loaded with six-million candlepower flares and accompanied by night attack aircraft, the Provider's crew first located targets with night vision devices, then dropped flares, and cleared the area for attack aircraft to roll in.

Most unusual about the C-123's association with the gunship program was that it had no guns. Nevertheless, when highly modified, it earned its reputation as a fearsome weapon among its brother cargo aircraft-turned-gunships flying combat missions in Southeast Asia.

The modification and evaluation of two C-123Ks proved tangible in the Air Force's quest to enhance night fighter capabilities. Early in the Southeast Asian conflict, Air Force tacticians realized that air interdiction was the most effective means of impeding the movement of troops and equipment along the Ho Chi Minh Trail. The enemy's use of darkness and foul weather made it imperative that Air Force planners shift their mindset of nuclear weapons and conventional ordnance delivery to all-weather and night attack in limited conflict. This change of strategy led to the establishment of *Operation Shed Light* during early February 1966 under the direction of Lt. Gen. James Ferguson, Deputy Chief of staff for Research and Development. *Shed Light* pooled the large number of USAF endeavors aimed at improving Air Force night fighting capabilities.

The project's initial goal was to identify requirements for communication and navigation systems, sensors, illumination and target-marking capabilities, specialized aircraft, and tactics. Thus began an extensive program of sub-projects that focused on a wide variety of systems. Projects *Red Sea* and *Lonesome Tiger* identified experiments with C/AC-47 and B-26K aircraft equipped with FLIR, while *Tropic*

Fairchild C-123Bs of the 311th Air Commando Squadron at Da Nang AB in 1966. (Tom Hansen)

The NC-123K, S/N 54-0698, during its evaluation period. (U.S. Air Force/Robert J. Mills Collection)

The largest number of Fairchild Providers were produced as C-123Bs. This example, S/N 56-4377, provided airlift for South Vietnam's army in 1962 as part of Operation Mule Train. Number 377 would do triple duty in Vietnam; first with Mule Train, then as one of 34 converted to UC-123K defoliant sprayers, and later with the VNAF. Camouflage had not been considered during the early 1960s. (Doug Janzen)

The NC-123K, S/N54-0691. The few C-123s converted for special operations were a significant deviation from its intended role as a cargo hauler. (Tom Brewer via David Menard)

Under Project Tropic Moon III, 16 Martin B-57Gs were modified with weapons and electronic equipment, becoming the only successful jet modification equipped with LLLTV to detect and track targets. The Air Force Shed Light panel preferred jet aircraft for night attack. Eleven of these began flying night attack missions in Southeast Asia in September 1970. Serial number 52-158 is seen here in night fighter camouflage during stateside evaluation. (Robert C. Mikesh)

This NC-123K, S/N 55-4528, wore the wrap-around camouflage familiar to the Black Spot NC-123K in 1971. With a radome above the cockpit and sensors on the nose and belly, it was used to detect trucks on the Trail. A removable U.S. insignia placard common to special operations aircraft, is seen on the fuselage. Even the serial number on the tail fin is on a "slipper plate" for easy removal to ensure plausible deniability. (Tom Hansen)

Seen at Davis Monthan AFB, Arizona, in July 1970, the AC-123K wears 140 red mission symbols on its nose, below which has been applied in yellow an AMARC storage code. The Provider's performance and ample fuselage made it ideal for special operation applications. (Bob Garrard via Stephen Miller)

The General Dynamics F-111A was preferred by the Shed Light panel as the self-contained night attack aircraft. Like others, it was scratched from the list of contenders when further studies revealed that its conversion to RF-111D was too costly and too difficult. (U.S. Air Force)

Moon identified the use of Low Light Level TV (LLLTV). An A-1E Skyraider was modified with the Tropic Moon I package, becoming the first LLLTV night search and attack platform. Although Air Force planners originally specified that the new night attack system be installed in jet aircraft, the Skyraider became the first to successfully employ the self-contained night attack system in combat. Concurrent with the special *Skyraider* project was the modification of three B-57Bs under *Tropic Moon II*. Before their deployment to Vietnam in December 1967, work had already begun on *Tropic Moon III*, which produced 16 B-57Gs modified with more sophisticated electronics and weapons. Eleven of these were sent to Ubon RTAFB in September 1970. Unsurprisingly, all of these aircraft and their systems were evaluated at Eglin AFB.

Flare studies conducted under *Shed Light* resulted in development of the *Briteye* flare, which led to development of the Battlefield Illumination Airborne System (BIAS). This system had 28 Xenon ARC lamps installed as a retractable unit in a C-123B's cargo compartment. Although the unit could produce instant daylight in an area two miles in diameter from 12,000 feet, it was pulled out of Vietnam since it proved too easy a target for enemy gunners.

The *Shed Light* task force deemed it necessary that aircraft fit into a self-contained night attack category, which meant they had to be able to find and strike targets at night without visible illumination. And they had to be large enough and powerful enough to carry the wide range of equipment necessary to carry out their mission. Such aircraft would essentially assume the hunter-killer role which prompted a search for available armed aircraft that could be modified with sensor and illuminator equipment. Only three aircraft then in Southeast Asia fit the bill—the McDonnell RF-4C Phantom II, the Martin RB-57E, and the Army's Grumman OV-1B

Mohawk. Additional research concluded that there were too few RB-57Es; Phantoms were destined for other attack roles; and planners realized all too well that selecting the Mohawk would only fan the embers of rivalry between the services over the use of their respective attack aircraft.

The sophisticated swing-wing General Dynamics F-111 was finally selected since it was large enough to carry all the necessary sensor, illumination, and ordnance systems, but since the F-111 had yet to become operational, the twin-turboprop North American OV-10 Bronco was proposed as an interim platform. *Shed Light* planners, however, had to resume their search when they discovered that the Bronco could not carry the night hunter-killer package. The F-111 itself was next to get the axe when studies revealed that it was not easily convertible to the RF-111D night fighter, and modification costs were prohibitive. The search for the ultimate night fighter continued.

Showing the most promise, believe it or not was the Navy's carrier-based Grumman S-2 Tracker, which could accommodate the three night sensors (LLLTV, FLIR, and FLR), plus it had a bomb bay for munitions dispensers and under-wing hard points for conventional ordnance. A bonus was the Tracker's searchlight, which could be slaved to the LLLTV. The aircraft was to be designated AS-2D, however, difficulty in acquiring the type from the Navy, funding problems, and looming modification delays caused the program's demise in 1968. Quickly running out of options, Air Force planners re-examined a project begun in 1965, before *Shed Light* had even been created. With their hopes for the AS-2D dashed, they considered the possibilities of a C-123K project, called *Black Spot*, as the *Shed Light* aircraft. The C-123K fit the basic requirements as a self-contained night attack platform; it had twin-engine power and safety (which was backed up by turbojets), it was large enough to carry all of the systems and ordnance, it was available, and, unlike jet aircraft originally sought, it had impressive loiter capability. The *Shed Light* panel became very interested.

Ling Temco Vought's (LTV) E-Systems was awarded a contract for modification, and in March 1966 took delivery of a pair of C-123Ks, S/Ns 54-691 and 54-698. Their most distinctive alteration was a nose extension of 58 inches to house an Autonetics R-132 forward-looking radar, Westinghouse LLLTV with automatic tracking and laser illuminator/rangefinder, Avco FLIR, and a Moving Target Indicator (MTI) with automatic tracking capability. Doppler navigation gear was added, along with ordnance release computers. The ordnance system comprised a 12-tube unit in the rear cargo area for dispensing BLU-3/B, BLU-26/B, or CBU-68 cluster bomb units. Two hand-operated flare launchers were eventually replaced by LAU-74/A automatic launchers. A Black Crow ignition sensor, then being developed for the AC-130, was also installed in aircraft number 698.

Designated NC-123Ks, number 691 arrived at Eglin AFB in August 1967, followed by number 698 in February 1968. Evaluation team crews trained with the *Black Spot* aircraft, and in July 1968 prepared for deployment to Korea. While sharing facilities with the 314th Air Division's reconnaissance element at Osan AB, the *Black Spot* duo

Barely visible in this NC-123K's lower rear fuselage are the 12 tubes through which cluster bomb ordnance was launched. Most unusual is the absence of number 698's under-wing turbojet engines. (U.S. Air Force/Robert J. Mills Collection)

flew missions against North Koreans attempting infiltration into South Korea by boat. North Korean boats hid among large fishing fleets, often dashing ashore to drop off or pick up agents. Missions proved troublesome since blacked-out boats tracked by Black Spot could not be identified as friend or foe, requiring that they be intercepted by South Korean Navy vessels. After 28 missions were flown between 19 August and 23 October, no enemy activity was detected, although operations were considered successful.

After troubleshooting and refining its equipment, the *Black Spot* task force was transferred to Vietnam in November 1968, arriving at Phan Rang AB on the 14th. The NC-123Ks averaged two missions per night, most of which were over the Trail and in the Mekong Delta region. Crews used the LLLTV to scrutinize targets detected by the FLIR unit and the Black Crow. The computer then took over to analyze range and ballistics data and then launch the cluster bombs. The computer's one glaring drawback, however, was its maximum range of only 5,000 feet, placing Black Spots within range of anti-aircraft weapons. Since the pair was designed as electronics test platforms, no threat warning or electronic countermeasure systems had been installed, nor had long-range navigational aids been included. Other problems with equipment surfaced, including difficulty in boresighting the sensor turret, the turret's tendency to freeze at altitude, and the FLIR's limited sighting range. In addition, exploding ordnance affected the highly sensitive LLLTV to the extent the system shut down, thereby disabling the firing system. The FLIR also proved overly sensitive by detecting VHF radio signals, and even heat emitted by the aircraft's windshield defrosters!

Despite such problems, Black Spots were killing trucks on the Ho Chi Minh Trail. They were escorted by night-flying F-4Ds of the 497th Tactical Fighter Squadron; however, their jet speeds made it difficult to stay with the slower NC-123Ks. By the time the last missions

were flown in early January 1969, Black Spots had racked up an impressive tally of 186 missions during which 415 trucks were destroyed and 273 damaged. In the delta region they had claimed 50 sampans and 24 damaged. The aircraft and crews returned to Hurlburt, where four new crews that had been trained in the systems at LTV's Greenville, Texas, facility were then trained in the aircraft by the original crews. The aircraft were upgraded with electronic countermeasure and radar homing and warning systems and re-designated AC-123Ks. In October the *Black Spot* task force flew to Ubon RTAFB, where they were supported by the 8th Tactical Fighter Wing. Since the majority of missions were flown over the heavily defended Trail, Thailand-based A-1 Skyraiders escorted the Black Spots and provided additional firepower. Again, two missions per night were flown, this time over Laos.

Black Spot missions ceased altogether in June 1970, and in July the aircraft arrived at the AMARC storage facility, where they were returned to C-123K standard. Reportedly, they were returned to Vietnam in their non-standard camouflage for airlift duty, although that is not supported by official records. In early September 1971, both aircraft went to Hayes Aircraft at Napier Field, Alabama, which performed modification services for the U.S. government. The reason for the transfer has not been substantiated. Supposedly, the Air Force did not originally intend to use Black Spots in actual combat; however, 20 production models were planned as early as 1966. It was also recommended that C-130s be included in the program and named *Black Spot II*; however, the AC-130 gunship program was more viable. The Black Spots had proven to be 50-percent successful in combat engagements which was more than other aircraft that saw combat under *Operation Shed Light*. Although left in the shadow of the gunship programs, *Black Spot* was responsible for the development of many of the gunships' advanced systems used in later years.

Black Spot's camouflage, which was typical of that applied to USAF special operations C-123s, was very effective. This photo of 54-0698 was taken during initial trials in the U.S. (U.S. Air Force/Robert J. Mills Collection)

Although its sensor equipment had been removed when 54-691 was photographed at the storage facility in 1970, 206 mission symbols proudly remained on the fuselage below the cockpit. (U.S. Air Force)

The AC-123K at Hurlburt during system improvements and the training of a second set of crewmen. The Black Spot is seen here in September 1969, one month prior to being deployed to resume combat missions. (Jack Morris via Stephen Miller)

Although both Black Spot aircraft were reverted to C-123K standard, they retained their distinctive special operations wrap-around camouflage. Following their attack role, they are reported to have assumed airlift duty. Serial number 54-0691 is seen here at Clark AB, Philippines, in March 1974. (David Menard)

A few years after flying combat missions, the Black Spot Providers remained a pair. Also still in its special operations guise is serial number 54-0698 in March 1974. (David Menard)

The cockpit of NC-123K, S/N 54-0698. Pilots favored the comfortable and practical arrangement. (Larry Davis Collection)

CHAPTER TEN

ASIAN GUNS

Since VNAF air operations were patterned after those of the USAF, psywar C-47s were used in conjunction with gunships. This TC-47B, S/N 44-76558, was converted to a Bullshit Bomber to drop leaflets and to broadcast surrender messages. Number 558 was acquired by the Philippine Air Force after the war. Unit tail markings, which included a national fin flash, indicate that this was aircraft V of the 415th Transport Squadron. (Norm Taylor)

Given the U.S. Government's ambitions to provide gunships and train personnel to continue the fight in Southeast Asia, it is important to examine all aspects of gunship operations undertaken by the governments of Cambodia, Laos, Thailand, and South Vietnam. As the 1975 communist takeover spelled the end of South Vietnam's air force, Cambodia and Laos suffered a similar fate. The government of Thailand, however, not only maintained its independence, it kept alive the gunship concept.

Cambodia

When French rule of Cambodia ended in 1953, new leadership under Khmer King Norodom Sihanouk came to epitomize non-alignment. For more than a decade, in an effort to maintain neutrality, the unpredictable political leader's alliance teetered between the communist bloc and the U.S. So pressured was Sihanouk by these governments, while trying to steer clear of wars in neighboring Laos and

The AC-47D, S/N 45-1079, of the Khmer Air Force, armed with the three-gun .50-cal. gun kit in June 1971, on the day prior to its delivery. (Doug Blair)

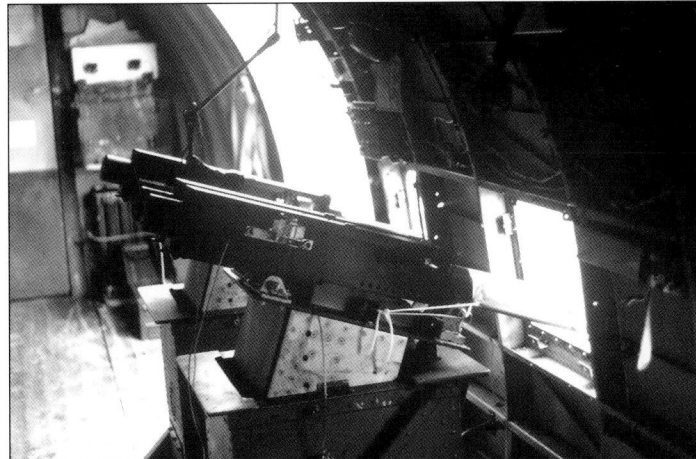

Interior view of the three-gun .50-cal. arrangement in a Khmer gunship. A single weapon occupied the window next to the doorway, while a twin set was mounted in the next forward window opening. It is almost hard to believe that in the late-1930s, the DC-3 airliner version of the C-47 carried up to 30 passengers in luxurious surroundings inside this same size cabin. (Doug Blair)

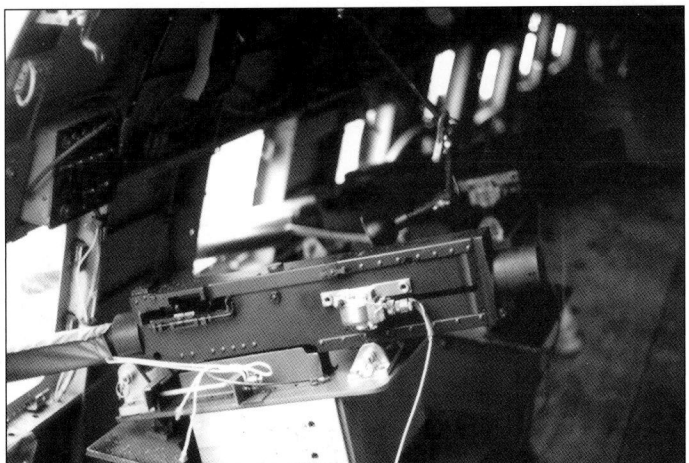

The three .50-cal. guns were installed in KAF gunships by USAF personnel of the Mobile Training Team (MTT), which was supported at by the 1st Air Commando Wing detachment at Udorn. A weapons mechanic assigned to the MTT recalls that Royal Laotian Air Force personnel also occupied the MTT's area, and that relations between them and the KAF were strained. (Doug Blair)

The Mobile Training Team at Udorn RTAFB comprised select USAF personnel who worked with Khmer Air Force units to maximize their capabilities. This building was used by the MTT section that worked with KAF C-47 transport and AC-47 gunship personnel. The Spooky emblem on the structure was commonly associated with all aspects of AC-47 operations. Below the sign is a C-47's forward cargo door section. (Doug Blair)

When the AU-24As of the Khmer Air Force were found to be too vulnerable to anti-aircraft fire, they were placed in storage at Davis Monthan AFB in June 1972. Serial number 72-1332 is seen here shortly after its arrival at the storage facility. The Stallions originally were intended for delivery to the Vietnamese Air Force. (Stephen Miller)

Of 15 Helio AU-24As received by the U.S. Air Force for transfer to the Khmer Air Force during 1972, S/N 72-1324, was retained at Eglin AFB for evaluation. (Peter Mancus via Stephen Miller)

A Royal Thai Air Force AC-47, S/N 45-1116, armed with the .50-cal. gun kit and a Madsen 20mm cannon on takeoff. This aircraft previously had been in the possession of the Khmer Air Force. (Sakpinit Promthep)

Emblem of Khmer Air Force AC-47 gunship crews. (Kenneth Conboy)

The patch worn by RLAF AC-47 gunship personnel. (Kenneth Conboy)

Wearing camouflage familiar to U.S. Air Force aircraft in Southeast Asia, AC-47s of the Royal Laotian Air Force at Wattay in 1971. The gunship in the foreground, S/N 43-48263, which is armed with minigun modules, was acquired from the Vietnamese Air Force. (via Larry Davis)

South Vietnam, that during the late 1960s he accommodated both North Vietnam and the U.S. Like a political referee, Sihanouk allowed U.S. air strikes against North Vietnamese bases that he himself had sanctioned. By March 1970 his countrymen, especially those of the Cambodian Army, had had enough and he was ousted and replaced by Gen. Lon Nol, commander of the Cambodian Army. Immediately, the Cambodian Republic became pro-western and the communist Vietnamese were ordered out of the country. Predictably, conflict intensified.

One week after Cambodian forces were forced to withdraw after moving against North Vietnamese Army positions, South Vietnamese and U.S. forces launched the Cambodian incursion. Support from the U.S. and other Free World countries had begun in earnest. Although communist forces staged offensives throughout Cambodia, the U.S. was forbidden by the 1970 Cooper-Church Amendment from direct involvement with the Cambodian military. That amendment was one small step in appeasing the American public, whose resentment of the Vietnam war had become pervasive. No strangers to side-stepping Congressional rulings, U.S. military leaders found other ways to support Cambodia's armed forces. Peripheral organizations were established including those aimed at bolstering the Cambodian Air Force.

Known as the Aviation Royale Khmere (ARK), Cambodia's air arm had officially been established in April 1955 with light aircraft intended for ground attack. When Lon Nol took command in 1970, the ARK became the Khmer Air Force (KAF), and its inventory was quickly enlarged with aircraft from the U.S. After the North Vietnamese destroyed almost the entire KAF with a ground attack at Pochentong Air Base in January 1971, the U.S. supplied aircraft to rebuild the air arm. Among 98 aircraft of various types in the KAF by the end of 1971, three were AC-47 gunships. The training of KAF air crew had begun during late 1970 at Udorn RTAFB by the U.S. Air Force's Detachment 1, 56th Special Operations Wing. The detachment had been training Laotian and Thai air crews since 1964. In

preparation for the acquisition of the KAF's first gunships, in May 1971 six KAF transport crewmen were flown to Udorn for AC-47 familiarization. These crewmen were experienced in the C-47, given the history of the type in Cambodian service. Since its inception, Cambodia's air arm had been in possession of at least 12 C-47s, which were a mix of A and B models acquired from the U.S., Great Britain, Australia, and France. These aircraft formed the KAF's 1st Transport Group. U.S. Air Force deliveries during 1970 of an additional eight C-47Bs brought the total to 20. Throughout August and September, six had been passed through the 6200th Air Base Wing at Clark Air Base, Philippines, one through the 635th COS Group at U Tapao RTAFB, and the remaining aircraft was transferred in August from the USAF 432nd Training Wing at Udorn. By February 1971, another seven had been supplied from the USAF inventory.

Doug Blair, a USAF "gun plumber," who had been involved with the AC-47D's gun systems from the onset, remembers:

"In the summer of 1971 I was in the AC-119K squadron at NKP. I was in Operations one Sunday morning when I got a call from headquarters asking me if I would volunteer for a special project. When I asked what it was, the officer said, 'We need a gun plumber to help install three .50-cal. machine guns in two C-47s for the Cambodian Air Force.' I left for Udorn Royal Thai Air Force Base that day by chopper. The rest of the team was on board; a pilot who I knew from a previous AC-47 tour at Nha Trang, and a navigator and a loadmaster. We were met by the detachment of the 1st Air Commando Wing.

"After a briefing we went to Tan Son Nhut where we stripped two 47s, and a RAM team [Rapid Area Maintenance] started the Mod, with us helping. The Mod is a gun installation kit that may still be in existence. The 47s were ferried to Udorn, where we were met by Major George Jenkins of the 1st Air Commando Wing Mobile Training Team [MTT].

An AC-47D of the RLAF undergoes maintenance at Don Muang RTAFB, Bangkok, Thailand, in July 1967. Don Muang served as a major overhaul dept for Allied aircraft operating in Southeast Asia. (Tom Hansen)

Included among the wide variety of weapons seen mounted in RTAF AC-47Ds was this combination, which comprised a twin .50-caliber system and a three-barrel M-197 20mm rotating cannon. (Royal Thai Air Force Museum)

"Major Jenkins had arranged some sheet metal and electric help, and the loadmaster, Bob Aaro, and I did the gun work. Some of the .50-cal. ammo was pretty old, and if not firmly clamped into links, could slow or stop its feed into the gun. So we had to reseat the rounds into the links using a hand-crank ammo-linking device borrowed from the bomb dump. It did not take long and one aircraft was ready to go. Then two full crews of Cambodian airmen arrived. The pilots were nearly fluent in English, as were the navigators. The flight engineer, loadmaster, and gunners did not speak a word of English. I had a French dictionary and we made out fine. Soon we started a ground school for the back-end guys. We covered emergency procedures, parachutes, gun maintenance, and flares. I wrote a checklist based on what I recalled from the Spookies, but it was in English so I will not swear to how much it got used after we turned them loose.

"We were flying and shooting in short order, using a range close to Udorn. The pilot was accomplished and did a damn good job with the front-end crew. And I think the loadmaster and I did a passing job with the guys in back. We only had to show them once and they did it after that. The Cambodians had no tactical experience and the banks the aircraft made were almost aerobatics, but they learned quickly. We stayed with them until they were fairly proficient and then we went back to NKP to finish our AC-119 tour."

The Tan Son Nhut-based pair of C-47s to which Blair refers were aircraft serial numbers 44-77152 and 42-93812. Both belonged to the 460th Tactical Reconnaissance Wing, which had opened its doors at Tan Son Nhut in February 1966. The 460th was the largest and most varied wing in Vietnam, flying seven different aircraft in various reconnaissance roles. The two C-47s were part of the wing's inventory since it flew RC/EC-47s and number 152 was first to have completed the conversion to gunship. When both arrived at Phnom Penh in June 1971, they were immediately put to work supporting a government garrison 40 miles southwest of the capital. As more AC-47s were acquired, they formed the KAF's 1st Gunship Squadron, 1st Intervention Group, called *Lougaru*, which, in French, meant "werewolf." True to the Spooky tradition, Khmer Air Force AC-47s flew

Khmer Air Force AC-47s

42-108865	received from France October 1955; to RTAF February 1971
42-93812	released from the 460th TRW at Tan Son Nhut AB to the MAP (Military Assistance Program) on 29 January 1971
43-15773	released from the 460th TRW at Tan Son Nhut AB to the MAP on 9 May 1971; converted to AC-47 July 1973
43-16254	released from the 635th Combat Support Group at U Tapao RTAFB to the MAP on 14 August 1970; crashed in Cambodia June 1974 and destroyed
43-48501	from VNAF
43-48492	released from the 6200th Air Base Wing at Clark AB to the MAP on 14 August 1970; converted to AC-47 in 1973; placed in storage at Udorn in June 1974, then transferred in November 1975 to the RTAF and serialed L2-49/18; displayed at Lopburi from 1988 to 2002; to Basler in late 2003 for conversion to BT-67; in service with RTAF in mid 2004
43-48805	taken out of storage at AMARC and loaned from WRAMA to KAF in 1973; crashed at Battambang on 6 November 1973 and written off
43-48908	taken out of storage at AMARC and loaned from WRAMA to KAF in 1973
43-49010	released from 432nd TRW at Udorn RTAFB to the MAP early June 1970 for delivery to RLAF; may have later been passed to KAF; escaped to Thailand in April 1975; transferred to RTAF at
	Udorn on 11 November 1975 and serialed L2-46/18
43-49254	delivered from USAF on 13 March 1973; escaped to Thailand April 1975; transferred to RTAF September 1975 and serialed L2-42/18
43-49516	transferred from VNAF to KAF in May 1974; escaped to Thailand April 1975, transferred to RTAF on 9 September 1975 and serialed L2-43/18
43-49572	released from 483rd TAW at Cam Ranh Bay AB to the MAP on 29 January 1971
44-76338	released from 6486th Air Base Wing, Hickam AFB, Hawaii, to the MAP on 2 February 1971
44-76657	released from WRAMA to the MAP on 16 September 1973
44-77152	released from the 460th TRW at Tan Son Nhut AB to the MAP on 15 January 1971; first AC-47 for the KAF; escaped to Thailand April 1975; transferred to RTAF September 1975 and serialed L2-44/18
45-1029	released from 6314th Support Wing at Osan AB, Korea, on 4 February 1971; destroyed during rocket attack at Battambang AB on 12 June 1973
45-1079	released from 6486th Air Base Wing at Hickam AFB, Hawaii, to the MAP on 2 February 1971; escaped to Thailand April 1975; transferred to RTAF on 14 November 1975 and serialed L2-47/18
45-1116	released from WRAMA to the MAP on 13 March 1973; escaped to Thailand April 1975; transferred to RTAF on 12 September 1975 and serialed L2-45/18

Number 876 was armed with three podded miniguns. Since the window modification placed gun number three clear of the cargo doorway, the forward section of the door was used. In this case, the door itself has been removed from its frame. Thai AC-47Ds were normally flown with the doors in place. (Phakphum Tangkijjarak)

The M-197 20mm side-firing cannon in the cabin area of RTAF Peacemakers was manned by a gunner. The first ten rounds of belt-fed ammunition fed into this cannon are tracer, not only having a psychological effect, but allowing the crew to check for target accuracy. (Royal Thai Air Force Museum via Sakpinit Promthep)

In 1982 the RTAF ordered 20 GAF N22B Nomads as replacements for the AU-23A, although both remain in service. The 12-passenger turboprop cargo aircraft was modified with the M-197 20mm cannon. (Sakpinit Promthep)

Initially supplied to the RTAF under Project Credible Chase, Fairchild's AU-23A Peacemaker proved ideal for operations in Thailand's permissive anti-aircraft environment. This example, S/N 74-2082, is complete with Southeast Asia camouflage and popular shark mouth markings. (Jirayu Hirunyawech)

This AC-47D, S/N 43-48876, was not converted to a gunship until the late 1970s. It would serve four squadrons of the Royal Thai Air Force before being placed in storage a decade later. (AAPP via Sakpinit Prompthep)

protectively over military bases. Night sorties by VNAF AC-119s and USAF AC-130s freed the KAF's pair of AC-47s so they could maintain a near-constant vigil of Pochentong Air Base.

By January 1972, two AC-47 sorties were flown every day, and the aircraft were operationally ready 67 percent of the time. Two more gunships were added in February, followed by another two in March. By the end of 1972, the KAF had 12 AC-47s, which were flying nearly 100 strike sorties per month. Although it was estimated that 16 pilots were required to make the AC-47 program efficient, only nine were assigned to the gunships. The experienced pilots were often diverted to fly C-47 and C-123 transport missions, further decreasing the gunship unit's effectiveness. During 1973 the KAF began providing air cover for river convoys from Phnom Penh to the east. The mission called for two Helio AU-24As and two UH-1 Huey gunships over convoys at all times, with three AU-24As, two Hueys, and one AC-47 standing alert.

The RTAF received this AC-47D, S/N 43-48501, from the Vietnamese Air Force in 1968. In the background is a standard USAF C-47. (Royal Thai Air Force)

Number 501 was armed with the .50-cal. gun kit. Like their USAF counterparts, RTAF gunships wore markings consisting of small national insignia, the serial number on the tail fin, and a unit emblem on the nose. (Royal Thai Air Force)

During 1974, KAF AC-47 strike sorties often averaged well over 100 per month, with a record 172 flown in November. The AU-24A Stallion, a turboprop-powered military variant of the famed light STOL utility aircraft originally known as the Courier, proved a superior performer for night missions, often flying twice the number of sorties flown by AC-47s. Despite numerous efforts by KAF leaders to improve tactical coordination with the Cambodian Army, ground commanders remained skeptical about the value of close air support by gunships. By the end of 1974 a total of 16 AC-47s would serve the Khmer Air Force. Not all were delivered as gunship conversions; some were converted long after they served in the transport role.

When American military assistance ceased in August 1973, the Cambodian Air Force had to go it alone. After a brief lull in operations and a slump in morale, KAF performance quickly improved.

By the end of 1974, U.S. Defense officials reported that Cambodian air crews were as proficient as their Thai and South Vietnamese counterparts. Unfortunately, by early April 1975, the Republic of Cambodia's demise at the hands of Khmer Rouge forces was imminent, as the KAF had depleted its entire supply of ordnance. When Phnom Penh fell on 12 April, much of the Khmer Air Force began escaping to Thailand, with the majority of aircraft landing at U Tapao RTAFB. When Cambodia came under Khmer Rouge control on the 18th, a total of 97 KAF aircraft had been flown to Thailand, including seven AC-47s; the six remaining gunships were captured by the Khmer Rouge.

Kham Phiou Manivanh, reflecting on his experience with the KAF, summarizes, "I was trained on the C/AC-47 in early 1970 by the Mobile Training Team at Udorn, and in the C-123K by Air

Mounted in the cabin doorway of this RTAF AU-23A is a crew-operated M3 .50-cal. gun. The RTAF experimented with a variety of door-mounted and under-wing weapons for its Peacemakers. (Royal Thai Air Force Museum via Sakpinit Promthep)

One of 15 Fairchild AU-23As for the RTAF is seen here at Eglin AFB, Florida. The crew-operated M-93 minigun in this Peacemaker was one of many weapons tested for the aircraft. Four 500-pound fire bombs on the wing stations nearly totaled the aircraft's maximum ordnance load of 1,925 pounds. (Royal Thai Air Force Museum)

Khmer Air Force AU-24As

72-1319 to USAF on 29 December 1971	72-1327 to USAF on 19 May 1972
72-1320 to USAF on 24 February 1972, escaped to Thailand April 1975; salvaged at Bangkok and transported back to U.S.; sold on civil market; crashed on 30 June 1988	72-1328 to USAF on 28 April 1972
	72-1329 to USAF on 22 May 1972
	72-1330 to USAF on 22 May 1972
72-1321 to USAF on 3 March 1972; escaped to Thailand April 1975; transported back to U.S. 1976; sold on civil market	72-1331 to USAF on 26 May 1972
	72-1332 to USAF on 26 May 1972; crashed in Cambodia August 1973 and not recovered
72-1322 to USAF on 8 March 1972; escaped to Thailand April 1975; transported back to U.S. 1976; sold on civil market	72-1333 to USAF on 9 June 1972
72-1323 to USAF on 17 March 1972	Serial number 72-1324 was delivered to the USAF on 24 March 1972 but was not passed from storage to the Khmer Air Force; it is believed to have been scrapped in storage at AMARC
72-1325 to USAF on 30 March 1972	
72-1326 to USAF on 12 June 1972	

An RTAF GAF N22B Nomad shows the configuration attributes that made this robust, yet maneuverable, little Australian-built aircraft such a good candidate for the gunship mission. (Sakpinit Promthep)

This war weary AC-47D, S/N 43-49503, was one of 16 gunships that formed the 817th Combat Squadron of the Vietnamese Air Force. Number 503, which wore VNAF tail code kF, departs Tan Son Nhut Air Base in December 1970. (Norm Taylor)

America at Vientiane. I flew the C-/AC-47 from 1970 until the communist government took over, and then flew for them both the C-47 and C-123K, until they sent me to a re-education camp. Sadly, that was the end of my flying career."

Khmer Air Force Light Gunships

With the experience gained from *Project Little Brother* during the 1960s, which evaluated light aircraft in the gunship role, a 1971 search for a light gunship for the South Vietnamese Air Force led USAF officials to the Helio AU-24A Stallion and the Fairchild AU-23A Peacemaker. Under a program called *Credible Chase*, which began in May 1971, both aircraft types were considered as light short takeoff and landing (STOL) gunships that would give the VNAF a manageable gunship capability in a short period of time. The 4400th Special Operations Squadron was created at Eglin AFB to perform the evaluation of *Credible Chase* aircraft. Unit personnel would determine the potential of the aircraft for a variety of missions, especially helicopter escort, close air support, outpost defense, re-supply of ground troops, armed reconnaissance, forward air control, and interdiction.

Although the XM-197 20mm Gatling gun was considered the standard armament of both aircraft, dual MXU-470/A minigun modules and a .50-cal. machine gun were also tested. Other weapons tested included 2.75-inch rockets, cluster bomb units, fire bombs, forward-firing minigun pods, and general purpose bombs. Additionally, flares, smoke grenades, and leaflet dispensers were tested on Eglin's ranges as well. The combat evaluation of both types was labeled *Project Pave Coin* and was conducted in Southeast Asia throughout June and July. Both types were found unsuitable for combat, with evaluators emphasizing their lack of sufficient power and extreme vulnerability to anti-aircraft fire. However, they recommended further testing if the aircraft could be brought up to combat standards.

Helio's Stallion was originally designed to fill the need for a single-engine turbine-powered STOL aircraft on the civilian market. It didn't take Air Force leaders long to recognize the type's potential in counterinsurgency roles. Powered by a United Aircraft PT6A-27 680 hp turboprop engine, the Stallion not only boasted a maximum speed of 228 mph, it was dive-tested to 282 mph and withstood more than 7 gs. Its maximum gross weight was 6,300 pounds, with a range of 386 nautical miles, and service ceiling of 25,000 feet. Four wing stations, along with a fuselage centerline rack, allowed for rocket, bomb and flare delivery. Foremost among the Stallion's armament systems was an XM-197 20mm, three-barrel Gatling gun mounted in the left rear compartment. Use of the gun, even in an aircraft this small, kept alive the side-firing concept proven by its big brother gunships.

For the second round of testing, which began at Eglin AFB in January 1972, the second prototype Stallion was leased from Helio and put through its paces. The Air Force had ordered 15 AU-24As, which were given serial numbers 72-1319 through -1333, and delivery of 14 AU-24As began on 4 March, with the last machine being delivered on 15 June. During the test period, VNAF crews were brought to Eglin to learn the aircraft and its systems. This was to be followed by their accompanying the aircraft to Vietnam for combat testing.

Other gunship support provided by the VNAF 415th Transport Squadron included flare drops. This C-47 had 100 flares on board when it was struck on Tan Son Nhut's runway by another VNAF C-47 on 8 August 1967. Below its cockpit is the emblem of the 33rd Tactical Wing. (Norm Taylor Collection)

When the AU-24As were again deemed too vulnerable to anti-aircraft fire, *Credible Chase* was ended. At the end of June 1972, pilots of the 4400th SOS flew the Stallions to the AMARC storage facility in Arizona. The Stallion's competitor, the Fairchild AU-23A, a U.S.-built version of the Pilatus Porter fared even less favorably, being slower and having less overall performance.

Since Cambodia's anti-aircraft environment was less severe than that of Vietnam and Laos, Cambodian government officials expressed their interest in the AU-24As and U.S. Air Force officials agreed that AU-24As could indeed serve the KAF well. Therefore, beginning in November 1972, the Stallions were taken out of storage, and by year's end, all had arrived at Takhli RTAFB. Throughout early 1973, KAF

Vietnamese Air Force AC-47D S/N 43-48929 of the 817th Combat Squadron undergoes maintenance at Tan Son Nhut AB in December 1970. The words Hoa Long *translate to "Fire Dragon," which VNAF gunship crews used to represent its AC-47Ds.* (Norm Taylor)

In the VNAF aircraft marking system, AC-47D gunships were identified by a two-letter tail code; the squadron was identified by the small letter "k," which was followed by a larger letter signifying the aircraft within the squadron. Like all VNAF AC-47D gunships, this aircraft, S/N 43-8801, was assigned to the 817th Attack (or Combat) Squadron. To identify squadrons, the VNAF used a three-digit number, the second two of which were odd if the first number was even, and vice versa. Heavy gunship units fell into the 800 category, with the three attack squadrons being the 817th, 819th, and 821st. Thus, the "kE" of this Fire Dragon identifies aircraft F of the 817th Attack Squadron. (Norm Taylor)

personnel trained with the AU-24As at Takhli. Training sorties were flown in Thailand, but some missions took place in Cambodia. In May, all 14 aircraft, along with 21 pilots, 21 gunners, and 36 maintenance personnel returned to Cambodia, forming the 1st Gunship Squadron of the 1st Intervention Group. Six sorties were flown daily, and a program was begun to team the Stallions with UH-1H Huey helicopters for convoy protection. Soon, two AU-24As and two Hueys accompanied every river convoy.

In the hands of skilled KAF pilots, the Stallions performed well in the light gunship and FAC roles, despite the aircraft's reputation for glaring control problems. Although the number of sorties neared 300 per month, that number plummeted after a crash on 10 August. Five persons on board were killed when the AU-24A experienced a control problem during a rocket pass. As a result, the KAF commander prohibited the AU-24As from firing rockets until October, when Helio representatives convinced him that the aircraft were mechanically sound. Morale in the KAF continued to improve and it got a tremendous boost in October when the KAF conducted its first offensive, called *Operation Thunderstrike*. For eight days, KAF gunships struck the enemy along routes south of the capitol. The AU-24As flew 24 sorties against 49 targets.

In December 1973, AU-24A and UH-1H crews began training for night operations. Night-vision devices, commonly called Starlight Scopes, reportedly were mounted atop XM-197 guns. Stallions flew 62 night missions in January 1974. In February, an AU-24A was shot down south of Phnom Penh, and another was lost due to enemy action in April. By mid 1974, Stallions were flying a record number of sorties, many at night, often in support of *Troops in Contact*. Problems with the 20mm cannon commonly arose, forcing the aircraft into an observation-only role. During October, Helio technical representatives considered modifying AU-24As to carry 1,000 rounds of 20mm ammunition, thereby doubling its standard load. Permanent night-vision devices were also considered. During late 1974, AU-24As maintained a high number of sorties, most of which were flown against enemy troop concentrations near the capitol. Stallions were armed with CBU-25 cluster bomb munitions and 250-pound bombs for use against enemy rocket sites.

During the communist takeover in April 1975, a Stallion crashed into the Gulf of Tonkin trying to escape. Three AU-24As did escape to Thailand, and the remaining six were captured by the Khmer Rouge. At least one of those is known to have been operated by the new regime until 1993.

A large number of Fairchild C-119s were transferred to the VNAF for both transport and gunship duty. This C-119G served the 413th Transport Squadron of the 33rd Tactical Wing at Tan Son Nhut Air Base in 1970. In the background are EC-47 Electric Gooneys. (Norm Taylor)

Royal Laotian Air Force AC-47s

While not all serial numbers are recorded in available documents, the following are known to have served as AC-47s with the RLAF:

43-16133	transferred from 432nd TRW at Udorn RTAFB on 8 June 1970	
43-48263	from VNAF	
43-48909	from VNAF	
43-49010	transferred from 432nd TRW at Udorn RTAFB on 8	June 1970; may have later been passed to KAF, then RTAF
44-76370	from VNAF	
44-76625	transferred from 432nd TRW at Udorn RTAFB on 8 June 1970	
45-1047		
45-1117		

Laos

Even before AC-47 gunships began flying over Cambodia, they had been fighting a war in neighboring Laos. Despite a 1962 peace agreement between communist factions and the Royal Lao government, fighting between them escalated to such an extent that in 1964, U.S.-supplied North American T-28 fighter bombers began flying ground attack missions against the Pathet Lao. In view of American foreign policy and objectives in Southeast Asia, U.S. military forces, especially the U.S. Air Force, became extensively involved. Since the Geneva agreement prohibited U.S. regular military forces from operating in Laos, a number of U.S. assistance programs were begun. It had become painfully clear that the war in Laos was not only a struggle for the nation's survival, but an extension of the war in South Vietnam.

In 1961, Russian Premier Khruschev and President Kennedy agreed on neutrality in Laos. Although a feeble ruse, a neutral stance remained paramount, giving rise to the covert nature of the war. In fact, airlift in Laos, as well as numerous other air operations, was carried out by contract firms funded by the CIA. What was billed as the "Secret War" could not possibly stay secret due to its pervasiveness, and eventually a watching world discovered that an air war of larger proportions than that taking place in South Vietnam was being waged in the unfriendly Laotian skies. Air operations were both supported and governed by the U.S. Air Force and the CIA. Two major air campaigns took place in Laos between 1964 and 1973. In northern Laos, *Operation Barrel Roll* supported ground forces of the Royal Lao government, while *Operation Steel Tiger* was in direct support of U.S. military aims in South Vietnam.

Laotian T-28 and AC-47 aircrew and maintenance personnel, along with those of the RLAF, were trained at RTAFB Udorn under *Project Waterpump*, which began in 1964. The USAF also provided aircraft maintenance to the RLAF, along with aerial reconnaissance, intelligence, interdiction, and close air support. By 1970, nearly 300 aircraft had been passed to the RLAF, with most pilots and maintenance personnel having received training in Thailand and the United States.

Early attempts were made by the RLAF to defend mountaintop bases and to attack North Vietnamese supply convoys. During the early 1960s, two C-47 transports were armed with .50-cal. machine guns for base defense, and although rudimentary, they were vital additions to the RLAF since the enemy exploited the cover of darkness and T-28s did not fly night missions. The commitment of RLAF leaders to employ gunships became evident in February 1965 when, to thwart a coup at Vientiane, a .50-cal. machine gun was rigged in the rear cabin of a de Havilland U-6 Beaver. While not precisely accurate, the ad hoc gunship served its purpose by intimidating rebellious forces.

As part of Project Enhance, which was intended to beef up the VNAF inventory, the C-119G, S/N 53-8089, was converted to an AC-119G gunship. Wearing squadron code HO, number 089 is seen here at Can Ranh Bay AB in March 1972. (James R. Wagner)

By the late 1960s, Gen. Vang Pao's guerilla army of Hmong tribesmen found itself hard-pressed to counter the much larger North Vietnamese Army. Despite the dire situation, Vang Pao vehemently resisted the introduction of RLAF AC-47s for support. Even the success of USAF Spookies deployed earlier for Laotian operations did not sway him, for mindful of a long-standing feud between fierce Hmong and the Laotians, the general envisioned the gunships being used against his Hmong troops. At the insistence of U.S. officials, and with no relief in sight, the RLAF began receiving AC-47s in late 1969. As more improved AC-119 and AC-130 gunships were committed to the war, plans were made to equip the VNAF and the RLAF with USAF AC-47s that were being phased out. Since the VNAF was scheduled to receive the majority of USAF AC-47s, three VNAF C-47s were selected for delivery to the RLAF. Following their conversion to gunships, the trio was delivered to Wattay airfield at Vientiane on 5 September 1969, and that night, the first aircraft cleared for combat, S/N 43-48909, flew a mission against a target in Military Region Five.

Initially, Vang Pao doubted the RLAF's ability to carry out precise night strike missions with AC-47s. After refusing to allow such missions, he relented after discovering that they proved superb at night close air support. One gunship was kept on alert at Vientiane to

support troops that made contact with the enemy. Whenever possible, this aircraft staged at Paksane. By the end of September 1969, the RLAF boasted five AC-47s, all armed with SUU-11/A minigun pods. In May 1970, these were supplemented by eight Vietnam-based USAF AC-47s armed with MXU-470/A minigun modules. These aircraft were drawn from the inventory of the disbanding 4th SOS in Vietnam after the ambassador to Laos notified 7th/13th Air Force staff of an urgent need for more gunships in Laos. In addition, three USAF AC-47Ds, which had been assigned to the 432nd TRW at Udorn RTAFB, were delivered to the RLAF on 8 June 1970 by crews of Detachment 1, 56th SOW. The 432nd's last Spooky mission was flown on 29 May to prepare the aircraft for delivery to the RLAF. Soon, RLAF Spookies were averaging about 50 sorties per month. Vang Pao's dim view of the AC-47s had changed drastically as RLAF Spookies repeatedly defended Lima Sites and supported Hmong forces throughout 1970. This success was attributed to French-trained Col. Thao Ly, who commanded the AC-47 unit, but in summer 1971 when RLAF Spooky operations were in full swing, Col. Ly was killed when his AC-47 was shot down.

All RLAF AC-47s, reportedly then numbering thirteen, were armed with MXU-470/A gun modules by mid 1971; however, problems with the guns persisted, prompting crews to fire them at their lower rate of 3,000 rounds per minute, which alleviated the problem. It's interesting to note that RLAF AC-47 crews had no qualms about adopting the Spooky name, but true to Laotian superstition, they drew the line at flying with seven crew members since Buddhist doctrine held that seven was an unlucky number. Hence, RLAF AC-47 crews always consisted of either six or eight men.

After the February 1973 ceasefire, most Laotian AC-47s had their guns removed and then served in the transport role. The last RLAF offensive was flown in April 1975, and in December, the Pathet Lao took control of the country, although without the carnage suffered by neighboring Cambodia and South Vietnam. It is estimated that between 15 and 20 C/AC-47s, along with C-123Ks, were taken over by the new regime and these survivors were

This sign at Da Nang Air Base in 1973 advertised the 18th SOS's mission of training members of the VNAF 821st Attack Squadron in the AC-119 gunship. (Author's Collection)

supplemented by seven Russian Antonov AN-24 and AN-26 transports. The C-47s and C-123Ks were removed from service during the mid 1980s due to fatigue, lack of parts, and the government's intent to standardize its Soviet aircraft fleet.

Thailand

The Royal Thai Air Force (RTAF) enjoyed a gunship capability, having obtained their AC-47Ds mainly by converting C-47 transports acquired from the French during the late 1950s, or through Military Assistance Programs. Throughout its long history, the Royal Thai Air Force operated nearly 60 C-47s of different configurations; 15 of which were AC-47D gunships. Most of the conversions were accomplished during the 1970s, while six were Khmer Air Force aircraft that had escaped to Thailand at the communist takeover of Cambodia. Although Thailand's piston-powered C-47 fleet was finally retired by 1997, Basler BT-67 turbo conversions began arriving in 1998, and as of this writing, nine BT-67s are in use.

Royal Thai Air Force AC-47Ds

42-108865/RTAF
L2-35/14   received from Khmer Air Force 16 February 1971; converted to AC-47 by February 1976; 42 Squadron; 603 Squadron; withdrawn from service February 1984; displayed at Lopburi as of November 1988

42-93224/RTAF
L2-36/14   received from U.S. MAP 16 February 1971; converted to AC-47D by May 1972; 42 Squadron; 603 Squadron; withdrawn from service February 1984; dumped at Lopburi 1989

42-93789/RTAF
L2-34/13   received 21 September 1970; 62 Squadron; converted to AC-47D by February 1976; 42 squadron; 603 squadron; written off following crash landing at Bangkok 8 February 1988, preserved at Don Muang

43-48501/RTAF
L2-32/11   received from VNAF through MAP as AC-47D 30 May 1968; 62 Squadron; 42 Squadron; 603 Squadron; in storage at Lopburi October 1986; Nakhon Phanom 2007

43-48876/RTAF
L2-19/00   converted from transport to AC-47D by March 1977; 62 Squadron; 42 Squadron; 461 Squadron; 603 Squadron; in storage at Lopburi April 1986

43-49010/L2-46/18
            former Khmer Air Force; 62 Squadron; 42 Squadron; 461 Squadron; 603 squadron; written off 23 April 1991; derelict at Don Muang 1995; displayed at Vietnam War Veterans Memorial Museum, Surasri Army Camp, Kanchanaburi

43-49254/RTAF
L2-42/18   former Khmer Air Force; 62 Squadron; 42 Squadron; 461 Squadron; 603 Squadron; operated by Royal Artificial Rainmaking Unit 1985-1995; Basler conversion to BT-67 by March 1999

43-49418/RTAF
L2-20/00   converted from transport to AC-47D by VNAF September 1967; 62 Squadron; on 13 December 1967 crashed on takeoff at Nakhon Phanom RTAFB when stolen by inebriated U.S. airman; written off March 1968

43-49516/RTAF
L2-43/18   former Khmer Air Force; 62 Squadron; 42 Squadron; 603 Squadron; display at Royal Thai Police Museum

43-49641/RTAF
L2-30/07   received through MAP 13 March 1964; UN aircraft in Korea 1964-December 1968; 62 Squadron; converted to AC-47D by September 1970; 62 Squadron; 42 Squadron; written off at Ubon 9 August 1983

43-49919/RTAF
L2-25/01   converted from transport to AC-47D by VNAF September 1967; 62 Squadron; 42 Squadron; 603 Squadron; written off due to corrosion October 1990; scrapped March 2000

44-76734/RTAF
L2-37/14   converted from transport to AC-47D by May 1972; 42 Squadron; 603 Squadron; withdrawn from service February 1984; in storage at Lopburi

44-77152/RTAF
L2-44/18   former Khmer Air Force; 62 Squadron; 42 Squadron; 603 Squadron; withdrawn from service 27 February 1984; preserved at Phitsanoluk

45-1079/RTAF
L2-47/18   former Khmer Air Force; 62 Squadron; 402 Squadron; written off due to corrosion September 1989; in storage at Lopburi; Basler conversion to BT-67 2004; dumped at Lopburi January 2005

45-1116/RTAF
L2-45/18   former Khmer Air Force; 402 Squadron; 461 squadron; withdrawn from service 23 April 1991; in storage at Lopburi; to Basler for conversion to BT-67 but not converted and stored at Basler

The few AC-47Ds in the RTAF inventory during the late 1960s and early 1970s were used mainly for base defense and protection of the country's borders along Laos and Cambodia. Since Thailand was not inundated with enemy air defenses during the 1970s, the gunships served mainly as base defense, sharing the gunship role with AU-23As and GAF N22B Nomads armed with 20mm cannons. In 1975, they formed 42 Squadron of the 4th Wing at Takhli RTAFB. In 1977, the unit was re-designated 402 Squadron. Other units to which the gunships were assigned were 62 Squadron, and later, 603 Squadron and 461 Squadron. Royal Thai Air Force AC-47Ds were armed with one of four major weapon combinations. Early versions had three minigun pods, some of which were updated to MXU-470/A modules. Another gun arrangement had dual .50-cal. machine guns in the sixth cabin window opening, with a single .50-cal. gun in the next aft window port. Another variation comprised the dual .50-cal. guns and one Danish Madsen 20mm cannon. At least one aircraft is known to have been armed with dual .50-cal. guns and one side-firing XM-197 20mm Gatling gun in a specially made mount near the aircraft's wing root. The RTAF flew its last AC-47 mission on 5 September 1985.

Royal Thai Air Force Light Gunships

During 1971, when American leaders expressed more than ever their intent to disengage from Southeast Asia, they were concerned about the ability of the South Vietnamese to counter a strengthening, relentless enemy. They needed a plan that provided the VNAF with more firepower and mobility in a short period of time. Foremost among the solutions proposed was a STOL light gunship. Although it was understood that such an aircraft could not match the ability of cargo aircraft turned into heavy gunships, U.S. officials believed it was a system the South Vietnamese could manage. Even before a light gunship was considered for the VNAF, it was seen as a possible counterinsurgency aircraft for the RTAF, augmenting, or even replacing, Huey gunship helicopters and T-28s. The idea seemed viable enough that in March 1971, Secretary of Defense Melvin Laird ordered that two STOL light gunship types be evaluated by the end of June.

The Aeronautical Systems Division set its sights on Fairchild's Peacemaker and Helio's Stallion, which, under *Project Credible Chase*, became the AU-23A and AU-24A, respectively. Both were turboprop, high-wing aircraft armed with a side-firing XM-197 20mm Gatling gun. The AU-24A, covered earlier in this chapter, went to the Cambodian Air Force, while the AU-23A, which was built by Fairchild under license, was earmarked for the RTAF. Based on the Pilatus PC-6 Turbo Porter, the AU-23A was powered by a 650 hp Garrett TPE 331-1-101F turboprop engine. Like its Helio counterpart, the Peacemaker featured four under-wing mounts for stores, along with a fuselage centerline station rated for 525 pounds. Carrying two pilots and a gunner, plus 1,900 pounds of ordnance, brought the AU-23A close to its maximum gross weight of 6,100 pounds.

During combat evaluation of both types in Southeast Asia during June and July 1971, the test unit noted multiple deficiencies. Such shortcomings, especially the vulnerability of both types to anti-aircraft defenses, fueled the political debate over supplying them to

With the AC-119K, S/N 53-7831, in the background, the 18th SOS Stinger Detachment at Da Nang AB poses with its VNAF charges in 1972. Posing prior to the first training flight are USAF trainers, from left to right; Maj. Robert Krueger (instructor pilot), SSgt. William Isham (gunner and illuminator instructor), and MSgt. Lee Kyser (flight engineer). VNAF personnel are; Maj. Nuoi (pilot and unit CO), Maj. Nhut (copilot and vice commander); and student illuminator operator and student flight engineer. (Lee Keyser Collection)

the South Vietnamese Air Force. More importantly, it fell upon VNAF leaders to determine if they could handle a force of 200 light gunships, which would form five new squadrons. In anticipation of a favorable outcome during a second round of combat tests, 15 of each type were ordered. Adding to everyone's concern, and wooing the skeptics, was a series of structural and performance problems that resulted in flight restrictions of both aircraft.

The negative aspects of the STOL light gunship became so prevalent that when *Project Credible Chase* ended in June 1972, the AU-23As and AU-24As were placed in storage. Neither type had received high marks from evaluators or from VNAF leaders involved with *Credible Chase* and *Pave Coin*, and production delays coupled with admissions from Vietnamese officials that they were reluctant to pit the light aircraft against enemy air defenses cinched the concept's demise—at least as VNAF aircraft. Cambodian Air Force and Royal Thai Air Force leaders, on the other hand, emphasizing the less threatening anti-aircraft environment in their countries, were happy to have the AU-23A and AU-24A. Accordingly, the Khmer Air Force got the AU-24A while the AU-23A went to the RTAF.

Of the 15 AU-23As allocated to the RTAF (serial numbers 72-1304 through -1318), 13 were actually delivered. Numbers 72-1304 and -1309 remained at Eglin AFB. Serial number 72-1306 was the first

aircraft delivered to the 4400th SOS on 2 January 1972, followed by -1304 and -1305 by the end of the month. Testing began immediately, although the first three were grounded on 4 February when cracks were found in their rudders. They were returned to Fairchild and delivery resumed during late April. The last AU-23A arrived at Eglin on 7 June. Another setback occurred on 10 May when number -1309 crashed after its engine failed on takeoff. Although the pilot escaped injury, the AU-23As were grounded until 22 May. Testing was then completed on 28 June and the aircraft were prepared for shipment to Thailand.

In RTAF service, the AU-23A Peacemakers formed 531 Squadron of the 53rd Wing at RTAFB Prachuap Khiri Khan. The squadron's parent designation was changed to the 5th Wing to honor its World War II origin. The Peacemaker soon earned the nickname "Mosquito" after Thai pilots realized it was a small airplane that could bite them. With the bugs worked out of the airplane and satisfied with the AU-23A's performance, the RTAF ordered an additional 20 aircraft, with deliveries beginning in October 1975. Number -1307, which had been retained by the USAF at Eglin AFB, was finally delivered to Thailand in 1977. In 1982, the RTAF ordered 20 Australian-built GAF N22B Nomads as replacements for the AU-23A. On 1 April 2007, the RTAF Mosquito unit was re-designated the 501st

Royal Thai Air Force AU-23As

72-1304/RTAF JTh2-01/15		72-1318/RTAF JTh2-13/15	damaged in accident 1973; civil registration N362F
72-1305/RTAF JTh2-02/15	written off January 1989		
72-1306/RTAF JTh2-03/15	written off July 1982	74-2073/RTAF JTh2-14/19	crashed on takeoff 18 August 1978, two killed
72-1307/RTAF JTh2-34/20	at Eglin AFB until 1977, then shipped to Thailand	74-2074/RTAF JTh2-15/19	
72-1308/RTAF JTh2-04/15	in storage at Prachuap Khiri Khan August 2004	74-2075/RTAF JTh2-16/19	storage at Takhli following accident February 2004; fuselage to Saraburi Aero Park early 2007
72-1309	retained at Eglin AFB, written off 10 May 1972 following crash due to engine failure on takeoff	74-2076/RTAF JTh2-17/19	
72-1310/RTAF-05/15	storage at Prachuap Khiri Khan August 2004	74-2077/RTAF JTh2-18/19	
		74-2078/RTAF JTh2-19/19	
72-1311/RTAF JTh2-06/15	written off April 1977	74-2079/RTAF JTh2-20/19	
72-1312/RTAF JTh2-07/15	crashed into sea 2 February 1978, seven killed; replacement 1312 crashed on 29 March 2006 when engine failed on takeoff, four killed	74-2080/RTAF JTh2-21/19	
		74-2081/RTAF JTh2-22/19	
		74-2082/RTAF JTh2-23/19	
		74-2083/RTAF JTh2-24/19	
72-1313/RTAF JTh2-08/15	written off 5 February 1973	74-2084/RTAF JTh2-25/19	written off April 1977
72-1314/RTAF JTh2-09/15	in storage at Prachuap Khiri Khan August 2004	74-2085/RTAF JTh2-26/19	
		74-2086/RTAF JTh2-27/19	
72-1315/RTAF JTh2-10/15		74-2087/RTAF JTh2-28/19	
		74-2088/RTAF JTh2-29/19	
72-1316/RTAF JTh2-11/15	in storage at Prachuap Khiri Khan August 2004	74-2089/RTAF JTh2-30/19	written off August 1978
		74-2090/RTAF JTh2-31/19	crashed and destroyed 6 September 2005
72-1317/RTAF JTh2-12/15	first built AU-23A; received civil registration N5301F June 2006 for Fairchild research and development	74-2091/RTAF JTh2-32/19	written off 21 January 1979
		74-2092/RTAF JTh2-33/19	

Attack Squadron, and now modern AU-23As fly unarmed and have been upgraded with FLIR systems for the reconnaissance role in southern Thailand.

South Vietnam

When the South Vietnamese Air Force (VNAF) was officially established in July 1955, more than one-third of its aircraft inventory consisted of C-47 aircraft. A total of 22 C-47s equipped two transport squadrons, which fulfilled the VNAF's transports needs until 1969. President Nixon first used the term "Vietnamization" in November 1969 when he called for expansion of Vietnamese forces as an alternative to a continued U.S. combat role in the war. Since a major goal of Vietnamization was to pattern nearly all aspects of the Vietnamese Air Force after those of the U.S. Air Force, it followed that gunships would become an important element in Vietnamese air operations. During 1967, consideration had been given to converting C-47s of the VNAF 417th Transport Squadron to gunships. Ten were to be completed by September, with six more converted by the end of the year. Since USAF AC-47Ds were scheduled to be upgraded with MXU-470/A gun modules, 7th/13th Air Force officials expected a sufficient number of minigun pods to be available for the VNAF conversion program. The plan was shelved, however, when the Air Force began upgrading to AC-119s, which would also be armed with minigun pods. Since there weren't enough minigun pods to go around, the VNAF would have to wait nearly two years to claim a true gunship capability.

The commander of the 7th Air Force, Gen. George Brown, grew impatient and in December 1968 ordered that steps be taken to provide the VNAF with enough AC-47Ds to form a gunship squadron. South Vietnamese crews, many of whom had a great deal of C-47 experience, began training on USAF AC-47Ds. As originally intended, the gunships were to replace C-47s of the 417th Transport Squadron. The first five AC-47Ds were turned over on 2 July 1969, and by October, the VNAF had 16 gunships, which came from the deactivating 4th SOS. When the changeover was complete, the Tan Son Nhut-based 417th became the 817th Attack Squadron (AS). When the 4th SOS was officially deactivated on 15 December, it still possessed 14 AC-47Ds, three of which went to the VNAF. The 817th Attack Squadron—which often went by the designation 817th Combat Squadron—fell under the 32nd Wing of the 5th Air Division (AD), which was VNAF headquarters at Tan Son Nhut AB. The VNAF numbered its other four air divisions to correspond with geographical corps identification. For example, the 1st AD was located at Da Nang in I Corps. The 5th AD controlled all other VNAF C-47 assets, including Special Mission VC-47s, reconnaissance RC-47s, and electronic intelligence gathering EC-47s.

Even before all 16 aircraft had arrived, the 817th, which was called Fire Dragons, became operational on 31 August. Experienced in the C-47, VNAF crews, after tutelage from their USAF gunship counterparts, soon began flying flare/minigun missions in defense of air bases. Those missions became secondary when the squadron was given the responsibility of supporting the hamlets populated by regional and popular forces. As the squadron grew, six aircraft and crews were detached to Binh Thuy for missions in IV Corps, and by the beginning of 1970, 817th gunships were flying nearly one-third of all gunship missions in South Vietnam. VNAF personnel had been unaccustomed to flying at night and in bad weather, and they had to become proficient with MXU-470/A gun modules, which were replacing minigun pods. However, experience soon overcame such obstacles and their kill ratios began to match those of USAF gunship crews. Vietnamese maintenance crews, many of whom, like the pilots, knew their way around the C-47, were able to keep gunship availability rates high. When the 817th was at full strength, detachments set up shop at Da Nang and Pleiku, providing support throughout South Vietnam. Until the VNAF's demise, a total of 29 AC-47Ds would fly in VNAF colors.

Transfer of the AC-47Ds to the VNAF was part of the rapid expansion of the Vietnamese Air Force, which was officially termed the Improvement and Modernization Program, or I & M. The goal of this program, which officially began in 1968, was to develop a self-sufficient Vietnamese Air Force. The modest first phase of the program, which called for strengthening the VNAF, quickly gave way to second and third phases, which focused on restructuring the VNAF to enable it to take over the air war. Such an alternative to a comprehensive U.S. combat role proved to be a mammoth task for the VNAF since USAF dominance of air operations had to be reversed, and the vast cultural gap and lack of time allotted for the changeover ultimately proved counterproductive to the I&M program.

Despite such obstacles, training Vietnamese aircrew was one of the U.S. Air Force Air Training Command's top priorities. Besides training VNAF personnel at stateside Air Force bases, the ATC sent field training detachments to Vietnam, one of which helped VNAF personnel at Tan Son Nhut AB transition from the C-47 to the C-119 in 1968. It was standard practice to establish VNAF training schedules to ensure that personnel were ready for the programmed activation of particular units.

Shortly after activation of the VNAF 817th AS, plans were laid for expanding Vietnamese gunship capability, and of particular interest was an Air Force Systems Command study aimed at supplying the VNAF with Lockheed EC-121 Constellations converted to gunships. Although the massive four-engine aircraft had ample room for weapons and ammunition, not only was it found to be too vulnerable to anti-aircraft fire, it lacked maneuverability, would be too costly to modify, and could prove to be a maintenance nightmare for the VNAF. Air Staff planners reverted to the programmed transfer of AC-119s to form a unit to replace the USAF 17th SOS. Accordingly, VNAF aircrews teamed with the 17th SOS to begin training. Vietnamese AC-119G crews attended a C-119 flight orientation course at Clinton County AFB, Ohio before undergoing training with the aircraft at the VNAF Air Training Center at Nha Trang. Meanwhile, 16 AC-119Gs were transferred during 1970. Despite expected problems with crew experience and coordination, the proficiency of VNAF AC-119G crews increased rapidly. Experiencing the least transition problems were VNAF gunners since they were already proficient with the MXU-470/A gun module, which was common to the AC-47D and AC-119G. The first VNAF Shadow class graduated in April 1971.

On 15 August 1971, VNAF crewmen assumed AC-119G operations, and on 1 September, the VNAF 819th Attack Squadron was activated, inheriting the facilities of the USAF's 17th SOS. The 819th, called *Hac Long,* meaning "Black Dragon," was one of four squadrons of the 51st Wing, 1st Air Division, which was located at Da Nang. After the last AC-119G was turned over to the VNAF on 24 September, the 819th began flying combat missions from Tan Son Nhut AB, freeing USAF gunships for missions over the Ho Trail.

While the priority remained making the VNAF strong enough to fight independently through a massive VNAF training program, plus pumping hundreds of aircraft into the air arm, it was mistakenly assumed that a mutual withdrawal of North Vietnamese and U.S. forces would occur. To ensure that Vietnamization under the I & M program succeeded, its gunship capability had to be improved. Subsequently, under *Project Enhance,* and its follow-on, *Project Enhance Plus,* additional AC-119s were supplied to the VNAF to offset attrition of AC-47s and AC-119s, replace AC-47s, and to form a new gunship squadron equipped with AC-119Ks. Beginning in October 1972, 16 AC-119K Stinger gunships were transferred from the USAF 18th SOS to the VNAF. These were joined by six transferred from the 1st SOW at Hurlburt. Prior to the deactivation of the 18th SOS on 31 December,

its personnel had established a 45-day training school for VNAF crews transitioning to the AC-119K. The VNAF 821st Attack Squadron with AC-119Ks was activated at Tan Son Nhut AB in December, with USAF Stinger crews remaining with the unit in the advisory role until March 1973. A Stinger loss on 1 March is reported to have caused the termination of *Project Enhance Plus.*

Although a cease-fire agreement had finally been signed on 27 January 1973, the VNAF had been so engorged with aircraft—more than 2,000 equipping 65 squadrons—that it proved impossible to operate. Subsequently, 34 VNAF AC-47 and AC-119 gunships were placed in storage during early 1974. Vietnamese aircrew and maintenance personnel did their best to go it alone as the U.S. pipeline of supplies and parts went dry, and few American advisors remained. Nevertheless, VNAF gunship crews fought battles on new fronts, facing ever intensifying enemy anti-aircraft fire, including SA-7 heat-seeking missiles. Bitter conflict marked the early months of 1975, yet VNAF gunship crews were unwavering in their support of ground troops. The North Vietnamese, however, continued to gain territory, and after they had overwhelmed defenders of the approaches into Saigon, the fate of South Vietnam was pretty much sealed.

The official VNAF inventory of September 1974 indicates that the VNAF had been given 56 AC-119G/K gunships, nine of which had been lost. Two were written off and eight were transferred back to the USAF. With the communist takeover in April 1975, 37 AC-119s were left in South Vietnam, three of which escaped to Thailand. A total of

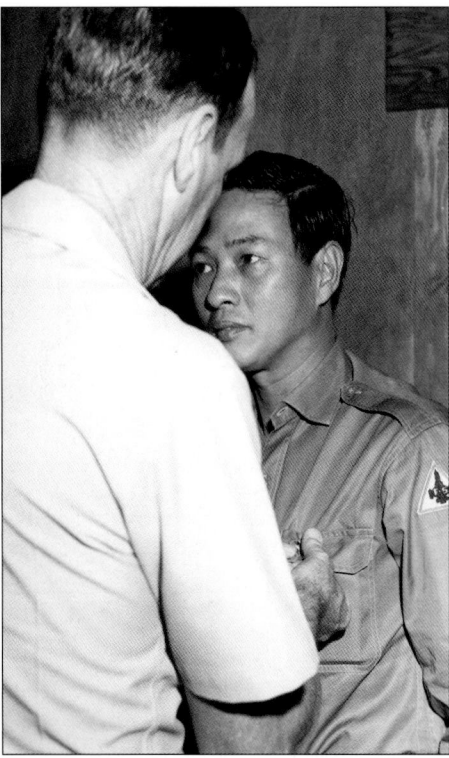

Upon graduation of the first AC-119G class on 13 March 1971, Col. Frank Eaton, 14th Special Operations Wing commander, awards a Shadow pin to Maj. Duc, commander of the 817th Attack Squadron. (U.S. Air Force)

At the AC-119G graduation ceremony on 13 March 1971, Col. Eaton officially passes the gunship squadron to Vice President Ky. Looking on is Maj. Gen. Tran Van Minh, Chief of Staff of the Vietnamese Air Force. (U.S. Air Force)

35 C-47s were left behind, including gunship versions. Sixteen escaped to Thailand, most of them loaded with families of VNAF personnel and refugees when they were flown out of the country.

The last aerial engagement of the war involved a VNAF gunship, testifying to the mettle of VNAF gunship crews. On 30 April, the day after President Ford ordered the evacuation of Saigon, Lt. Thanh and fellow pilot Lt. Tran Van Hien and their AC-119K crew made a night takeoff from Binh Thuy AB to fly against North Vietnamese divisions surrounding the capitol. Joined by a pair of VNAF Skyraiders, the Stinger dropped flares for the A-1s and fired throughout the night upon enemy forces attacking Tan Son Nhut AB. Two days earlier, three defecting VNAF pilots flying A-37s had attacked Tan Son Nhut, damaging three AC-119s. Thanh landed before dawn to rearm and refuel, ignoring pleas by the operations officer of the 821st not to go up again. Again, the valiant crew took off, laying down minigun fire on troops advancing on the base until tragedy struck. While in a gun pass at about 3,000 feet, an SA-7 Strela missile streaked wide of the gunship, but a second one found its mark on the aircraft's right engine. As the aircraft came apart, a gunner bailed out only to have his chute become entangled in the Stinger's tail as it plummeted to the ground in flames.

Vietnamese Air Force AC-47Ds

VNAF tail codes, where known, follow the aircraft serial number.

43-16065	written off 16 August 1969
43-16140	later to Philippine AF
43-16368/kT	
43-48263	later to RLAF
43-48491	
43-48501	later to RTAF
43-48686	
43-48701	damaged at Da Nang 17 September 1971
43-48801	
43-48909	later to RLAF
43-48929/kL	
43-49211	damaged at Quang Ngai 9 June 1973
43-49339	
43-49495	later to Philippine AF
43-49503/kF	
43-49516	
43-49517	later to Colombian AF
43-49524	
43-49770	
44-76354	
44-76370/kD	
44-76394	
44-76558	later to Philippine AF
44-76606	written off at Binh Thuy 5 September 1969
44-76626	
44-76643	destroyed ground attack at Tan Son Nhut 20 February 1968
44-76717	
45-0919/kC	
45-0927	
45-1047	
45-1057/kJ	written off following crash 24 November 1972; two killed
45-1121	

Vietnamese Air Force AC-119G/Ks

VNAF tail codes, where known, follow the aircraft serial number.

52-5864 (K)	
52-5889 (K)	
52-5910 (K)	
52-5911 (K)	
52-5926 (K)	
52-5938	
52-5940 (K)	destroyed 24 May 1973; seven killed
52-5945 (K)	
52-9982 (K)	
53-3154 (K)	
53-3170	destroyed 20 June 1972; eight killed
53-3187 (K)	
53-3197 (K)	
53-3211 (K)	
53-7830 (K)	
53-7831 (K)	
53-7839 (K)	on VNAF training flight on 1 March 1973, unable to land due to weather, ran out of fuel and crew bailed out over South China Sea; one VNAF crew man killed
53-7850 (K)	
53-7877 (K)	
53-7879 (K)	
53-7883 (K)	
53-8069	
53-8089	
53-8121 (K)	
53-8145 (K)	
53-8148 (K)	

CHAPTER ELEVEN

BASLER TURBOS:
THE LEGEND CONTINUES

The first two AC-47T gunships built by Basler for the Colombian Air Force, numbered 1681 and 1686, fly over Wisconsin farmland prior to delivery. (Basler Turbo Conversions, LLC)

A few years ago, while visiting Wittman Field at Oshkosh, Wisconsin, I looked up to see the unmistakable silhouette of a Douglas DC-3 high above the field. While watching the aircraft go through various maneuvers, it became obvious that this was no ordinary Gooney. It was more agile, almost to the point of being aerobatic, than the Douglases I remembered from my youth. And the airplane sounded different—quieter, and not emitting the typical drone of the old girl's recips. It wasn't until I began the research for this book that I realized the mystery plane I had been observing was a Basler Turbo.

Presumably, the venerable C-47 had its swansong during the Vietnam War, having had its already long life extended, proving its value in the gunship, transport, psywar, and electronic roles. True, the Gooney still thrived in many parts of the world, but as time marched on, its numbers dwindled. Finally, in an era when more remain earthbound than flyable, the C-47 has all but been relegated to history. Although a few of these stalwart transports still fly profitably for small cargo operators in the U.S., most of the C-47s in existence languish in boneyards, fly the warbird circuit, serve as displays, or fly scattered routes in Third World countries. But, there's more.

Warren Basler had a vision. He made clear his conviction by stating, "The DC-3 was a beautiful, stable, and virtually indestructible airframe going to waste. We realized that by turbinizing and modernizing the airplane it would go on for many years." Long before Basler embarked on his endeavor, others had similar thoughts, giving DC-3s turbo power, but with less favorable results. These turboprop conversions either strictly satisfied engineering goals, or were aimed at commercializing turbine-powered air transportation.

The first conversion was accomplished in Great Britain in 1949 when Rolls-Royce installed its Dart turboprop engines on a Dakota. Another British experiment that same year had Armstrong Siddeley Mamba Mk3 and Mk6 turboprops installed on a Dakota. In 1951, Field Aircraft Services modified two Dakotas of British European Airways with the Dart engines as a test-bed for the Vickers Viscount, but after an 18-month evaluation period, the Dakota was reverted to its radial engine configuration. Commercial aviation just wasn't ready for the turbine, having too many skeptics who refused to believe that a departure from radial engine design could economically benefit air travel.

Twenty years would pass before experiments with turbo-powered DC-3s began again in the United States. On 13 May 1969, Jack Conroy's *Turbo Three* first flew with Dart 510 engines borrowed from a former United Airlines Viscount. Interest in the concept was

Evident here is the extent to which Basler prepares a C-47 for re-manufacture. All major components are removed and the airframe is reduced to ribs and skin. The large gap forward of the wing indicates the 40-inch fuselage stretch to compensate for a center-of-gravity shift caused by the turbo engines. This aircraft, under construction in spring 2008, was destined for the U.S. State Department for logistical work in Afghanistan. (Basler Turbo Conversion, LLC)

This striking view of an AC-47T on takeoff from Wittman Field shows to good effect the front profile of its PT6A-67R engines. Wittman Field at Oshkosh, Wisconsin, is home to Basler's facility. (Basler Turbo Conversions, LLC)

short-lived with only one other conversion completed, a Super DC-3 also modified with Dart turboprops. Although the aircraft was intended for use by Pilgrim Airlines in New England, it never reached the certification phase and was abandoned. The last experimental and most radical turbo conversion was completed for Specialized Aircraft, Inc. Aircraft Technical Services Corp. modified Conroy's *Turbo Three* with three United Aircraft PT-6A-45 engines, one of which occupied the DC-3's nose section. Although this version showed promise with a marked increase in payload and speed, it too would fade into obscurity, ending up at Basler's facility. A more recent modification program undertaken by South Africa's Wonder Air, and reportedly Simera, resulted in a number of turbo DC-3/C-47s for that country's civil and military fleets. Beginning in the late 1980s, PT6 engines were installed in at least two dozen aircraft, and possibly more, the majority of which were delivered to the South African Air Force (SAAF). Labeled C-47TP, the design was poorly executed, with much of the fleet grounded and then sold. Those remaining in SAAF service equipped the 35 Squadron for maritime and reconnaissance work.

Although they displayed great ingenuity, the designers of these aircraft could not match Basler's fortitude and level of passion for breathing new life into the classic airframe. So extensive is Basler's work with the DC-3/C-47 that its president, Tom Weigt, asserts, "We don't just rebuild the airplane; we re-manufacture it. We take it down to the ribs and skin. This is a new airplane." A tour of Basler's facility reveals not only the thoroughness of the company's work, but the independent nature of its re-manufacturing process. Highly skilled technicians completely strip the aircraft to a bare fuselage with much of its framing exposed. Just forward of the wings, a 40-inch extension is added to compensate for a shift in the airplane's center of gravity as a result of the new engine installation.

A pair of Douglas DC-3s at Basler's facility in 2008 await conversion to BT-67s. The foreground aircraft, registered N8187E, was one of six acquired when Miami Valley Aviation, Inc., went out of business. (Author)

Replacing the original radial engines are Pratt & Whitney PT6A-67R turboprops. Proven in the commuter airline industry for more than two decades, the PT6 is rated at 1,424 shaft horsepower on takeoff, allowing a cruise speed of 215 knots. Enclosed in wide, streamlined composite nacelles, the engines drive five-bladed, aluminum Hartzell reversible propellers. Basler's turbos even enjoy a stealth quality since engine exhaust heat is cooled by augmenters before being directed into the propeller wash, thereby greatly diminishing infrared signature.

Outer-wing sections are given a new leading-edge camber to maximize low speed stability, and originally rounded wing-tip shapes are changed to sharp, obtuse angles. Completing Basler's new wing package is reinforcement of the center and outer wings to reduce loads on lower wing-attack angles, and to support the aircraft's increased maximum gross weight of 28,750 pounds. Fabric control surfaces on the rudder and elevator are replaced with metal, and new electrical, fuel, hydraulic, and avionics systems are installed.

Aircrews who flew the C-47 would barely recognize the turboprop's new interior, which is designed for comfort and efficiency. Basler moved the cockpit bulkhead forward five feet to increase cabin space, and insulated the interior to minimize noise levels. Everything in the cockpit is new, right down to the flight-control yokes, along with a modern digital "glass" instrument suite. A new lightweight, but rugged, cabin floor incorporates cargo rollers and a cargo winch is installed at the forward end of the cabin.

The result is a new aircraft whose payload and performance surpasses that of the standard DC-3/C-47. Not only are Basler Turbos reliable and easy to maintain, but operators find them economically feasible, getting a *new* aircraft for the fraction of the cost of a new mass production transport. Thanks to a variety of optional equipment, versatility is a byword of the Basler Turbo. Basler's Tom Weigt states, "All of our aircraft are used for special operations, whether military or civilian." Those used for civilian applications are labeled BT-67s, which stands for Basler Turbo, engine model 67. These, typically, are used for spray work, fire fighting, geographical survey, rainmaking, research, and cargo hauling. Military versions, which are called C-47Ts, serve as troop and cargo transports, reconnaissance, and paratroop operations. The turboprop DC-3/C-47 became so successful that on 21 April 1994, the Department of the Air Force approved the designation C-47T as applied to Basler's BT-67. Gunship variants, accordingly, are designated AC-47Ts.

Under contract from the U.S. government, Basler converts C-47s to gunships, which are operated by the air arms of Colombia and El Salvador. Besides various types of side-firing weapons, AC-47Ts are equipped with FLIR and a Night Vision Imaging System (NVIS), both of which allow imagery surveillance and dark cockpit operations during night missions. Basler's gunship is complete, right down to the gun mounts and gun sight, with the only exception being weapons, which are installed by the using country. The AC-47T's gun sight is the same used in the original USAF Spookies. Older .50-cal. machine gun sets used in the gunships are being replaced by General Dynamics-produced GAU-19/A Gatling guns. Also a .50-cal.

weapon, the three-barrel GAU-19/A has a firing rate of 1,000 or 2,000 rounds per minute. In 1999, the U.S. Government sent 28 GAU-19/As to the government of Colombia.

The government of El Salvador was actually the first to take delivery of the AC-47T gunship, followed by Colombia. Other Latin American countries that received Basler Turbos are Guatemala and Bolivia, although these were placed in service as cargo and troop transports. The single C-47T flown by the Bolivian Air Force is no longer in service. Basler C-47Ts also serve with the Mali Air Force, Mauritania Air Force, and the Royal Thai Air Force which took advantage of having an abundance of C-47s stored in Thailand. The RTAF turned to Basler to transform them into new economical aircraft.

The Thai government also took delivery of nine Turbos between 1998 and 2004, all of which were assigned to 461 Squadron, Wing 46 at Phitsanoluk in northern Thailand. Initially used for rain-making and fire fighting, the Thai turbos reportedly have had their roles expanded to include transport and reconnaissance, and even an electronic warfare capability. In 2008, a similarly equipped turbo, Basler's 52nd conversion, was being prepared for the U.S. State Department to be used for logistical work in Afghanistan.

El Salvador

To counter overwhelming rebel forces during El Salvador's civil war, U.S. advisors in 1981 strongly urged El Salvadorian leaders to place greater emphasis on counterinsurgency warfare. They needed no more persuasion after a guerilla attack on the Ilopango airfield on 27 January 1982 resulted in the destruction of fourteen aircraft, three of which were C-47s. Another three were badly damaged, reducing the FAS C-47 fleet to 11 aircraft. U.S. assistance in bolstering the small and poorly equipped El Salvador Air Force, or Fuerza Aérea Salvadoreña (FAS or FAES), included two AC-47 gunships. The pair was converted from transports and delivered during December 1984. Both were armed with .50-cal. machine guns.

During 1985 the gunships were regularly engaging rebel forces, and proved to be El Salvador's most effective aerial weapon. During the late 1980s, U.S. Air Force aid intensified under *Project Asp*, with low-profile training taking place at Eglin's Duke Field. The same Air Force personnel responsible for training El Salvadorian airmen had trained Latin America-bound CIA personnel in the AC-47 during the early 1980s. After the war ended, both FAS gunships were rebuilt into Basler AC-47Ts to maximize their effectiveness. El Salvador became Basler's first customer when the pair was delivered during 1990, and so successful were the AC-47Ts that additional aircraft were ordered, with the FAS boasting four AC-47Ts by 1992.

Painted overall camouflage green, the gunships are assigned to the Transport Group of the 1st Air Brigade at Ilopango Air Base. Their serial numbers are FAES 116 through 119, the latter having been lost in a crash on 19 November 2000.

Colombia

Colombia has long been one of the major operators of the C-47 in South America. The Colombian Air Force, or Fuerza Aerea Colombiana (FAC), received its first C-47s in 1944. Thereafter, more were acquired through assistance programs and from civilian sources. As the C-47 was withdrawn from U.S. Air Force service, many were

Rear facing view of the interior of AFSOC's C-47T. Basler's military turbo has 40 fold-up troop seats in the spacious cabin, which can hold more than 10,000 pounds of cargo. Near the aft bulkhead, which provides access to lavatory facilities, a stepladder is attached to the rear cargo door. Overhead is the static line for paratroopers. (Basler Turbo Conversions, LLC)

The cabin bulkhead was moved forward five feet to increase cabin space. An electric cargo winch at the forward end of the floor roller system eases cargo loading. Basler's new interior includes complete soundproofing. (Basler Turbo Conversions, LLC)

passed down to the FAC beginning in 1964, and by 1978, nearly 60 C-47s were listed on the FAC inventory. Most were used in the transport role with the 1st Transportation Squadron, although some wore camouflage for tactical roles.

Despite the politically sensitive nature of U.S. military support of Colombia's armed counter-drug operations, U.S. Air Force involvement gained momentum, capping with the establishment in September 1987 of a Mobile Training Team. Concurrent with the Asp program in El Salvador, *Operation Peace Emerald* focused on training FAC personnel in the AC-47. The team was comprised of three pilots, three copilots/FLIR operators, two flight mechanics, and two gunners, all of whom were assigned to the 1st Special Operations Wing. In preparation for *Peace Emerald*, a training aircraft (FAC C-47, S/N

The nose section of Basler's AC-47T includes a new composite radome and the optional FLIR unit. Original divided windshields are replaced by one-piece glass. The gun-sight mount is visible in the pilot's window. (Basler Turbo Conversions, LLC)

The AC-47T gun sight in the pilot's left window. (Basler Turbo Conversions, LLC)

An AC-47T of the Colombian Air Force prepares for departure from Basler's Wittman Field facility. The long range oxygen system being loaded is one of Basler's many options. (Basler Turbo Conversions, LLC)

The mission operator/FLIR operator's station. Mounted on the wall to its right is an oxygen system, which serves a crew of three. (Basler Turbo Conversions, LLC)

An AC-47T of El Salvador's Air Force in 1993. (Author's Collection)

FAS 118 is one of the first two AC-47Ts Basler delivered to El Salvador in 1990. The FAS replaced its original overall dark gray scheme with this white over light gray livery. The third cabin window space is occupied by a push-out air inlet for the smoke-clearing system, which was part of the original USAF AC-47 tech order. Immediately aft of the fourth window are two chaff dispensers. (Luc Hornstra)

Of the eight AC-47Ts built for the Colombian Air Force, later deliveries were given a two-tone gray paint scheme. This example goes through an engine run-up at Basler's facility prior to delivery. (Basler Turbo Conversions, LLC)

Before being transformed into a gunship, this C-47, S/N 41-38745, had a long history of civilian ownership since World War II. Basler's 40-inch fuselage stretch is evident in this view of FAS 119. The AC-47T shows wear from action during El Salvador's civil war. This gunship was lost in a crash on 19 November 2000. (Luc Hornstra)

El Salvador's AC-47T number 118. Basler's redesigned wing tips and outer wing leading edge droop is clearly seen. A cockpit observation window replaced the astrodome common on standard C-47s. The engine exhaust area was treated with black non-skid material. (Luc Hornstra)

This AC-47T of the Colombian Air Force wore a grim reaper on its vertical fin. Four pressure plates were attached forward of the cargo door to create a reduced pressure area to assist smoke removal. The gunship is armed with two .50-cal. GAU-19/A Gatling guns. (Basler Turbo Conversions, LLC)

Five members of the USAF Mobile Training Team organized for training Columbian Air Force AC-47D crews pose with a FAC gunship in fall 1987. Back row, left to right, are Lorin Siron and Tom Sprauge. In the front row, shown with a .50-cal. machine gun, are Jesse Wise, Ed Thien, and Mister Gunship himself, Ron Terry. (Ed Thien Collection)

Former Spooky pilots would barely recognize the modernized cockpit of the C-47T of the 6th SOS. All components are either new or rebuilt. (Basler Turbo Conversions, LLC)

since parts had to be flown from Madrid AB, Bogota. Munitions availability also affected training; Colombia's stock of 1.2 million .50-cal. rounds produced by Winchester during the 1950s had deteriorated and was deemed unsafe. New ammunition was obtained, and in 1988 the FAC 214th Tactical Squadron took delivery of five AC-47s, although one was lost in August of that year.

In 1991 the FAC commander visited the U.S. with hopes of acquiring the AC-130. When it became apparent that the Spectre could not operate from many of Colombia's crude airstrips, the FAC opted for Basler turbo conversions in 1992. With U.S. State department approval, four C-47s were transformed by Basler into AC-47T gunships. Called *Fantasma*, meaning "Phantom," the gunships were assigned to the Tactical Air Squadron at Palanguero. Four more were converted, one of which became a combat loss. Painted overall dark gray, the AC-47Ts are used mainly for anti-terrorist and counter-drug missions. Colombia not only exploits the AC-47T's short-field capability, but finds Basler's long-range fuel system especially useful for long distance flights over Colombia's vast territory. Colombia's AC-47T serial numbers are FAC 1654, 1658, 1659, 1667, 1670, 1681, 1683, and 1686.

The Air Commando Legend

Unique among the aircraft that have been rolled out of Basler's facility is the turbo its employees call AFSOC, which stands for Air Force Special Operations Command. Many a bar bet could be won arguing that the U.S. Air Force flew a C-47 in the twenty-first century. Re-manufactured by Basler into a C-47T in 2000, the 1943-vintage aircraft held the distinction of being the oldest airplane in the Air Force inventory. It is one of a handful of unique aircraft operated by

1650) had undergone modifications by E-Systems at Greenville, Texas, and AFSC's Detachment 2. Modification consisted of adding weather/mapping radar, FLIR, an Omega navigation system, a Mk-50 decoy flare system, a 32-tube LUU-2A/B flare unit, the .50-cal three-gun system, and IR-resistant paint.

All training of two AC-47D crews was conducted at German Olano Air Base, Puerto Salgar, but logistical support was a problem

Study of the Peace Emerald *insignia showing the inimitable plan view of the C-47 and crossed machine guns with an Emerald in the center.* (Ed Thien Collection)

Shell casings from its two GAU-19/A guns litter the floor of this AC-47T. The weapons are belt-fed from ammunition storage containers in the foreground. (Basler Turbo Conversions, LLC)

Basler-built AC-47Ts of the Colombian Air Force originally wore an overall dark gray paint scheme, with only their FAC numbers on the tail. (Basler Turbo Conversions, LLC)

the 6th Special Operations Squadron based at Hurlburt Field, long the hub of Air Commando operations. The 6th SOS is the only U.S. military unit with a wartime mission to assist and train Allied air arms to defend their countries, and to become coalition partners against global terrorism and insurgency. Its volunteer members undergo an intense training regimen, where they learn not only the specialized aircraft, but foreign language, survival, weapons, tactics, combat search and rescue, and medical and mission planning. The air commandos then deploy to host countries, reporting their assessments to special operations offices and the U.S. embassy. Their training concept is the aviation version of that used by the U.S. Army Special Forces to train ground forces.

The unit also parallels Mobile Training Teams that trained Allied air arms during the war in Southeast Asia, and later in South America. The modern military term used to describe the squadron's mission is Foreign Internal Defense, an office which was created with an aviation detachment in early 1991. While training foreign allies to use air power and fight their own battles, the air commandos operate in the most dangerous parts of the world where terrorists, warlords, and criminals thrive, and due to the nature of their work, members of the 6th SOS prefer to keep a low profile. Usually under a veil of secrecy, the squadron's teams have trained and assisted air arms in El Salvador, Ecuador, Peru, Venezuela, South Korea, Indonesia, Oman, Jordan, Tunisia, Sri Lanka, Eritrea, Uzbekistan, Poland, Slovenia, and the Philippines.

The C-47T flown by the 6th SOS, named *Goon 76*, is at home among the unusual variety of aircraft operated by the unit. These include Russian Antonov transports, Mi-8 series helicopters, Bell UH-1 helicopters, and CASA 212 Aviocars. The unit also flies C-130s of the 16th Special Operations Wing. Like many of the unit's aircraft, the C-47T is leased, bearing Basler's name and wearing the civil registration of N40386. Originally a C-47D given S/N 43-48859, this aircraft has a long and proud history, having served not only with the U.S. Army Air Force and U. S. Air Force, but with the U.S. Marine Corps and the Vietnamese Air Force as well. It was placed in storage at AMARC in 1968 and later ended up on the civilian market. Old timers in the Air Commando community claim that before Basler acquired the aircraft, it had been in the hands of the Drug Enforcement Agency, which had captured it from drug runners. After Basler rebuilt the C-47 in 2000, the company used it as a demonstrator in Europe. While with the 6th SOS beginning in 2003, its primary job was to enhance Colombia's ability with its AC-47Ts to combat revolutionary armed forces. In 2006 it went back to Basler for two weeks before going to the Antarctic for logistical work.

So important was the C-47T's mission with the 6th SOS that the unit was slated to again acquire a C-47T in 2008. Such importance reinforces Basler's claim that its turbo DC-3/C-47 is the world's most experienced all-purpose aircraft, and that is a claim not to be taken lightly.

Goon 76, the Air Force Special Operations Command C-47T, flies a para-cargo mission. Since the aircraft is leased for use by the 6th Special Operations Squadron, it wears Basler's title and civilian registration. The tail emblem is highly symbolic of the proud tradition of the Air Commandos, which traces its origin to the 1st Air Commando Group, formed in 1944. The Commandos began operations during World War II with a handful of C-47s, alluding to their secrecy with an unofficial emblem; a black question mark on a white circle. (Basler Turbo Conversions, LLC)

A sampling of aircraft used by the 6th SOS to assist and train Allied air arms poses at Hurlburt Field, Florida. Present is a pair of Bell UH-1N Huey helicopters, the C-47T, a Soviet bloc Mi-17 helicopter, and an Antonov An-26 transport. Besides its leopard camouflage scheme, which was introduced in 1978, the Huey at left wears five white diagonal stripes, reminiscent of markings worn by aircraft of the 1st Air Commando Group during World War II. (U.S. Air Force)

CHAPTER TWELVE

WORLDWIDE GUNSHIPS

The South African Air Force flies a number of C-47TPs, called Turbo Daks, the gunship version of which was called Dragon Dak. Converted by Aero Modifications, this example, number 6877, is seen at East London in June 2007. (Gary Shephard)

An Aero Modifications C-47TP of the South African Air Force flies formation with a standard SAAF C-47 in November 2003. (Fanie Kleynhans)

Besides turbo-powered AC-47T gunships, lesser known radial-engine AC-47s have been operated, or remain in operation, worldwide, armed with a wide variety of weapons. The conversions to gunship were often accomplished with .50-cal. modification kits provided by the U.S. government, while South African Air Force Dragon Daks are known to have used 20mm cannons. Of the 25 Dakotas flown by the Rhodesian Air Force's No. 3 Squadron, several were configured as unmarked gunships during the 1970s or 1980s. Among six C-47s flying with the Honduras Air Force, or Fuerza Aérea Hundureña (FAH), is a single AC-47 attached to the Transport Squadron at San Pedro Sula, and during the late 1970s, when civil war raged in Nicaragua, the U.S. transferred two C-47s, one of which had been converted to an AC-47D gunship. The Dominican Republic Air Force, or Fuerza Aérea Dominicana (FAD), had seven C-47s in its inventory, wearing S/Ns 3401 through 3407, five of which were still in service during the 1980s. Some of these airplanes were converted to gunships with the .50-cal. modification kit.

Like many Third World countries, political unrest drove the development of the Indonesian Air Force, or Tentara Nasional Indonesia—Angkatan Udara (TNI-AU). The government acquired a number of C-47s from former Dutch colonial rule and from the U.S. and Australian air forces. During the first half of 1971, the U.S. government supplied the Indonesian Air Force with modification kits to convert two of its six C-47s into gunships. Although the conversions were completed by July 1971, the pair was not used in combat until October 1975. Accompanied by two Douglas B-26 Invaders, these gunships supported troops fighting Fretilin guerillas along the Indonesian border with Portuguese Timor. The aircraft saw a few weeks of combat before their weapons were removed early in 1976, after which they assumed the straight transport role.

Since the Vietnam war, the U.S. has supplied a .50-cal. gun-modification kit in support of Allied air arms. The kit was used to convert this C-47 of the Dominican Republic Air Force into a gunship during the 1980s. (Larry Davis Collection)

BIBLIOGRAPHY

The best primary source a writer can hope for when conducting research for a book such as this is input from numerous individuals who had hands-on involvement with the subject. There is no substitute for their profound insight and often remarkably clear recollection. Second to their experiences are literary works that have been thoroughly researched by skilled, seasoned writers. Such research is evident in Gradidge's DC-3 tome, which is considered the bible of the DC-3/C-47 aircraft. Equally valuable are governmental and manufacturer documents written as systems were designed and developed, evaluated, and operationally deployed. Since not all material gathered during research can be accepted as gospel, it falls upon the writer's diligent and often exhaustive research, tact, and skill in composition and transition to create an accurate and readable account. Those who have designed, tested, and taken gunships into battle deserve nothing less.

Books

Ballard, Jack S. *Development and Employment of Fixed-Wing Gunships.* Washington, D.C.: Office of Air Force History, 1982.

Conboy, Kenneth, and Kenneth Bowra. *The War in Cambodia 1970—75.* Osprey, 1989.

Davis, Larry. *Gunships: A Pictorial History of Spooky.* Carrollton: Squadron/Signal Publications, Inc., 1982.

Drendel, Lou. *C-130 Hercules In Action.* Carrollton: Squadron/Signal Publications, Inc., 1981.

Gradidge, J.M.G. *The Douglas DC-3 and its Predecessors.* Air-Britain, 1984.

Martin, Patrick. *Tail Code: The Complete History of USAF Tactical Aircraft Tail Code Markings.* Atglen: Schiffer Publishing Ltd., 1994.

Mikesh, Robert C. *Flying Dragons: The South Vietnamese Air Force.* Osprey, 1988.

Mutza, Wayne. *The A-1 Skyraider in Vietnam: The Spad's Last War.* Atglen: Schiffer Publishing Ltd., 2003.

Magazines

Aceto, Guy. *The Night Shift.* Air Force Magazine, December 2006.

Aviation Week & Space Technology. *Gunship Project Reflects New Approach.* June 26, 1972.

Brownlow, Cecil. *AC-47 Broadens Viet Attack Envelope.* Aviation Week & Space Technology, April 17, 1967.

Casey, William R., Major, USAF. *AC-119: USAF's Flying Battleship.* Air Force/Space Digest, February 1970.

Citizen Airman. *Against the Odds.* April 1988.

Colucci, Frank. *Night Spectre.* Sentry Books, n.d.

Dorr, Robert F. *AC-130 Gunship Has a Place in Modern War.* Air Force Times, May 21, 2001.

———. *AC-130 Gunship in the 21st Century.* Air Forces Monthly, 2002.

———. *AC-130 Spectre Gunship.* Combat Aircraft, n.d.

———. *AFSOC Gunship Force at a Juncture.* Armed Forces Journal, 2005.

———. *The Lockheed C-130 Hercules.* World Airpower Journal, 1993.

Katz, Samuel M. *USAF Special Ops.* Air Forces Monthly, March 2000.

Lessels, Robert J., SSgt. USAF. *Shadow.* Air Force Magazine, 1971.

Marshall, Michel. *The Birth of Spooky.* Air & Space, June/July 2002.

Rucker, James. *Son of Spooky.* Air Combat, n.d.

Schanz, Mark V. *Special Operations Heads West.* Air Force Magazine, March 2008.

Warnes, Alan. *A Legend Modernised: Basler BT-67s.* Air Forces Monthly, April 2006.

Government Publications

Anthony, Victor B., Maj., USAF. *Tactics and Techniques of Night operations 1961–1970.* U.S.A.F. History Office, March 1973.

Bowman, Alfred C., Maj., USAF. *AC-47 Navigation.* The Navigator, USAF ATC, Summer 1968.

Harvell, John F., Capt., USAF. *Development Test of the SUU-11/A 7.62mm Gun Pod. APGC Technical Documentary Report No. APGC-TDR-64-19.* Air Proving Ground Center: USAF, April 1964.

Harvell, John F., Capt., USAF. *Engineering Evolution of the SUU-11/A Gun Pod.* USAF, April 1965.

Harvell, John F., Capt., USAF. *First Article Test of the SUU-11/A Gun Pod.* USAF, July 1966.

Harvey, Jack B., Capt., USAF. *AC-47 Side Firing Gunnery.* USAF, 1966.

Hildebrandt, Herbert C., Capt., USAF. *History of the 14th Special Operations Wing 1 October—31 December 1969.* USAF, n.d.

Kimberlin, Ralph D., 1st Lt. USAF. *Engineering Evaluation of the Prototype MXU-470/A Machine Gun Module in the AC-47D Aircraft.* USAF, October 1966.

Masko, David P., TSgt., USAF. *First Lady retires, Era Ends.* Air Force News Service, n.d.

Noble, Richard J., Capt., USAF. *History of the 4th Air Commando Squadron 29 Aug. 1965–31 Dec. 1965.* USAF, 1966.

Stephens, Douglas W., SSgt., USAF. *History of the 6250th Combat Support Group July–December 1965.* USAF, n.d.

Trexler, Walter L., Jr., 2nd Lt., USAF. *First Article Test of the 7.62mm MXU-470/A Machine Gun Module.* Air Proving Ground Center: USAF, October 1967.

Air America Phnom Penh Station Monthly Reports. Various excerpts November 1973 to June 1974.

Fact Sheet AC-130H/U Gunship. 16th SOW Public Affairs Office, n.d.

Fact Sheet 4th SOS. 16th SOW Public Affairs Office, n.d.

Fact Sheet 16th SOS. 16th SOW Public Affairs Office, n.d.

Flight Manual; USAF NC-123X Aircraft. USAF, 15 May 1967.

Happy Valley Weekly. Phan Rang AB, South Vietnam: various excerpts 1969.

Newsreview. Air Force Systems Command, January 1966.

7th Air Force News. *Crews Mount Impressive Totals.* July 15, 1970.

7th Air Force News. *Spooky Crew Joins Navy to Sink Enemy.* October 29, 1969.

Project CHECO (Contemporary Historical Examination of Current Operations) Report: Fixed-Wing Gunships in SEA July 1969—July 1971. HQ, PACAF, 30 November 1971.

Stars and Stripes. Various excerpts, n.d.

TAC Oplan, Final Report Combat Introduction/Evaluation AC-119K, Gunship III (Combat King). USAF, August 1970.

Technical Order 1C-119K-1 Flight Manual. USAF, 1967.

Technical Order 1C-119K(A)G-2-1 General Maintenance Instructions. USAF, n.d.

Other Documents

Dorr, Robert F. *Special Ops C-130's Flight at the Tip of the Spear.* Special Ops Yearbook, 2004.

Kimberlin, Ralph D. *The Development and Combat Evaluation of the AC-47 Gunship.* American Institute of Aeronautics and Astronautics, Inc., 2002.

Lockheed-Georgia Company Newsbureau Release. *Twenty Years Later, Number 1 Hercules Still at Work.* December 9, 1976.

Lockheed Star. *First Gunship Readied for Ontario Mod.* March 17, 1968.

Rockwell International Gunship Litho. *USAF AC-130U Gunship.* January 1993.

Zeybel, Henry, Lt. Col., USAF. *Truck Count.* Air University Review, January/February 1983.

INDEX

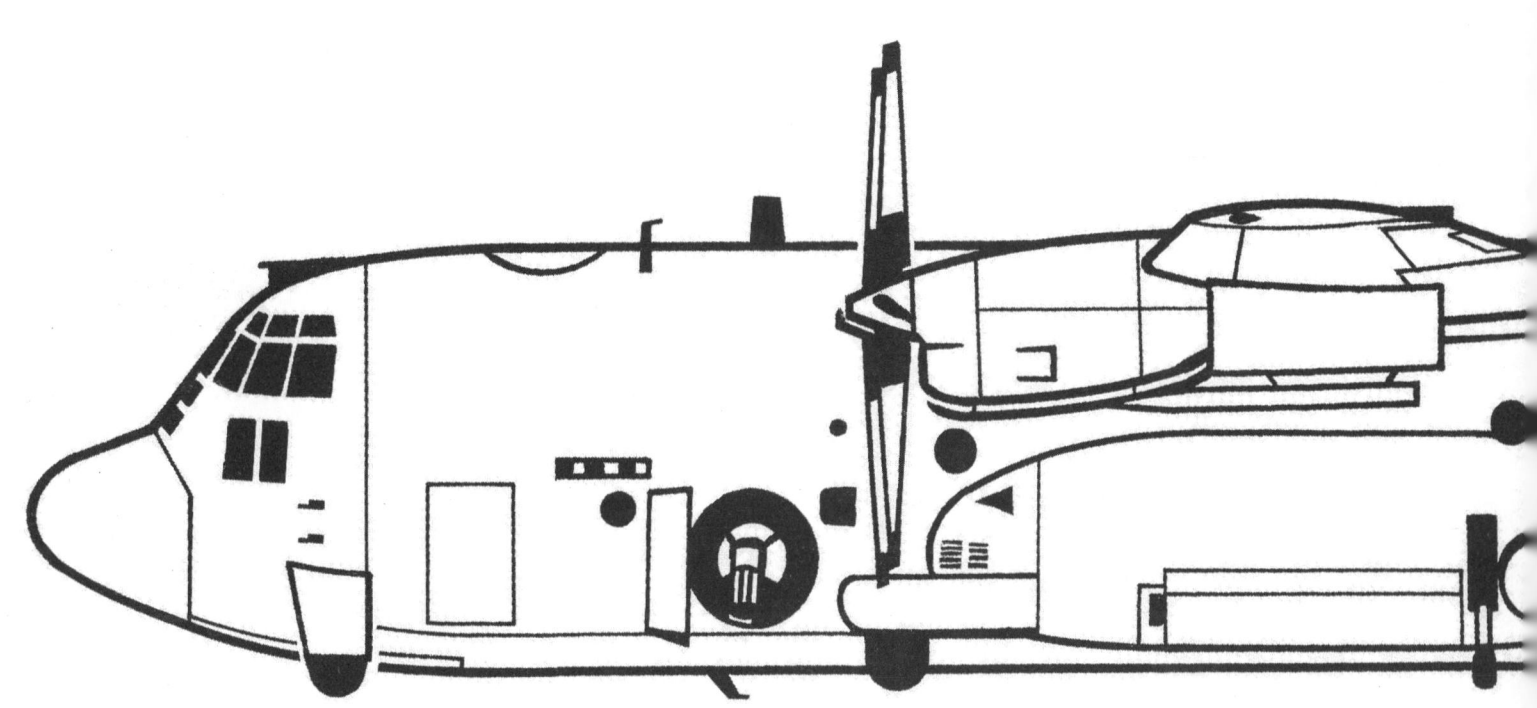